AF352441

Language, Culture, and Knowledge in Context

Language, Culture, and Knowledge in Context
A Functional-Cognitive Approach

Brian Nolan

SHEFFIELD UK   BRISTOL CT

Published by Equinox Publishing Ltd.

UK   Office 415, The Workstation, 15 Paternoster Row, Sheffield,
      South Yorkshire S1 2BX
USA   ISD, 70 Enterprise Drive, Bristol, CT 06010

www.equinoxpub.com

First published 2022

British Library Cataloguing-in-Publication Data

A catalogue record for this book is available from the British Library.

ISBN-13   978 1 80050 191 1   (hardback)
          978 1 80050 192 8   (paperback)
          978 1 80050 193 5   (ePDF)
          978 1 80050 194 2   (ePub)

Library of Congress Cataloging-in-Publication Data

Names: Nolan, Brian, 1952- author.
Title: Language, culture, and knowledge in context : a functional-cognitive
  approach / Brian Nolan.
Description: Sheffield, South Yorkshire ; Bristol, CT : Equinox Publishing
  Ltd, 2022. | Includes bibliographical references and index. | Summary:
  "The purpose of the book is to draw a comprehensive and representative
  picture of the dimensions of meaning, emerging from the
  interrelationship between these domains of language, culture, knowledge,
  and context"-- Provided by publisher.
Identifiers: LCCN 2021042107 (print) | LCCN 2021042108 (ebook) | ISBN
  9781800501911 (hardback) | ISBN 9781800501928 (paperback) | ISBN
  9781800501935 (pdf) | ISBN 9781800501942 (epub)
Subjects: LCSH: Language and culture. | Knowledge, Theory of. |
  Functionalism (Linguistics) | Cognitive grammar.
Classification: LCC P35 .N65 2022 (print) | LCC P35 (ebook) | DDC
  306.44--dc23/eng/20211130
LC record available at https://lccn.loc.gov/2021042107
LC ebook record available at https://lccn.loc.gov/2021042108

Typeset by Sparks – www.sparkspublishing.com

Contents

List of figures

1   Introduction

1.1   The complicated relationship between culture and context

Over the years of my linguistic research, I have become increasingly intrigued and fascinated by the nature and function of culture and knowledge, and the role that context plays in informing language use. This book seeks to tease out the sets of relationships that might be found across and within these domain areas. The theme of this book is that there is a rather complicated set of relationships between the domains and that these relationships can be tricky to characterize. The premise is that we can shed some clarity and light on the dimensions of the construction and organization of meaning at the interfaces between these domains. Specifically, this study examines the nature of the relationship between language, culture, and context, and looks at the definitions of each to see what the connections are between them. One of the issues that we need to grapple with is: "what exactly is culture?" We examine the application of language in the service of culture, including language-based artifacts such as art, paintings, poetry, and text, using examples from within a cultural narrative and the language-based artifacts of the linguistic landscape. Our cultural sense entails our knowledge about cultural norms, beliefs, and values of human society, a community, a nation, and our generalized knowledge about the language system that we use in our social and communicative interactions. We all have a sense of what culture is, but sometimes this relates to cultural artifacts rather than the notion of culture itself. Is culture different to civilization? Is culture the glue that holds a civilization together in meaningful ways?

As part of its *purpose*, the book attempts to elaborate on the nature of language, culture, knowledge, and context, and their interrelationships. We look to define each, in terms of their relationship to language in particular, and for each, to identify their respective properties. We also look to find, for example, what exactly is meant by the term "knowledge" and what are the different kinds of knowledge? How might this be shared in a dialogue between two interlocutors, within a shared common ground, in the realization of successful speech acts? Cultural and other knowledge is also found within the linguistic landscape and the artifacts within our environment. As a purpose, we want to explore the ways that language is central to expressions of knowledge and culture. The purpose of the book is also therefore to draw a comprehensive and representative picture of the dimensions of meaning, emerging from the interrelationship between these domains of language, culture, knowledge, and context.

The *aim* of the study then is to advance the discussion on these sets of relationships and how they might influence and inform language in interaction. We intend to do this through detailed theoretical characterization of the thematic domains of interest. As such, the general objective is to bring new focus and a fresh perspective to these complicated sets of relationships across language, culture, and knowledge, and to do this through studying language in the linguistic landscape, the language found on artifacts and in art (as a special kind of artifact), knowledge and context, and the pragmatics of language in interaction. We adopt a functional-cognitive approach within the study.

Our *hypothesis* is that meaning in culture is facilitated by language and that language draws on context and shared knowledge, the cultural common ground, while the cognitive processes that retrieve a meaning from language use are argued to be exactly those that apply to retrieving meaning from art, music, poetry, and language-based artifacts found within the linguistic landscape. We take the view that language is not an autonomous system, and that its interactions with the domain areas, heretofore mentioned, and the linguistic landscape of our environment, are actually more wide-ranging and multifaceted than had been previously considered. Our view of culture is that it includes, at least, artifact, language, worldview, and the cultural models/ way of life of a community. The question "What is culture?" is not the only important question, by any means. The role of artifacts as cultural objects, and public signs (and graffiti) in the linguistic landscape have a sociocultural dimension. We can ask: "What exactly is an artifact, and its function, in a discussion on culture?" and "How is culture manifest within the linguistic landscape?" We can also ask: "How do we retrieve meaning in context from language in interaction and use?"

As we progress, we will highlight a number of approaches to characterizing language in the functional-cognitive space that are sensitive to issues of culture. In many ways, the question of "What is the relationship between culture and language?" can be reformulated as: "What is the relationship between knowledge and language?" This itself is rather a tricky question. The representation of knowledge requires us to consider the nature, and structure, of our shared mental ontology as a repository for our cultural knowledge. This ontology provides a shared and common understanding of the world, which advances onwards into language by informing the lexicons in our language grammars. Therefore, our cultural knowledge includes ontology, representation, reasoning, cultural schemata, cultural metaphors, and cultural conceptualizations. Many artists use language in the service of their art, and visual artists frequently use text directly in paintings as a cultural visual-linguistic semiotic.

The *key questions* for us, therefore, in this study are:

i. What is CULTURE and cultural knowledge?
ii. What is WORLDVIEW and way of life of a community, and how are these motivated by cultural models?
iii. What are (cultural) ARTIFACTS and their function, and what cultural knowledge do they instantiate?
iv. What language artifacts are found in the LINGUISTIC LANDSCAPE?
v. What are the various kinds of KNOWLEDGE and their forms, and how might these be represented?
vi. What is the relationship between language and CONTEXT?
vii. How does context and COMMON GROUND inform utterance meaning in discourse?

We support our study with evidence from four case studies, from across the overlapping domains of language, culture, knowledge, and context. The case studies are:

1. The linguistic landscape and cultural identity (in Chapter 4, *The linguistic landscape*)
2. Meeting the challenges of context in linguistic analysis (in Chapter 8, *Context, situation, and common ground*)
3. Bloomsday as evidence of cultural systematicity (in Chapter 10, *Culture and language in interaction*)
4. The pragmatics of Irish tea culture (also included within Chapter 10, *Culture and language in interaction*).

Taking a stance within the functionalist-cognitive space, we argue that language is a system of communicative social action in which grammatical structures are employed to express meaning in context. In the broad sense of this discussion, context can be considered to be the cultural context, and is that subset of context relevant to discourse that resides in a dynamic and emergent common ground. Here, common ground operates as a shared distributed context space between discourse interlocutors, allowing situations of interest to be discussed, and thereby providing cognitive and computational processing economy over the management of a discourse. We propose a tentative structure for common ground and the various kinds of knowledge contained within it. The knowledge in common ground, informed by the surrounding culture of the speech community, gives us a dynamic set of beliefs, desires, and intentions (BDI) that we manage appropriately within a discourse. The set of beliefs, desires, and intentions is informed and influenced by cultural knowledge and mediated via language and reasoning.

All around us, language transforms our world and provides us with meaning in context. To successfully manage common ground, at the intersection of culture and language, requires a shared ontological commitment in discourse. We argue for a view of culture as the set of values shared by a community. The relationship between these values, along with all the knowledge (language, grammar, stories, sounds, meaning, and signs) shared by a community of people, form a particular worldview, transmitted according to their traditions. We propose that meaning in culture is facilitated by language while the cognitive processes that people employ to retrieve a meaning are precisely those characterized within relevance theory (Sperber and Wilson 1995). According to this theory, an input is relevant to an individual when, and only when, its processing yields such positive cognitive effects. Typically, the greater the positive cognitive effects achieved by processing an input, the greater its relevance will be. The greater the effort of perception, memory, and inference required, the less rewarding the input will be to process, and thus less deserving of attention. Relevance therefore may be assessed in terms of cognitive effects and processing effort. The view we take here is that these cognitive processes also apply to retrieving meaning from art, music, poetry, and artifacts within the linguistic landscape. Human cognition tends to be geared to finding meaning and the maximization of relevance, but an informed and mutually agreed common ground is necessary before any communication or dialogue can effectively take place. We argue that, in finding meaning, there is a deep connection between language, cognition, communication, and culture. Language, common ground, and our cognitive processes allow us to retrieve a relevant meaning with least cognitive cost. It's complicated, of course, and very interesting, while also very human, and very worthy of our attention.

1.2   Culture and civilization

While we more or less freely use the word "culture" today, it is not widely known that the word "culture" itself, with its modern, technical, or anthropological meaning, was only established in English in 1871 by Tylor's publication *Primitive Culture*.

> CULTURE or Civilization, taken in its wide ethnographic sense, is that complex whole which includes knowledge, belief, art, morals, law, custom, and any other capabilities and habits acquired by man as a member of society. The condition of culture among the various societies of mankind, in so far as it is capable of being investigated on general principles, is a subject apt for the study of laws of human thought and action.
>
> Tylor (1871: *Primitive Culture*. Volume I, chapter 1)

The word "culture" does not seem to have entered to any British or American dictionary until over fifty years later (Kroeber and Kluckhohn 1952: 12). Apparently, Tylor, after some hesitation against using the term "civilization", borrowed the word "culture" from German, where it had become well recognized with the meaning here under discussion. Civilization is considered to be all of human society with its well-developed social organizations, including the culture and way of life of a society at a particular period in time. Civilization is therefore the condition that exists when people have developed effective ways of organizing a society and care about art, science, and such like – it is the social process whereby societies achieve a stage of advanced development and cohesive organization. Clearly, there is some overlap between culture and civilization and it would be useful to define culture before we start our exploration.

The notion of what constitutes "CULTURE" is slippery and tricky. We argue that it has at least four major senses and, as such, includes (1):

---

(1)   The constituents of culture

1.   [ARTIFACT]: A body of artistic and intellectual work.
2.   [LANGUAGE]: A means of spiritual and intellectual development.
3.   [WORLDVIEW]: The values, customs, beliefs, and symbolic practices by which people live as a community.
4.   [CULTURAL MODELS/WAY OF LIFE]: A whole way of life viewed at some moment in time.

The term "Irish culture", for example, can mean the poetry, music, and dance of the people who inhabit the island of Ireland; or it can include the kind of food they eat, the music and literature they create, the sort of activities they engage in, and the type of belief systems they observe. The poet T.S. Eliot in his book *Notes Towards the Definition of Culture* (Eliot 1973), took culture to include "all the characteristic activities and interests of a people". We might say that civilization is to do with facts within a society, while culture is to do with the values of a society. Civilization, then, is necessarily the precondition of culture. Civilization refers to a world that is manufactured, fabricated, and built by people working together. There can be no distinctively human activity without signs and values. We use the notion of a sign as a technical term whereby a sign maps form with meaning. Roughly speaking, to amplify the difference between civilization and culture, we say that post-boxes are part of civilization, but the color one paints them (green in Ireland, for example, while red in Britain, blue in other countries, etc.) is a matter of culture. We need traffic lights in modern societies, but red does not have to signal "Stop" and green "Go" but by conventional agreement internationally, this is the case and it represents an organized and civilized way of doing things. Culture is about shared meanings, and language is the privileged medium in which we make sense of things, in which meaning is produced and exchanged (Hall 1997: 4–5). Meaning can only be shared through our common access to language. Language, as a means of communication, is essential to this. Indeed, language is central to the construction of meaning and has always been regarded as the key repository of cultural values and meanings. Language is able to do this because it operates as a representational system. Through the signs and symbols that we use (sounds, text, images, musical notes, objects – artifacts of various kinds) we express our concepts, feelings, and ideas to other members of our society, especially so when we do this via language. Language is therefore a channel through which our thoughts, emotions, and ideas are expressed in culture. Expression of this knowledge through language is central to the construction of meaning. Culture is many things but is especially concerned with the production, expression, and exchange of meaning between members of a social group, ranging over artifact, language, worldview, and way of life. Again, language, as a means of communication, is essential to this. We will speak more on language later.

1.3   Culture, worldview, common ground, and language

Culture can be viewed as a kind of social-collective-cognitive background in which we wrap our knowledge, beliefs, instincts, prejudices, sentiments, opinions, and assumptions. Embedded within a culture is a worldview, and every language gives voice to the distinctive worldview of a specific people. A worldview is a theory of the world, used for living in the world. Our worldview is a mental model of our reality – a framework of ideas and attitudes about the world, ourselves, and of life. Is a worldview important? Yes, of course it is. We might compare the worldview of Europeans of 100+ years ago to that of Europeans today. Of course, it is clear that much has changed in the worldview of people. There is a rich diversity of cultures (and languages) in our world, and a culture is at its finest when language successfully expresses and reveals the common general experience of the people of the community. In this way, language and culture distil the intrinsic nature, character, and essence of a people. What is shared in a community of speakers within a culture?

Cultural knowledge, residing in artifacts, language, worldview, and lifestyle, is shared. For members of the same community, culture exposes the shared knowledge, that common ground that is the repository of our shared knowledge. Common ground provides the contextual glue between language and culture. As a living thing, culture is always a work in progress. In this view, common ground acts as a kind of decentralized knowledge system supporting the cognitive activation of a subset of relevant contextual knowledge. The types of knowledge characterized in common ground are of various kinds and include, for example, declarative, procedural, heuristic, meta, and structural knowledge, and cultural knowledge, along a scale from volatile and dynamic to less volatile and less dynamic. Specifically, common ground contains relevant knowledge on local dialogue, language, environment, recent events, historical knowledge, common sense, cultural knowledge.

What about language? Language is a tool with wide-ranging usefulness and a multiplicity of purpose, with function and form established and refined by humans to satisfy their social need for meaning. The things in the world, entities and actions, are communicated via language as part of our everyday interactions. In fact, language represents our greatest demonstration of human cognitive power. It is the basis for mathematics, science, philosophy, art, music, poetry, and literature. All human languages exist to solve the human problems relating to communication and social cohesion. Language is crucial for making sense of the world. In particular, we use language for categorizing and classifying the components of the world around us. A language, therefore, as well as being a cognitive tool, is a repository of the riches of highly specialized cultural experiences. Language in interaction is fundamentally a cultural activity and, at the same time, language is also an instrument for organizing our cultural domains. Functionalist-cognitive approaches to linguistics understand language structures as supporting language in use within a community of speakers and, as such, is sensitive (to varying degrees) to culture. Many linguists then, broadly view language as a communicative tool (Nolan 2012) used to relate our experiences and mental representations to the external world. Functionalist-cognitive approaches to linguistics, when they are sensitive to the cultural connection, equate cultural cognition with socially situated activity mediated by language.

Linguists working with the cultural linguistics approach (Sharifian 2011, 2015a, 2015b, 2015c, 2017; Sharifian and Palmer 2007) consider that language is used to maintain cultural conceptualizations through time whereby people use the narrative of oral traditions to connect people, place, history, and culture. This involves cognition and conceptualization. As humans, we have evolved to create and store concepts through signs and to recognize relationships between the signs we create. A sign maps form with meaning. Each culture determines which conceptualizations, categorizations, and cultural generalizations are the most important to it, and the vocabulary and grammar of the languages spoken within that community reflect its priorities of knowledge. It has been argued that the emergence, transmission, disturbance, and perpetuation of cultural conceptualizations are phenomena best understood as constituting a complex adaptive system. Understood as a complex adaptive system, both language and culture can be conceptualized as forming a complex intertwined nexus while allowing us to appreciate the structural connections between them. Cultural artifacts such as paintings, rituals, language, and gesture are all instantiations of cultural conceptualizations and, as such, have a cognitive dimension. The points of intersection between culture, cognition and language all relate to common ground and are therefore concerned with the nature of cognition within the community group. In this regard, common ground acts as a kind of decentralized knowledge system supporting distributed cognition within a community supporting speech acts.

Nothing has more to tell us about what it means to be human than the forms and uses to which we put language. Languages are central to our achievements in art and science, and give us access to all the knowledge and skills learned by humans. We have, in a cultural community, the shared knowledge of that community (called the shared common ground), organized through language. In this sense, culture is at the interface of knowledge and language. We find examples of this readily in the arts and in poetry. The artist Cy Twombly often quoted the poets Stéphane Mallarmé, Rainer Maria Rilke, John Keats, as well as many classical myths and allegories in his works. In contrast to Cy Twombly, Jean-Michel Basquiat's visual art focused on elements of contemporary culture and civilization. In his painting, Basquiat appropriated poetry, drawing, and painting, and conflated text and image, abstraction, and human figures, with various kinds of textual information mixed freely in his work. In this way, Basquiat used textual commentary in his paintings to better comprehend truths about the individual, as well as society and its culture. Another use of words is found in poetry (recognizing, of course, that this is a special genre), where the selection of knowledge from broad context to process the poem creates appropriate cognitive effects with minimal processing effort. We will not spend too much time on poetry, but suffice it to say that common ground is crucial for the retrieval of meaning from a poem. Language is a powerful thing and a rich, shared common ground is necessary to allow us to find meaning in poetry.

The linguistic landscape of our environment, considered in its broadest sense, is a particularly rich context area in which we can explore the connection between culture and language, through instances of language found on, and with, artifacts of various kinds in our environment. The linguistic landscape, and the artifacts that populate it, all play a role in this cultural narrative and contribute to our sense of our culture, our connection to place, our sense of identity within a culture, and who we are. The study of the linguistic landscape therefore advances our understanding of the relationship between culture, context, and common ground, as languages are part of the cultural heritage and, as such, are reflective of our linguistic and cultural diversity.

One example of a cultural artifact, a book, that contributed to the Irish and indeed European (if not world!) cultural narrative through language is *Ulysses* (1922) by James Joyce (Joyce 2008 edition), a novel about a day in the life of ordinary people in Dublin on 16th June 1904. By way of background to the book, it was written by Joyce in Trieste, Zurich, and Paris between 1914 and 1921. It tells in great detail many incidents of the life of Leopold Bloom and those around him over the span of that single day, and into night. Each year, the book is celebrated as the cultural event of Bloomsday. As a conceptual schema, Bloomsday organizes actions and experiences, and structures our individual perception of events, building frames, and basic cognitive structures to guide one's perception of reality. Every year in Dublin on that date, hundreds of Dubliners re-enact the day dressed as characters from the book to assert a connection with the text and its events. The Bloomsday schema is culturally motivated and shares a common understanding amongst its participants – a shared common ground. Context has a central role in Bloomsday, including as it does a set of cultural knowledge, general knowledge and shared communal beliefs, and the experience that arises from the resulting interplay of culture and social community. We treat this later, in more detail, as one of our case studies.

Culture provides the invisible color and texture of our everyday lives. It is a kind of social-collective-cognitive background in which we wrap all our beliefs, instincts, prejudices, sentiments, opinions, and assumptions. Embedded within culture is a worldview, and every language gives voice to the distinctive worldview of a specific people. A worldview is a theory of the world, a cultural model, used for living in the world. A worldview is a mental model of reality, a framework of ideas and attitudes about the world, ourselves, and through our cultural models, influences our way of life. Language and culture distil the essential essence of a people as a living community and act as the repository of our shared knowledge. As a living thing, culture is always a work in progress.

1.4   The organization of the chapters

In Chapter 2, *Language and culture*, we examine a number of approaches to characterizing language. We argue that language is a tool that can be put to many useful and creative tasks, and the things in the world, entities and actions, are reflected in language. We mentioned already that language allows us to communicate regarding the "things" of interest to a community. In this sense, language can be considered as a cognitive instrument for capturing the shared knowledge ontology of a speech community. Also examined is the notion of culture, and how one might seek to define it in some appropriate way. Culture is quite an abstract, and complex, term that has been defined in many ways over the years. However, there is still no unifying definition of culture. Typically, culture is considered to concern the beliefs, values, rules, norms, symbols, and traditions that are common to a group of people.

In Chapter 3, *The nature of worldview*, we examine the notion of worldview, its importance to how we perceive, conceive and experience, and act in the world. A worldview is the fundamental cognitive orientation of an individual and society encompassing the whole of the individual's or society's knowledge. We touch upon the relationship between language and worldview. We discuss the use of the term worldview as introduced by von Humboldt, the German philosopher. Many linguists believe that each language system opens up a new world for us, in which the concepts with which we speak and think, are shaped differently. This is controversial and not yet proven by any means. We briefly survey what evidence might provide support for this perspective, and offer relevant definitions of the term world-view, and examine the functions a worldview provides to us.

In Chapter 4, *The linguistic landscape*, we discuss the linguistic landscape as an environment where public displays, that incorporate language, act and function as a form of sign. The visible use of language on signs in the public environment constitutes the linguistic landscape of a place. We examine the functions of the linguistic landscape as supporting cultural identity and providing important identity markers of communities. As signs in the linguistic landscape consist of a mix of visual and textual elements, we explore the linguistic and visual structures within the realm of visual communication and visual semiotics. People inhabit this human linguistic landscape in time and space. Language on these public signs is a specific type of language use which is distinct from other forms of written and spoken communication. We include a case study on the linguistic landscape and cultural identity,

Chapter 5, *The nature of cultural artifacts*, examines the circumstance that, in our environment, we are surrounded by the artifacts of our society and our culture. We interact with our world via artifacts and, in many ways, they enhance the quality of our lives, and often have significant culture value. These artifacts have a function, purpose, and a utility of some kind. In virtue of their ability to retain a cultural significance, the artifacts we value are important because they have the potential to reveal distinctive features of the human mind. Our judgment about the nature and identity of an artifact is sensitive to the context in which we use it, or indeed to the task at hand.

In Chapter 6, *Cultural models and way of life*, we discuss how way of life is defined as the habits, customs, and beliefs of a particular person or group of people. It is a style of living that reflects the attitudes of a person or group, and thereby reflects the cultural models of that society. What then are individual lifestyles, and a way of life, and how do these relate to cultural models? Within cultural and social frames, people develop individual lifestyles, and a way of life. The notion of lifestyle therefore motivates the individual's active choice of cultural expressions. An individual's choice of lifestyle, along with their normal everyday activities, is broadly determined by the society and culture in which they belong and the positions occupied within that society and culture. We find, however, that the beliefs, desires, intentions, worldview, and life goals of people are not fully governed by their social or cultural membership. A way of life is developed and maintained by people. However, social and cultural structures intersect with an individual's own actions and life choices.

In Chapter 7, *Knowledge and its representation*, we delve into elements of the theory of knowledge, and look at some of the characteristic questions including: What is knowledge? And what types of knowledge are there? We can distinguish, for example, between knowledge of propositions, or propositional knowledge, and know-how, or ability knowledge. The goal of a theory of knowledge is to clarify what knowledge involves, how it is applied, and to explain its characteristic features. Any discussion of knowledge must recognize some basic linguistic facts about the way that the verb *know* and its cognates function in discourse. In particular, it is important to recognize that to *know* has both a propositional and a procedural sense. This contrast is found in the matter *of knowing that something is the case* (THAT-knowledge) versus the practical knowledge of *knowing how to perform some action* to realize some end result (HOW-TO-knowledge). There are in fact more fine-grained insights into the many different kinds of knowledge. Declarative knowledge is to do with concepts, facts, and entities. This type of knowledge describes what is known and includes simple statements that are asserted to be either true or false. This also includes a matrix of attributes and their values so that an entity or concept may be fully described. Procedural knowledge is to do with processes, rules, strategies, agendas, and procedures. This type of knowledge describes how something operates or how a problem is solved, and provides directions on how to do something. Heuristic knowledge describes our experiential knowledge that guides the reasoning process. It is empirical and represents the knowledge compiled through the experience of solving past problems. Meta-knowledge is high-level knowledge about the other types of knowledge and how to use them, and describes knowledge about knowledge. We use this type of knowledge to guide our selection of other types of knowledge for solving a particular issue. This type of knowledge is used to enhance the efficiency of our reasoning by directing the reasoning processes into the most promising area. Structural knowledge is to do with our sets of rules, concept relationships, and concept to entities relationships. It describes actual knowledge structures within our overall mental models. Our mental model of concepts, sub-concepts, and entities with all their attributes, values, and relationships is typical of this type of knowledge.

In Chapter 8, *Context, situation, and common ground*, we address how context and situation are important notions within pragmatic analysis. Within a dialogue, context helps to differentiate, for example, between *what is said* vs. *what is meant*. The nature of the contribution of context, therefore, is a central area of research interest within pragmatic analysis. We also examine context and its relation to discourse. While theories of speech acts have accounted for some of the properties of speakers and hearers, such as their knowledge, intentions, or beliefs, to formulate appropriateness conditions, in many instances they have not pursued a systematic analysis of contextual conditions. Context draws on knowledge of the world and, as almost anything may become relevant for discourse, a theory of context risks becoming too large and unmanageable. However, not everything that can be understood as a knowledge background to discourse is necessarily part of its context. Developing a theory of context means selecting those elements of a communicative situation that are systematically relevant for the discourse situation. This means that there is a need to examine how situations are defined and determine criteria for what must be included in a theory of context. Context models must inform us as to how participants produce and understand discourse, and enable participants to adapt discourse to the communicative situation at the moment of communicative interaction. We also examine context and common ground, and the way in which common ground mediates the multifaceted relationship between culture and language in interaction, and communication, and how culture informs language usage. Common ground is considered to be a complex distributed structured entity important to the interface between culture, language, and knowledge, where knowledge includes ontology, knowledge representation, reasoning, cultural schemata, cultural metaphors, and cultural conceptualizations. We address the question of how theories of language might effectively characterize contextual knowledge and the cultural connection. One way that functionalist approaches do this is through examining performatives and speech acts, that is, language in interaction and use within a specific culture. We include a case study addressing how we might meet the challenges of context, in a linguistic analysis of two speech acts.

In Chapter 9, *Salience, context, and common ground,* we discuss the nature of salience and its relationship to context and common ground. The factors that correlate with salience are examined. Salience has a special significance in a consideration of the dynamics of the construction and maintenance of common ground, and the management of knowledge and information flow. Some knowledge can become readily available in cognition, more so than other elements of knowledge, in the communicative process. Salience can occur for both a speaker and a hearer and, when convergence occurs for both, the salient "thing" enters common ground and the co-construction of common ground is established. Salience therefore selects contending entities of various kinds as candidates for inclusion into common ground.

Chapter 10 examines *Culture and language in interaction.* We look at language in culture, art, and artifact, and find that there are several ways in which visual artists use words or text in visual art. Words can be used explicitly when they are included in, or on, the visual artwork. We are all familiar with this explicit use of words within medieval art where the words assume a core prominent position. In particular, medieval illuminated manuscripts are a key example of an art form that relies on the cohesive interdependence of graphics and language where words and image contribute equally to the overall reading. In visual art forms, the explicit words are easily recognized, and are widely accepted while generally understood in virtue of the contribution they make. Indeed, as a more contemporary example, we can consider pop art, modern cartoons, and MEMES where words are used as a visual semiotic linguistic device that has a cohesive interdependence with the images displayed. We also focus on an empirical analysis and characterization of elements of the Irish cultural narrative. In this, we are again concerned with the relationship between culture and language, and how culture informs language usage. We posit that common ground mediates this relationship. We examine the application of language in the service of culture, and how we relate to our world through language. Using authentic data (art, artifact, linguistic landscape, and language), we present empirical case studies of facets of culture as a systemic model whose dimensions encompass culture, worldview, common ground, and language. Specifically, as case studies, we examine and analyze: a) the conceptualization of the cultural schema for the celebration of the Joycean Bloomsday in Dublin, as a language related ritual, and its connection with the linguistic landscape, and b) the cultural pragmatic schema and pragmeme of "offers and refusal" relating to tea drinking in an Irish social interaction context. Overall, in the characterization of elements of a particular cultural narrative, we apply a functional-cognitive approach sensitive to cultural issues.

Finally, in Chapter 11, *Some final comments*, we provide a summarizing discussion to this study.

2   Language and culture

2.1   Characterizing language

In this chapter, on language and culture, we characterize language and approaches to its linguistic study. We lay a foundation for examining the relationship between culture, context, and language and make reference to the important linguistic work of Malinowski and Firth. Systemic Functional Linguistics is one linguistic model that takes culture, context, and situation into consideration and we review that approach. We examine the relationship between culture and language and explore the notion of culture, and how it might be defined. It is accepted generally that language is a tool with wide and creative utility that can be put to many useful tasks. The things in the world, entities and actions, are reflected in language. Indeed, language allows us to communicate regarding the collection of "things" of interest to a speech community. In this sense, language can be considered as a cognitive instrument for capturing the shared knowledge ontology of a speech community. Different words and terms can mean different things in different contexts. Cultural misunderstanding, and the possibilities of misinterpretation in discourse, happen because of contexts that are not aligned, the failure to construct a shared common ground, and from cultural differences that occur as the result of differing relations between a language and objects postulated to be in "existence" by that language. How might we usefully define language? One useful definition of language is provided in (1).

---

(1) Definition of language

Merriam-Webster's online dictionary defines language as "a systematic means of communicating ideas or feelings by the use of conventionalized signs, sounds, gestures, or marks having understood meanings."

This definition has value to us for our present purposes. A language is a repository of the riches of highly specialized cultural experiences. Common sense would seem to tell us that if we have a theory of language that begins with the assumption that culture plays no role, then we are not likely to actually notice a role for culture, or any evidence or connections that might exist between language and culture.

2.2 Approaches to linguistics

Functionalist, and indeed cognitive, approaches to linguistics broadly characterize language use within a community of speakers, based primarily on discourse pragmatics and speech acts, from use to lexicon. Functional linguists view language as a communicative tool that is used within a community of speakers to relate experience and mental representation of the external world. How can theories of language characterize the cultural connection? One way that functionalist approaches do this is through examining speech acts, that is, language in interaction and use, and the way that culture and contextual knowledge informs speech act meaning across a discourse.

Views of language have ranged from language as a cognitive system or faculty of the mind, to language as action, as social practice, or as a complex adaptive system (Sharifian 2015a: 20). Culture has similarly been viewed differently by different schools of thought. It has been seen, for example, as a cognitive system, as a symbolic system, as social practice, or as a construct. Cultural Linguistics examines the relationship between language and cultural cognition, and in particular cultural conceptualizations. The major assumption underlying the Cultural Linguistics approach is that many features of language encode cultural–conceptual structures such as cultural schemas, cultural categories, and cultural metaphors. Sharifian (2015a: 33) argues that the semantic and pragmatic meanings that underlie the use of language largely dwell within cultural conceptualizations.

The relationship between language and meaning and its relationship to culture is discussed in Halliday and Hasan (1989) in the context of the SFL approach.

> Linguistics, then, is a kind of semiotics. It is an aspect of the study of meaning. There are many other ways of meaning, other than through language. Language may be, in some rather vague, unidentified sense, the most important, the most comprehensive, the most all-embracing; it is hard to say exactly how. But there are many other modes of meaning, in any culture, which are outside the realm of language.
>
> These will include both art forms such as painting and sculpture, music, the dance, and so forth, and other modes of cultural behaviours that are not classified under the heading of forms of art, such as modes

of exchange, modes of address, structures of the family, and so forth. These are all bearers of meaning in the culture. Indeed, we can define a culture as a set of semiotic systems, a set of systems of meaning, all of which interrelate.

But to explain this general notion, we cannot operate with the concept of a sign as an entity. We have to think rather of systems of meaning, systems that may be considered as operating through some external form of output that we call a sign, but that are in themselves not sets of individual things, but rather networks of relationships. It is in that sense that I would use the term "semiotic" to define the perspective in which we want to look at language: language as one among a number of systems of meaning that, taken all together, constitute human culture.

Halliday and Hasan (1989: 10)

The relationship between language and culture is discussed by Kecskes (2015: 130) from the perspective of context. Adopting a socio-cognitive perspective within an intercultural pragmatics, Kecskes explores the relationship between language, culture, and context, and views culture as a set of shared knowledge structures that capture the norms, values, and customs to which the members of a society have access.

Language reflects the ways that members of a speech community think about the world, their environment, and their contexts. Language, culture, and context are intertwined and inseparable. Both language and context are rooted in culture, and they both are "carriers" of culture and both reflect culture but in a different way. What is encoded in language is a part of culture as well as our past experience with different contexts, while actual situational context represents our distinct, present experience (Kecskes 2015: 131). People who share the same background knowledge will better comprehend each another than interlocutors who do not. For Kecskes, culture in intercultural pragmatics is seen as a socially constituted set of various kinds of knowledge structures that individuals turn to as relevant situations permit, enable, and usually encourage. It is a system of shared beliefs, norms, values, customs, behaviors, and artifacts that the members of society use to cope with their world and with one another. Within the framework of Kecskes' socio-cognitive approach, meaning is the result of the interplay between these two forms of context. An important characteristic of culture is that it is differentially distributed, and that not all the members of a given social or cultural group reflect their common culture in a similar way in every moment and every circumstance. Culture has fuzzy boundaries, and it is considered not rigidly stable but ever-changing over time. It has both a priori and emergent features. Culture changes slowly through the decades, and emerges in real time in the moment of speech.

Language functions to channel our thoughts into linguistic signs by formulating utterances, and at the same time it helps speakers shape their thoughts by offering a variety of linguistic options for foregrounding or backgrounding as suits the context. No linguistic sign or expression can be independent of context because they carry prior context, they encode the history of their prior context in a speech community (Kecskes 2015: 132). Furthermore, the socio-cognitive approach of Kecskes (2003, 2010, 2013) argues that context is a dynamic construct that appears in different formats in language use both as a repository and trigger of knowledge. As such, in this approach, context represents two sides of world knowledge: one that is in our mind as prior context and the other, as actual situational context, out there in the world (Kecskes and Mey 2008). Prior experience that becomes declarative knowledge is tied to the meaning values of lexical units constituting utterances produced by interlocutors, while current experience is represented in the actual situational context (procedural knowledge) in which communication takes place, and which is interpreted (often differently) by interlocutors (Kecskes 2015: 133).

Therefore, language encodes prior contexts and is used to make sense of actual situational contexts, so language is never context-free. As such, there are no meanings that are context-free because each lexical item is a repository of context itself and is always implicitly indexed to a prior recurring context of reference. Even when an actual situational context is not available, one is constructed from stored knowledge originating in prior experience during the process of comprehension (Kecskes 2015: 135–136). Each culture organizes their background knowledge differently. The act of translating from one language to another requires that we formulate a reconstruction of cognitive and cultural configurations prompted by the source language, with a determination of how the target language would set up similar configurations with an appropriate meaning.

2.3   Culture, context, and language

In this discussion, we set the background for showing how linguistics is engaging with the idea of culture, context, and knowledge. Discourse is viewed as language in the contexts of its use, broadly above the level of the sentence and as a system of knowledge and beliefs.

Language is the expression of a speech community. Language is a cultural achievement and a cultural tool (Senft 2009a:6). Language is a mirror of the culture of its speech community. Humboldt emphasized the strong interrelationship between language, culture, and cognition. Indeed, Humboldt (1830–1835: 426) considered language as the "creative organ of thought". The difference between languages represents a difference in worldviews (Humboldt 1820: 20), and in every language rests a specific worldview (Humboldt 1830–1835: 224, 434).

For Malinowski, language meaning is its function within context (Senft 2009a:7). Malinowski bound language to the situational moments and cultural contexts of use in his theory of "context of situation". His approach tried to ground the idea of context and make it operationally usable. Malinowski (1935: 58) understood language "in its primitive function" as a mode of behavior, as a mode of action, rather than as a countersign of thought. For him language is not only an instrument of thought, but first and foremost a tool for creating social bonds and accountability relations in more or less ritualized forms of social interaction. In his pragmatic theory of meaning the insight that the meaning of a word lies in its use is central. Thus, to study meaning one cannot examine isolated words but one must consider sentences or utterances in their situational context; the real understanding of words is always ultimately derived from active experience of those aspects of reality to which the words belong.

This consideration is echoed by Silverstein (1975: 167) when, in a paper on Linguistics and Anthropology, he identified one of the aims of (anthropological) linguistics to be the conduct of research into the function of speech behavior. He makes the following programmatic statement:

>…the study of grammar cannot in principle be carried on in any serious way until we tackle the ethnographic description of the canons of use of the messages corresponding to sentences. Reformulating this result, we may say that grammar is open-ended, not closed, and a part of the statement of the total meaning of a sentence is a statement of the rules of use that are involved in proper indexicality of elements of the message. This means, again, that if we call the "function" of a sentence the way in which the corresponding message depends on the context of situation, then the determination of the function of the sentence, independent of its propositional value, is a necessary step in any linguistic analysis. Thus a theory of rules of use, in terms of social variables of the speech situation and dependent message form, is an integral part of a grammatical description of the abstract sentences underlying them.

> Rules of use depend on ethnographic description, that is, on analysis
> of cultural behavior of people in a society. Thus, at one level we can
> analyze sentences as the embodiment of propositions, or of linguistic
> meanings more generally; at another level, which is always implied in
> any grammatical description, we must analyze messages as linguistic
> behavior which is part of culture…a valid description of a language by
> grammar demands description of the rules of use in speech situations
> that are structured by, and index, the variables of cultures.
>
> Silverstein (1975: 167)

As well as his work on context of situation, Malinowski (1923) was also interested in practical or pragmatic uses of language, the functions of language.
On the one hand, he subdivided pragmatic uses of language into active and
narrative and, on the other hand, the category of ritual or *magical* uses of
language that were associated with ceremonial or religious activities in a culture (Halliday and Hasan 1989: 15). Senft (2009b: 210–225), in reviewing
the influence of Bronislaw Malinowski on linguistics research, points out
that language is best understood as a tool for creating social bonds, a mode
of communicative behavior, and the meaning of an utterance is constituted
by its pragmatic function.

2.4   Malinowski and Firthian linguistics

Malinowski (1935), in his research work, considered language as a seamless part of everyday life, and he created his theory of "context of situation"
around this view, whereby language is bound to situational moments and
cultural contexts of its use (Ager 2009: 111). Firth was heavily influenced
by Malinowski's work on language within the social process and created a
model of language where context is shown to have a central role. In Firth's
view, meaning is function within context. The characterization and contextualization of an utterance in the context of a situation must be embedded
in the context of culture. Situations take their meaning from the cultural
context.

The foundation of what has become known as Firthian linguistics (Östman & Simon-Vandenbergen 2009) was created by Malinowski (1923) with
his article, "The problem of meaning in primitive languages". In this, he
tried to characterize the interaction between meaning and culture. His concern was with discourse as it functions in a particular situation. He was led
to the conclusion that one cannot understand the meaning of language unless

the situation in which an utterance was made is considered. Malinowski emphasized the crucial importance of context of situation within a culture.

Firth abstracted a number of features (2) within a contextual frame of reference within his theory.

(2) Firth's features within a contextual frame of reference

1. The relevant features of participants and their roles
    a. The verbal action(s) of the participants
    b. Non-verbal actions[1]
2. Relevant objects
3. The effect(s) resulting from the verbal action

To make this operationally usable in theory development and linguistic characterization, it is necessary to ground such factors including background knowledge, framing devices, schemata and scripts, and the interrelationship between linguistics of cognitive structure. These are problems of contemporary pragmatics.

2.5 Culture, context, and situation in Systemic Functional Linguistics

Context of situation is viewed as a construct encompassing meaning relations and, as such, contains features that inform meaning in a dialogue. These contextual features are dynamically updated and realized by specific language utterances in a given situation. For Halliday (2014: 51), language operates in context, and language is always characterized within an environment of meanings: "a given language is thus interpreted by reference to its semiotic habitat". In this, Halliday is influenced by Malinowski and Firth. In particular, Halliday notes that:

---

[1] Examples of nonverbal communication cues would include body language such as facial expressions, posture and gestures, eye contact as people typically look for information in the eyes, one's distance from people during communication, nonverbal use of the voice such as a gasp or a sigh, and a touch such as a handshake or "high five".

The contextual potential of a community is its culture – what we call the context of culture. The context of culture is what the members of a community can mean in cultural terms. We interpret culture as a system of higher-level meanings, as an environment of meanings in which various semiotic systems operate, including language, paralanguage (gesture, facial expression, voice quality, timbre, tempo, and other systems of meaning accompanying language and expressed through the human body) and other human systems of meaning such as dance, drawing, painting and architecture.

Halliday (2014: 52)

Operationally, however, as Halliday (2014: 52) observes, describing the culture of a community is a huge undertaking and it is easier to take on the task of describing a particular cultural domain based on evidence gathered from the various contexts of situation operating within that domain. While there are still no comprehensive descriptions of the context of culture, of specific cultures, within Systemic Functional Linguistics (SFL), the general categories of context (3) have been explored under the headings of FIELD, TENOR, and MODE, and any situation type has the potential to be characterized in these terms within SFL (Halliday 2014: 52–54).

Specifically, MODE is glossed as "the nature of contact", while TENOR is glossed as "the nature of social relation", and FIELD is glossed as "the nature of social activity". Bowcher (2018) characterizes FIELD as concerning the nature of the activity and its content, with MODE to do with the nature of the means of communication in the situation and how this affects the language used. TENOR then is about the nature of the participants with respect to one another in the situation. In this model, FIELD, TENOR, and MODE are sets of related variables, with ranges of contrasting values that define a multi-dimensional semiotic space – the environment of meanings in which language, other semiotic systems and social systems operate. The combinations of FIELD, TENOR, and MODE values are held to determine the different uses of language and so form the basis for any attempt to develop a taxonomy of situations.

Halliday (2014: 54) considers the activity that constitutes a situation as either one of behavior or one of meaning such that a) "DOING": a situation is constituted in some form of social behavior, involving one or more people. Language, or other semiotic systems such as gesture, gaze, and facial expression, may be engaged to facilitate the performance of the activity, or b) "MEANING": the situation is constituted in some process of meaning.

Halliday (2007: 275) diagrammed the dual set of perspectives on context and situation, and the relationship between these two (Figure 2.1), as characterizing the foundations of a functional semantics: a theory of meaning relevant to applied linguistic concerns.

---

(3)   Halliday's characterization of situation types via terms of field, tenor and mode (based on Halliday 2014)

- FIELD – *what's going on in the situation:*
    - (i)   the nature of the social and semiotic activity; and
    - (ii)   the domain of experience this activity relates to ("subject matter" or "topic")
- TENOR – *who is taking part in the situation:*
    - (i)   the roles played by those taking part in the socio-semiotic activity –
        - (1)   institutional roles,
        - (2)   status roles (power, either equal or unequal),
        - (3)   contact roles (familiarity, ranging from strangers to intimates),
        - (4)   sociometric roles (affect, either neutral or charged, positively or negatively);
    - (ii)   the values that the interactants imbue the domain with (either neutral or loaded, positively or negatively)
- MODE – *what role is being played by language and other semiotic systems in the situation:*
    - (i)   the division of labor between semiotic activities and social ones (ranging from semiotic activities as constitutive of the situation to semiotic activities as facilitating);
    - (ii)   the division of labor between linguistic and other semiotic activities;
    - (iii) rhetorical mode: the orientation of the text towards FIELD (e.g. informative, didactic, explanatory, explicatory) or TENOR (e.g. persuasive, exhortatory, hortatory, polemic);
    - (iv)   turn: dialogic or monologic;
    - (v)   medium: written or spoken;
    - (vi)   channel: phonic or graphic.

It has been argued that the concepts of Malinowski and of Firth only become powerful, abstract tools with Halliday's theorization in SFL and its semiotic dimensions, and with his elaboration of relations between text, context, and register.

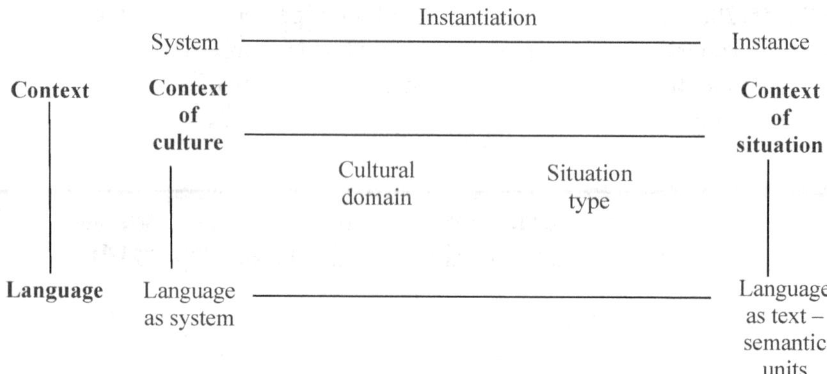

Figure 2.1 Language and context; system and instance (adapted from Halliday 2007: 275).

Halliday and Hasan characterize text within a functional social-semiotic perspective:

What do we mean by text? We can define text, in the simplest way perhaps, by saying that it is language that is functional. By functional, we simply mean language that is doing some job in some context, as opposed to isolated words or sentences that I might put on the black-board. [...] So any instance of living language that is playing some part in a contest of situation, we shall call text. It may be either spoken or written, or indeed in any other medium of expression that we like to think of.

Now, with the sort of social-semiotic perspective that we are adopting here, we would see text in its "process" aspect as an interactive event, a social exchange of meaning. Text is a form of exchange; and the fundamental form of a text is that of a dialogue, of interaction between speakers. Not that dialogue is more important than other kinds of text; but in the last resort, every kind of text in every language is meaningful amongst speakers, and ultimately to ordinary everyday spontaneous conversation. That is the kind of text where people exploit to the full the resources of language that they have; the kind of situation in which they improvise, in which they innovate, in which changes in the system take place. The leading edge of unconscious change and development in any language is typically to be found in its natural conversational texts – in this context of talk as the interpersonal exchange of meanings.

Halliday and Hasan (1989: 13)

Additionally, Halliday and Hasan view the context of situation and the wider context of culture, as follows:

> The context of situation and the wider context of culture make up the non-verbal environment of a text. We have spoken here of these as "determining" the text. Stressing the predictability of the text from the context; and this is an important perspective, since it helps us to understand how people actually exchange meaning and interact with one another. But in fact the relationship between text and context is a dialectical one; the text creates the context as much as the context creates the text. "Meaning" arises from the friction between the two. This means that part of the environment for any text is a set of previous texts, texts that are taken for granted as shared amongst those taking part. Again, the school provides very clear examples. Every lesson is built on the assumption of earlier lessons in which the topics have been explored, concepts agreed upon and defined; but beyond this there is a great deal of unspoken cross-reference of which everyone is largely aware.
>
> This kind of INTERTEXTUALITY, as it is sometimes called, includes not only the more obviously experiential features that make up the context of a lesson but also other aspects of the meaning; types of logical sequencing that are recognised as valid, even interpersonal features such as whether a question is intended to be answered or is being used as a step in the development of an argument. There are also likely to be "coded" expressions that are carried on from one text to another, more or less formulaic sequences that may signal what is happening, or what is going to happen next.
>
> Halliday and Hasan (1989: 31)

However, van Dijk (2008: 44–45) offers a critique of SFL as a model that directly concerns itself with a theory of context, and in which context is an analytical level of description available in the scientific investigation of language, as system and social activity (see also Halliday 2014, Butler 2003: vol. 1 and 2). SFL has been influenced by both Firth and Malinowski. The notion of context was introduced in Firthian linguistics as the context of situation, where this should be understood as situational context, rather than the narrower linguistic context of words and sentences. Notwithstanding SFL's notion of context, van Dijk (2008: 45) criticizes the model as having significant limitations which are due to theoretical defects within its general approach to language and discourse. He summarizes these defects as:

...too much linguistic ("lexico-syntactic") sentence grammar; too few autonomous discourse-theoretical notions; anti-mentalism; a lack of interest in cognition; limited social theory of language; too much esoteric vocabulary; too little theoretical dynamism, development and self-criticism.

van Dijk (2008: 45)

While, as we mentioned, the theory of SFL was influenced by the thinking of Malinowski and Firth, and as such rejected any form of mentalism and cognitive accounts of discourse, van Dijk (2009: 25) observes that, notwithstanding the influence of Malinowski and Firth on SFL, notions such as knowledge, and the idea of shared knowledge and common ground which are crucial in context and the definition of presupposition, coherence, and semantics, cannot be defined in the SFL framework. That is, despite its functional and semiotic aims, SFL fails to provide an explicit theory of communicative situations. As a theory of language use, it does not offer the necessary levels and structures of discourse needed to be related to such communicative situations. In his account of the context of situation, Halliday (1978), following Malinowski and Firth, lists the following properties (4) of context (van Dijk 2008: 53):

---

(4)   Halliday's properties of context

(a)   Language is used, and must be studied, in relation to its social environment.
(b)   Contexts only feature relevant aspects of situations.
(c)   Contexts are learned as general and abstract types of situation.

Van Dijk (2008: 58) asks the question: What does SFL offer for a theory of discourse that goes beyond the traditional distinction between syntax, semantics and pragmatics with which it partially overlaps, and should the SFL theory not introduce more fundamental functions, including cultural functions? Van Dijk considers it odd that SFL ignores these fundamental functions of language, each of which can be systematically associated with language use or discourse structure. Contexts are assumed by van Dijk (2008: 62) to be dynamic participant constructs, that is, mental models, continually updated by language users. A theory of context as an abstraction cannot account for such dynamics – unless it is done in some kind of formal pragmatics, but that is not what SF offers. The SFL view of context indicates that the non-cognitive stance of SFL does not allow for the representation of the mental properties of contexts, such as the knowledge, and the beliefs, desires, and intentions of the participants. Therefore, they cannot define the appropriateness conditions of speech acts, or speaker knowledge (van Dijk 2008: 234). In SFL, context itself is defined by the three notions of FIELD, TENOR, and MODE, which appear to be vaguely and inconsistently defined so as to not be insightful into language use. According to van Dijk (2008: 46), the serious consequence of these defects for SFL is that despite its claim to provide a functional theory of language, the limited social theory and non-existent cognitive theory do not meet the levels of adequacy needed for a robust functional theory of language use and discourse.

2.6   The relationship between culture and language

The relationship between culture and language is a long-standing topic of inquiry reaching back to the Humboldtian tradition where the language and culture link found expression in grammatical terms, worldview, and ideas of nationhood and national characteristics. Intercultural communications is about what happens when one language-culture meets with another. Culture in intercultural communication is not clearly defined yet within intercultural communication research and its associated scientific community. Our understanding of culture, according to Serangi (2009: 82), has transformed from something to do with cultivation of the human mind to something to do with a way of life. Kroeber and Kluckhohn (1952) offer a taxonomy of definitions of culture organized along descriptive, historical, psychological, and structural lines. These definitions of culture draw attention to a) the totality implied in the culture concept in that every aspect of a community's social life is absorbed in culture, and b) the organizing principle underpinning the social structure of a community where culture is synonymous with social system.

Many definitions, however, do not articulate the relationship of cultural elements to one another and their relationships to non-cultural elements in a society (Serangi 2009: 84). The interrelationships between a person and their society are an important aspect of culture as individuals inhabit their culture and the culture comes alive through people. Notwithstanding the many different properties of culture found across the many definitions, for Serangi (2009: 84–86), there are three main approaches to characterizing culture. The mentalist approach defines culture as "that complex whole which includes knowledge, belief, art, morals, law, custom, and any other capabilities, and habits acquired by man as a member of a society" (Tylor 1871). Culture is a precondition for an individual's membership of a societal group. Individual actions are executed according to various cultural scripts and schemata. Equating cultures with an individual's thoughts, feelings, beliefs, and values, has the effect of making this notion of culture abstract and it conflates various aspects of human capabilities to do with knowledge, belief, and worldview. The behaviorist approach to understanding culture characterizes it as a learned behavior in the absence of explicit teaching, such that members of a group have a choice of selection that is constrained by what counts as acceptable practice socially. Such an approach recognizes the importance of human agency and the possibility of social change, and that patterns of behaviors reflecting beliefs and values are not always fixed but contextually and socially shaped. Serangi (2009: 86) puts this very well: Culture is viewed as a map *for* behavior rather than a map *of* behavior. The semiotic approach to culture views culture as a system of symbolic meanings. Culture is used to consolidate sameness and distinctive forms of identity within sub-groups as a source of identity construction.

To demand of a grammar that it represent language use in context is often argued to be unreasonable because to do so would lead us "into a maze of more and more elaborate and complex analytic procedures that will fail to provide answers for many important questions about the nature of linguistic structure" (Chomsky 2002: 52–53). This is undoubtedly one of the reasons why the notion that syntax is autonomous is so attractive. Such a stance prevents theoretical models from becoming too complicated (De Busser 2015: 9), and consequently, in many linguistic theories, the non-linguistic context is often largely excluded from grammatical description and interpretation as a working assumption. However, De Busser argues that there is an ever-growing mountain of evidence which suggests that there are plenty of complex interactions between language and its environment, and that in certain cases these interactions have a measurable influence on language and its structures.

Dik (1987: 83) had an instrumentalist view on language as a tool used in the establishment of complex patterns of social interaction, realized through the interaction of syntax, semantics, and pragmatics that can be encoded in a formal-logical model. Davidse (1987: 47–49), discussing Halliday's Systemic-Functional model, argues that linguistic structure arises from environmentally imposed constraints on a speaker's creative potential and takes the form of "systematic relations [...] between semantic system networks and behavior patterns on the one hand and between semantic networks and the lexicogrammar on the other". Accordingly, for De Busser (2015: 30), language should not be considered to be an autonomous system, as its interactions with its environment are more varied and complex than we had previously assumed. One example of this is found with Daniel Everett (2005) in his description of Pirahã, a language isolate spoken in the Brazilian Amazon. Everett noted the absence of several linguistic features that are often considered as basic to any human language, such as a counting system, color terms, and grammatical embedding and recursion (two of the pillars of formal linguistic theory). He argued that this is due to the world view of the Pirahã people, with the implication that, cross-linguistically, "some of the components of so-called core grammar are subject to cultural constraints" (Everett 2005: 622). The views of Everett, that culture exerts an influence on linguistic structure of the Pirahã, proved to be very controversial as it attacked some of the basic assumptions of formal theories of languages.

The concept of linguistic relativity was originally formulated by Whorf (1940), but the idea itself was probably best expressed by Sapir (1921: 221), who stated that "language does not exist apart from culture, that is, from the socially inherited assemblage of practices and beliefs that determines the texture of our lives" (De Busser 2015: 10). A weak form of the Sapir–Whorf hypothesis is that language facilitates one's perceptions and experience of reality. The strong version is that language in a community determines how native speakers codify, categorize, and create their cognitive structures and so determines our perception of reality (Sapir 1921: 578). It has been observed that the Sapir–Whorf hypothesis searches for isomorphisms between grammar and culture, and views language as providing the means for thought, perception, and worldview. Language is a dimension of culture, as we argue, because it is through language that our culture is learned, explained, and perpetuated across time. Language is not just a carrier of culture values and norms. It plays a direct role in maintaining cultural practices. Hall (1959: 53) suggests that "culture hides much more than it reveals, and strangely enough, it hides most effectively from its own participants". This captures the elusive quality of culture from the perspective of cultural agents in given societies.

We will here assume, as with De Busser (2015: 11), that a weak interpretation of linguistic relativity is appropriate, with the implication that culture does exert some influence on, but does not fully determine, linguistic structure, and that the interaction between culture and language is actually bidirectional. For De Busser, a basic assumption is that every single element in the extralinguistic environment, whether it is cognitive, social, cultural, biological, or physical, should be treated as a potential factor of influence on the structure of languages.

We still have the difficulty in showing how communication at a given time is bound by culture, or how culture finds continuous expression in communication. The term "cultural communication" suggests two separate entities whereas they really are actually bound together integrally such that culture is found within the use of language. For Wittgenstein, *Lebenswelt* "way of life" of the speaker has embedded within it the *Sprachspiel* (language game). When Wittgenstein uses the term "form of life" *Lebensform*, he indicates the "intertwining of culture, worldview, and culture" (Glock 1996: 124). Further, Wittgenstein (2009 edition) was of the considered opinion that language-games are "part of", embedded in, a form of life (from Philosophical Investigations §§23–5).

We next present one definition of culture, due to Ward H. Goodenough. There are many other definitions of culture, as we will see in the next section on the notion of culture.

A society's culture consists of whatever it is one has to show in order to operate in a manner acceptable to its members, and to do so in any role that they may accept for any one of themselves. Culture being what people have to learn as distinct from biological heritage, and must consist of the end product of learning: knowledge in a most general if relative, sense of the term [...] Culture is not a material phenomenon: it does not consist of things, people, behaviours, or emotions. It is rather an organisation of these things. It is the form of things that people have in mind, their models for perceiving, relating and otherwise interpreting them. As such, the things people say and do, their social arrangements and events, are products or by-products of their culture as they apply it to the task of perceiving and dealing with their circumstances

Goodenough (1964: 36)

2.7   The notion of culture

In this section we examine in some more detail the notion of culture, and how one might seek to define it in some appropriate way. Culture is quite an abstract, and complex, term that has been defined in a large multitude of ways by various scholars over the years. Typically, culture is defined as somehow concerning the beliefs, values, rules, norms, symbols, and traditions that are common to a group of people. However, as we will see, it seems there is (still) no unifying definition of culture. In 1952, Alfred Kroeber and Clyde Kluckhohn compiled a list of 164 definitions of culture in *Culture: A*

Critical Review of Concepts and Definitions. This list was, even then, non-exhaustive! We will examine some of these definitions here, following.

These definitions of culture are grouped by similarity or relatedness by Kroeber and Kluckhohn (1952) under various cluster headings (Table 2.1). In undertaking this review, Kroeber and Kluckhohn (1952: 8) remind us that Malinowski (1931: 588) referred to culture as the most central problem of all social science. Noting that culture is not unconditionally interchangeable with civilization, Kroeber and Kluckhohn (1952: 12) posed the simple but actually very tricky question: *What do we mean by culture?*

In that same review, with respect to culture, Kroeber and Kluckhohn (1952: 45) remind us that all definitions are constructed from some particular point of view but which point of view is very often left unstated. Not all definitions of culture are substantive and some of the definitions are functional in intent. Others are characterized as epistemological in that they point to the phenomena and process by which we gain our knowledge of culture. Some definitions of culture look to the actions of the individual as the start point of generalizations. In this section, then, we provide a representative selection of these definitions from within each of the groupings of Kroeber and Kluckhohn (1952), while drawing on a few points of interest. The reader will be pleased to know that we do not rehearse each individual definition here from the 164 definitions, just a representative selection across each cluster group, with discussion – the interested reader is recommended to consult the Kroeber and Kluckhohn (1952) work.

Table 2.1 Grouping of definitions of culture in Kroeber & Kluckhohn (1952)

Group	Clustering of definitions of culture	Definition in
A	Emphasis on enumeration of content	1952: 46
B	Emphasis on social heritage or tradition	1952: 50
C	Emphasis on way of life	1952: 53
D	Emphasis on psychological dimension of culture	1952: 58
	i. Emphasis on learning	
	ii. Emphasis on habit	1952: 61
	iii. Purely psychological definitions	1952: 63
E	Structural dimensions of culture, art, artifact, and activities	1952: 64
F	Culture as a product or artifact	1952: 67
	i. Emphasis on ideas	1952: 69
	ii. Emphasis on symbols	1952: 72
	iii. Residual category definitions	1952: 73
G	"Incomplete" definitions	1952: 75

The first group identified by Kroeber and Kluckhohn (1952: 46) is to do with gathering definitions that emphasize the enumeration of cultural content. Kroeber and Kluckhohn make the comment that these definitions seem to have been influenced by Tylor (1871: 1).

---

(5)   Group A: Definitions with emphasis on enumeration of content

a.   Culture, or civilization[2],... is that complex whole which includes knowledge, belief, art, law, morals, custom, and any other capabilities and habits acquired by man as a member of society.
        Tylor (1871: 1) (Kroeber and Kluckhohn 1952: 46)
b.   Culture in general as a descriptive concept means the accumulated treasury of human creation: books, paintings, buildings, and the like; the knowledge of ways of adjusting to our surroundings, both human and physical; language, customs, and systems of etiquette, ethics, religion, and morals that have been built up through the ages.
    Kluckhohn and Kelly (1945: 96) (Kroeber and Kluckhohn 1952: 47)

The second group identified by Kroeber and Kluckhohn (1952: 50) relates to groupings of definitions that place emphasis on the historical basis of the tradition of social heritage. Kroeber and Kluckhohn (1952: 51) note that these definitions select one feature of culture, social heritage, or social tradition, rather than trying to define culture substantively.

---

(6)   Group B: Historical emphasis on social heritage or tradition

a.   Culture, that is,...the socially inherited assemblage of practices and beliefs that determines the texture of our lives...
    Sapir (1921: 221) (Kroeber and Kluckhohn 1952: 50)
b.   This social heritage is the key concept of cultural anthropology. It is usually called culture... Culture comprises inherited artefacts, goods, technical processes, ideas, habits, and values.
        Malinowski (1931: 621) (Kroeber and Kluckhohn 1952: 50)

---

[2] Both British and American spelling are to be found within these definitions, depending on the original author. We leave these spellings as in the original source.

The third group used by Kroeber and Kluckhohn (1952: 53) gathers those definitions that emphasize mode or way of life, and the social rules governing behaviors. Kroeber and Kluckhohn (1952: 54) note that Wissler's (1929) statement regarding the *mode* or *way of life* followed by the community is actually the concept of the customs of a community raised into a totalizing generalization, where the word "mode" or "way" can imply: (a) common or shared patterns; (b) sanctions for failure to follow the rules; (c) a manner, or *how* to behave; (d) social blueprints for action.

(7)   Group C: Emphasis on rule or way of life

a.   The mode of life followed by the community or the tribe is regarded as a culture… [It] includes all standardized social procedures…a tribal culture is…the aggregate of standardised beliefs and procedures followed by the tribe.
Wissler (1929: 15, 341) (Kroeber and Kluckhohn 1952: 53)

b.   Culture applies to that whole *way of life* which is determined by the social environment. To paraphrase Tylor, it includes all the capabilities and habits acquired by an individual as a member of a particular society.
Klineberg (1935: 233) (Kroeber and Kluckhohn 1952: 53)

c.   Culture: the behaviour patterns of all groups, called the *way of life*: an observable feature of all human groups; the fact of "culture" is common to all; the particular pattern of culture differs among all. "A culture": the specific pattern of behaviour which distinguishes any society from all others.
Bennett and Tumin (1949: 209) (Kroeber and Kluckhohn 1952: 54)

The fourth group of Kroeber and Kluckhohn (1952: 58) concerned those definitions with a psychological dimension where the emphasis is on learning or habit, culture as a problem-solving device.

(8)   Group D: Definitions with a psychological dimension

a.   Through this process of inventing and transmitting symbols and symbolic systems and technologies as well as their non-symbolic counterparts in concrete tools and instruments, man's experience and his adjustment technique become cumulative. This societal behaviour,

> together with its man-made products, in their interaction with other aspects of human environment, creates a constantly changing series of phenomena and situations to which man must continually adjust through the development of further habits achieved by the same process. The concrete manifestations of these processes are usually described by the vague word culture.
>
> > Lundberg (1939: 179) (Kroeber and Kluckhohn 1952: 58)
>
> b. Culture consists in behaviour patterns transmitted by imitation or tuition. … Culture includes all behaviour patterns socially acquired and socially transmitted.
>
> > Hart and Pantzer (1925: 703, 705) (Kroeber and Kluckhohn 1952: 61)
>
> c. Culture is the sum total of integrated learned behaviour patterns which are characteristic of the members of a society and which are, therefore, not the result of biological inheritance.
>
> > Hoebel (1949: 3, 4) (Kroeber and Kluckhohn 1952: 61)
>
> d. Culture is generally understood to mean learned modes of behaviour which are socially transmitted from one generation to another within particular societies and which may be diffused from one society to another.
>
> > Steward (1950: 98) (Kroeber and Kluckhohn 1952: 61)

The fifth grouping relates to structural considerations within the definition of culture (Kroeber and Kluckhohn 1952: 64). These definitions involve reference to material and non-material dimensions of culture, as well as art, artifact, and activities.

> **(9)   Group E: Definitions of structural dimensions of culture, art, artifact, and activities**
>
> a. A culture consists of inventions, or culture traits, integrated into a system, with varying degrees of correlation between the parts. … Both material and non-material traits, organized around the satisfaction of the basic human needs, give us our social institutions, which are the heart of culture. The institutions of a culture are interlinked to form a pattern which is unique for each society.
>
> > Ogburn and Nimkoff (1940: 63) (Kroeber and Kluckhohn 1952: 64)
>
> b. An organisation of conventional understandings manifest in act and artefact, which, persisting through tradition, characterises a human group.
>
> > Redfield (1940, quoted in Ogburn and Nimkoff 1940: 25)
> > (Kroeber and Kluckhohn 1952: 64)

The sixth grouping gathers those definitions that Kroeber and Kluckhohn (1952: 67) consider to reflect culture as fabrication, reflecting a sense of man, the maker of culture, with an emphasis on ideas, symbols, and material culture and artifacts. Kroeber and Kluckhohn (1952: 70) note that, strictly speaking, there is no such thing as material culture: A pot is an artifact, not culture itself – what is culture is the *idea* behind the artifact.

---

(10) Group F: Culture as fabrication, idea, symbol, or artifact

a. The term culture is used to signify the sum-total of human creations, the organised result of human experience up to the present time. Culture includes all that man has made in the form of tools, weapons, shelter, and other material goods and processes, all that he has elaborated in the way of attitudes and beliefs, ideas and judgments, codes, and institutions, arts and sciences, philosophy and social organization. Culture also includes the interrelations among these and other aspects of human as distinct from animal life. Everything, material and immaterial, created by man, in the process of living, comes within the concept of culture.

> Reuter (1939: 19) (Kroeber and Kluckhohn 1952: 67)

b. By culture we mean every object, habit, idea, institution, and mode of thought or action which man produces or creates and then passes on to others, especially to the next generation.

> Huntington (1945: 7-8) (Kroeber and Kluckhohn 1952: 68)

c. Culture is an organization of phenomena – material objects, bodily acts, ideas, and sentiments – which consists of or is dependent upon the use of symbols.

> White (1943: 335) (Kroeber and Kluckhohn 1952: 72)

d. 'Culture' is the name of a distinct order, or class, of phenomena, namely, those things and events that are dependent upon the exercise of a mental ability, peculiar to the human species, that we have termed "symbolling". To be more specific, culture consists of material objects – tools, utensils, ornaments, amulets, etc. – acts, beliefs, and attitudes that function in contexts characterised by symbolling. It is an elaborate mechanism, an organization of exosomatic ways and means employed by a particular animal species, man, in the struggle for existence or survival.

> White (1949: 363) (Kroeber and Kluckhohn 1952: 73)

Exosomatic memory is the recording of memories outside the brain and, as used in White's definition of culture (10d), is defined as being from outside of the body. Kroeber and Kluckhohn (1952: 73) comment that a common view is that the true nature of man is a symbol-using animal, rather than a rational or a culture-building animal. There is therefore much to be said for referring to the use of symbols in a definition of culture (Kroeber and Kluckhohn 1952: 73). The earliest forms of symbolic behavior, that of scratching marks on bones, are generally considered as instances of exosomatic memory.

The final, seventh, grouping of definitions (Kroeber and Kluckhohn 1952: 75) serves as a catch-all for definitions that do not easily fit into any other the other groupings, even though many definitions could actually, and easily, appear in several other clusters.

---

(11) Group G: "Incomplete" definitions

a.   Culture may be defined as *what* a society does and thinks.
                          Sapir (1921: 233) (Kroeber and Kluckhohn 1952: 75)
b.   Culture will be conceived of as comprising the actual artefacts, plus any ideas or behaviour of the people who made them which can be inferred from these specimens.
                          Osgood (1942: 22) (Kroeber and Kluckhohn 1952: 75)

Kroeber and Kluckhohn (1952: 86–127) summarize their discussion of culture in terms of culture and civilization, along with some general features of culture in terms of what they call integration, historicity, uniformities, causality, significance and values, values and relativity.

---

(12) The nature of culture

a.   [Culture includes] on the one hand, the whole of man's *material* civilisation, tools, weapons, clothing, shelter, machines, and even systems of industry; and, on the other hand all of *non-material* or spiritual civilisation, such as language, literature, art, religion, ritual, morality, law, and government.
                          Ellwood (1927: 9) (Kroeber and Kluckhohn 1952: 86)
b.   [Culture] may be defined as the artificial objects, institutions, and modes of life or of thought which are not peculiarly individual but

which characterize a group; it is "that complex whole…" [repeating Tylor]. (9)

Culture is the life of a people as typified in contacts, institutions, and equipment. It includes characteristic concepts and behaviour, customs and traditions. (13)

Culture, then, means all those things, institutions, material objects, typical reactions to situations, which characterise a people and distinguish them from other peoples. (32)

Wallis (1930: 9, 13, 32) (Kroeber and Kluckhohn 1952: 86)

c. Most modern authors are agreed, whether explicitly or not, upon certain very general assumptions about the nature of the material they study. They consider the acts of individuals not in isolation but as members of society and call the sum total of these modes of behaviour "culture". They are impressed also by the dynamic interrelationship of items of a culture, each item tending to vary according to the nature of the others. They recognise too that in every culture there are certain features common to all: groups such as the family, institutions such as marriage, and complex forms of practice and belief which can be aggregated under the name of religion. On the basis of this they argue for the existence of universally comparable factors and processes, the description and explanation of which can be given in sociological laws or general principles of culture.

Firth (1939: 18–19) (Kroeber and Kluckhohn 1952: 88)

d. The word "culture" has many different meanings. As a psychologist I would define culture in accordance with its dictionary meaning in English, as the process by which a human individual acquires, through contact with other individuals, or from such things as books and works of art, habits, capabilities, ideas, beliefs, knowledge, skills, tastes, and sentiments; and, by an extension common in the English language, the products of that process in the individual.

Radcliffe-Brown (1949: 510–11) (Kroeber and Kluckhohn 1952: 88)

It is observed by Kroeber and Kluckhohn (1952: 95) that, in their definitions of culture, both Firth (1939) and Radcliffe-Brown (1949) stress the dynamic interrelations of activities within a culture. In addition, Radcliffe-Brown actually narrows the concept of culture, to be the process by which language, beliefs, usages, etc., are handed on, and cultural tradition is a social process of interaction of persons within a social structure.

---

(13) The components of culture

a. The stuff of which culture is composed is capable of analysis into the following categories: Speech – Material traits – Art – Mythology – Knowledge – Religion – Family and Social systems – Property – Government and War. Any of these components of culture does not by itself, however, form an independent unit, but is closely bound up with the rest through many ties of association.

Bose (1929: 25) (Kroeber and Kluckhohn 1952: 97)

---

(14) Distinctive properties of culture

a. Culture consists essentially in the external storage, interchange, and transmission of an accumulating fund of personal and social experience by means of tools and symbols... Culture is the unique, distinctive, and exclusive possession of man, explainable thus far only in terms of itself.

Case (1927: 920) (Kroeber and Kluckhohn 1952: 101)

---

(15) Culture and psychology

a. Cultural configurations stand to the understanding of group behaviour in the relation that personality types stand to the understanding of individual behaviour. ... It is recognized that the organization of the total personality is crucial in the understanding or even in the mere description of individual behaviour. If this is true in individual psychology where individual differentiation must be limited always by the cultural forms and by the short span of a human lifetime, it is even more imperative in social psychology where the limitations of time and of conformity are transcended. The degree of integration that may be attained is of course incomparably greater than can ever be found in individual psychology. Cultures from this point of view are individual psychology thrown large upon the screen, given gigantic proportions and a long time span.

Benedict (1932: 23, 24) (Kroeber and Kluckhohn 1952: 198)

(16) Culture and language

a. Of all forms of culture, it seems that language is that one which de-
    velops its fundamental patterns with relatively the most complete
    detachment from other types of cultural patterning. Language is pri-
    marily a cultural or social product and must be understood as such.

    Sapir (1929: 211–214/1949: 164–66)
(Kroeber and Kluckhohn 1952: 119)

b. Every language serves as the bearer of a culture. If you speak a lan-
    guage you take part, in some degree, in the way of living represented
    by that language. Each system of culture has its own way of looking
    at things and people and of dealing with them. To the extent that you
    have learned to speak and understand a foreign tongue, to that extent
    you have learned to respond with a different selection and emphasis
    to the world around you, and for your relations with people you have
    gained a new system of sensibilities, considerations, conventions, and
    restraints.

    Bloomfield (1945: 625) (Kroeber and Kluckhohn 1952: 120)

c. When we hear the statement that "language is a part of culture", it is
    in fact meant that utterances are correctly understood only if they are
    symbols of cultural phenomena. This implies that since experience
    is communicated by means of language, a person speaking any lan-
    guage participates to some degree in the ways of life represented by
    that language. These verbal symbols are not loosely joined, but co-
    ordinated by means of a system that expresses their mutual relations.
    Language is thus the regular organisation of series of symbols, whose
    meanings have to be learned as any other phenomenon. The implica-
    tion of this is that as each culture has its own way of looking at things
    and at people and its own way of dealing with them, the encultura-
    tion of an individual to a foreign body of customs will only be possible
    as he learns to speak and understand the foreign language and to re-
    spond with new selection and emphasis to the world around him – a
    selection and emphasis presented to him by this new culture.

    Silva-Fuenzalida (1949: 446) (Kroeber and Kluckhohn 1952: 123)

(17) Relation of culture to society, individuals, environment, and artifacts

a. Culture is concerned primarily with the way people act. The actions,
    then, of manufacture, use, and nature of material objects constitute

> the data of material culture. In their relation to culture, artefacts and materials are to be classed in the same category as the substances, such as minerals, flora, and fauna, which compose the environment in which people live. Artefacts themselves are not cultural data, although, to be sure, they are often the concrete manifestations of human actions and cultural processes. The cultural actions of a people cannot even be inferred from them without extreme caution, for a number of reasons. Chief among these are the following: (1) instead of being a product of the culture the artefact may have been imported; (2) the process of manufacture is frequently not implicit in the artefact itself; and (3) the use or function of the artefact is not deducible from the object alone.
>
> Ford (1937: 226) (Kroeber and Kluckhohn 1952: 129)
>
> b.   Culture cannot be inherent in the artefacts. It must be something in the relationship between the artefacts and the aborigines who made and used them. It is a pattern of significance which the artefacts have, not the artefacts themselves. Culture, then, is merely a single one of a group of factors which influence the artisan's procedure in making an artefact… Culture may be the most important of the interplaying factors. Nevertheless, it would not seem justifiable to consider the artefacts themselves to be equivalent to culture.
>
> Rouse (1939: 16, 18, 19) (Kroeber and Kluckhohn 1952: 130)

It turns out that both Ford (1937) and Rouse (1939) share agreement that artifacts are not culture, per se. Ford's position is that culture is concerned with the way in which people act. How people make, and use, artifacts is part of culture and the artifacts themselves are cultural data, but not culture itself. Artifacts stand in the same kind of relationship to culture as does environment. Rouse characterizes this insight somewhat differently, in that culture cannot be inherent in artifacts but the relationship between artifact and the artifact user, and the pattern of significance of artifacts, is cultural and not the artifacts as such (Kroeber and Kluckhohn 1952: 140).

The earliest definition of culture is due to Tylor in 1871, as we have seen. Tylor, during the course of his research and thinking, wavered between the terms culture and civilization, and eventually considered the term culture as more appropriate, with a connotation of high degree of advancement. Nonetheless, in many of the usages, the two terms have continued to be near-synonymous. We have cited Kroeber and Kluckhohn (1952) as critically reviewing 164 definitions of culture, and summarized part of their discussion and definitions. An observation in Kroeber and Kluckhohn (1952: 148) is that civilization has been identified with the objective, technological, and informational activities of society, but culture is associated with subjective elements, such as religion, philosophy, and art. Civilization is accumulative while the cultural component is highly variable and unique. As regards the general features of culture, according to Kroeber and Kluckhohn (1952: 159), there seems to be broad agreement that every culture possesses a considerable degree of integration of both its content and its forms. In terms of historicity, Kroeber and Kluckhohn (1952: 160) make the comment that, while Malinowski was holistically interested in culture, he compared very little, but tended to proceed directly from the functional exposition of one culture to formulation of the principles of all culture. The result was that Malinowski's theory of culture is in many ways a set of permanent, autonomous principles whose acceptance makes observed historical change seem superficial and unimportant in comparison. Culture includes both modalities of actual behavior and a group's *designs for living* that may be conscious, partly conscious, and unconscious. According to Kroeber and Kluckhohn, there are at least three different classes of data that constitute materials from which one may abstract the conceptual model of the culture. In their view, culture is not a point but a complex of interrelated things:

<table><tr><td>

(18) Abstracting the conceptual model of the culture (Kroeber and Kluckhohn 1952: 162)

1)   A people's notions of the *way things ought to be*;
2)   Their conceptions of the way their group actually behaves;
3)   *What does occur*, as objectively determined.

</td></tr></table>

The author of *The Silent Language*, Edward T. Hall (1959/1973), one of the most influential anthropologists of our time, made the important point that *culture is communication and communication is culture*. Culture is essentially about values of a community, and significance and values are of the essence of the organization of culture (Kroeber and Kluckhohn 1952: 171). They write that while it is true that human endeavor is directed toward ends; those ends are shaped by the values of culture; and the values are felt as intrinsic, not as means. The values are variable not predetermined, though certain universals of human biology and of human social life appear to have brought about a few constants or near-constants that cut across cultural differences. The values are part of the products of people in community, and living in societies, and reflect the structural essence of the culture of these societies of people. In turn, these values and their significances are subjective intangibles that they can be experienced, but are also objective in their expressions, embodiments, or results. The understanding of cultures involves recognition of their particular value systems. Comparison of cultures (Kroeber and Kluckhohn 1952: 174) leads to recognition of the relativity of their values as cultures have different sets of values, are differently structured, and differ in their functioning. Cultures are distinct, yet similar and comparable (Kroeber and Kluckhohn 1952: 179). Comparisons of cultures must not be simplistic in terms of an arbitrary or preconceived universal value system, but must be multiple and diverse, with each culture first understood in terms of its own particular value system and structure. The concluding assessment of Kroeber and Kluckhohn (1952: 185) regarding culture is that it is a general category of human nature. In this regard, culture cuts across communities, societies, and nations. Every scientist, linguist, and anthropologist concerned with culture realizes that cultural *situations* make more sense, and reveal more meaning, the more we know of their cultural antecedents, and cultural *context*. In other words, cultural forms or patterns gain in intelligibility as they are set in context in relation to other cultural patterns. Context informs us. The definitions presented here encompass, in one way or another, societal and cultural knowledge, worldview, artifacts and social/institutional artifacts, art, way of life, the experiences of people in a societal group, sets of beliefs, and patterns of behaviors (what we would today call scripts and cultural models), and language. We advance our understanding of the nature and significance of each of these in the following chapters. We next examine the nature of worldview in Chapter 3, followed by, in Chapter 4, an examination of language in use in the environment of the linguistic landscape and the various language-based artifacts that it contains. The nature of cultural artifacts, technical artifacts, institutional artifacts, and art as an artifact, is explored in Chapter 5.

3   The nature of worldview

3.1 Introduction

As individuals in a society, our worldview guides us in how we perceive, imagine, and experience our world. Every day, our worldview guides our actions. What then is a worldview? A worldview is the essential cognitive orientation of an individual and a society encompassing the whole of the individual's or society's knowledge. In this chapter we are concerned with the notion of worldview and the different ideas relating to it. Our discussion will lead us to a consideration of the relationship between language and worldview. We will discuss the term "worldview" as used by Wilhelm von Humboldt, the German philosopher, and several other scholars. Many linguists believe that each language system opens up a new world for us, in which the concepts with which we speak and think, are shaped differently. In this regard, the term "worldview" has become somewhat associated with the Sapir–Whorf hypothesis, which we mentioned previously, by some linguists and anthropologists. We briefly survey what evidence might provide support for this view. We offer some definitions of the term *worldview* and examine the functions that a worldview provides to us. Connections will be made between worldview, imagination, art, artifacts, and our involvement in the world around us. In particular, we summarize the nature of a worldview as a frame of reference, and how we create and maintain worldviews. We start by examining the notion of worldview.

3.2 The notion of worldview

In the notion of worldview, two basic factors are at play, that of world-perceiving, for the perception we have of the world, and world-conceiving, for forming concepts to represent our experience of the world and the things in it. This distinction covers our ability to perceive the world and our cognitive activity of organizing the world we perceive via our senses. Underhill (2009: 147–148) suggests that, as part of our worldview, we each have a "cultural mindset, personal world and perspective".

A cultural mindset is that essential conception of the world which frames our perception and conception of politics, society, history, behavior, the individual's place in the world and the organizing frameworks of social relations. The personal world is our individual perception and conception of the world, and is the individual's own version of the mindset that they observe, consciously and unconsciously. A perspective provides for the changing nature of the way each person dynamically perceives and conceives the world. This perspective changes as one moves through the world, interacting and experiencing others. With age and experience, we naturally adopt new ideas and expressions, which alters the way we view the world.

A mindset is a mental attitude that determines how we interpret and respond to situations while a cultural mindset is the thought processes characteristic of an individual, as part of a cultural group or community, that determines how and why particular life choices get made. A mindset is a set of beliefs, ways of doing things, and mental representations held by people, and can be indicative of a person's worldview. It may be so deeply embedded that it creates a strong incentive within people or groups to act in a certain way. A mindset represents the cognitive processes activated in response to a given task or situation. The term "worldview" is useful for characterizing the personal and individual, but also the shared vision of reality.

Underhill (2011: 18) provides the following (1) taxonomy of a worldview. An important question is: What is the relationship between language and worldview? Worldview and language are important concepts and the relationship between them necessitates that we consider at least three dimensions (2). Each language opens up to us a world. When we speak our language with others, each language system opens up a realm of creative conceptual thought. Individuals can accept or modify the concepts that are provided via their language and cultural mindset.

---

(1)   The worldview taxonomy

1. WORLD-PERCEIVING, designating the frameworks which mediate our perception of the world.
2. WORLD-CONCEIVING, identifying the conceptual frameworks via which we communicate and interact with others.
3. CULTURAL MINDSET, describing the worldview specific to a group.
4. THE PERSONAL WORLD designating the system of concepts organizing and structuring the worldview.
5. PERSPECTIVE defining the conceptual and emotional response in interacting with the world, whose shape we constantly reinvent.

> ## (2)   The relationship between language and worldview
>
> 1.   The worldview of the language system which provides us with con-
>   cepts and organizes the relationships between concepts.
> 2.   The worldview of each cultural mindset, a worldview which is ground-
>   ed within a given linguistic worldview but which can migrate between
>   language systems.
> 3.   The worldview of the individual which finds its expression in the works
>   of great writers who cultivate their language.

Cultural mindsets are maintained by people, and by people alone. Worldviews facilitate individuals in giving expression to their thoughts and feelings, whereby they can live together within communities with broadly shared
worldviews. Worldview has been used to imply an essential conception of
the world which envelops the rational person, and an implication of the term
"worldview" is that it foregrounds a visual aspect of perception while backgrounding all other forms of knowing the world in context.

A quote from Wittgenstein's (1969: 64, proposition 5.6), from the *Tractatus Logico-Philosophicus* (Treatise on Logic and Philosophy), neatly captures the sense of worldview and its relationship to language: "The limits of
my language mean the limits of my world".

3.3   The term worldview and the Sapir–Whorf hypothesis

For Crystal (2014: 49), a language represents a guide to understanding a
community's worldview and different languages represent different worldviews such that, according to this hypothesis, we conceptualize the world
around us in virtue of using our language and the way we experience the
world is (somehow) related to the way we speak of it. Worldview has come
to denote the perspective of a culture. Language is a human cognitive system which has evolved over time to give verbal expression to a people's
culture, and their way of life. Language allows us to take the world into our
consciousness, and, we represent the world in our minds as a cultural mental
model.

It is worth noting that there are estimated to be 7,000 or so languages now
spoken in the world, and only about half of these will survive the twenty-first
century. Historically, this idea that there is a relationship between language
and culture has its origins in the work of Franz Boas (1930, 1938) and his
ethnological exploration of Amerindian cultures. His work caused linguists

to re-evaluate some of their fundamental premises about language. Indeed, many linguists consider that each language system opens up a new world for us, in which the concepts with which we speak and think are shaped differently.

In this regard, the term "worldview" has become somewhat associated with the Sapir–Whorf hypothesis, which posits that thought is language-dependent. According to the Sapir–Whorf hypothesis, a language's difference results in a different intellectual and structuring for the mind of the speaker of a language community. This claim is that that different languages enabled different ways of describing reality. However, this is rather controversial and a very strong claim to support! However well-intentioned they may be, defenders of linguistic diversity have tended to assume that each language is a worldview, but that such an assumption is rarely backed up with any profound experience of the worldview in question. The advocates themselves are unlikely to have any real knowledge of the language they are defending. Importantly, the intuition that each language allows its speakers entry into a unique worldview remains substantially unproven. We share this opinion and, consequently, do not defend any strong version of the Sapir–Whorf hypothesis here but, instead, explore the relationships, connections, and links between worldview, culture, and language.

3.4 Humboldt and worldview – *Weltansicht*

Use of the term "worldview" has first been attributed to Wilhelm von Humboldt (1820, 1830–1835). He insisted that, in order to understand the worldview of a foreign language, a linguist must understand the way that a language employs and organizes concepts. For example, how is the concept of SPACE used to construct TIME, or the concept of LOCATION used to construct STATE (as in, "I'm in a good place now", meaning "all is well"), in different languages? This requires us to understand the degree to which our worldview is linguistically constructed. Ultimately, only a linguistic community can keep alive a worldview.

Humboldt had views which are, in fact, not very distant from those of Sapir and Whorf. Indeed, Humboldt believed that each language explores reality in a manner which is essentially specific to it, and he attempted to characterize the nature of different languages, and the worldviews that language unlocks to its community of speakers. For Humboldt, worldview is our fundamental processing of the world by the mind through the faculty of language. It is the primary conceptual tool for understanding and classifying languages. The concept of *Weltansicht* was developed by Humboldt to refer to the way that the language system shapes both the perspective and conception we have of the world. Indeed, this notion seems to have anticipated the Sapir–Whorf hypothesis! *Weltansicht* was considered by Humboldt to shape the way we mediate our way through life as we interact with others, such that each speaker of a language is led by its structure and by the particular modes in which meaning is put into form in that language, to categorize a speaker's experience in a certain manner.

Humboldt's conception of *Weltansicht* as worldview connects language, culture, and people in a conceptual framework with the organization of ideas in the form of language. This *Weltansicht* notion of worldview implies the socially constructed formation of the individual's mind and his linguistic capacity and further implies that language discloses the way individuals and linguistic communities think. Through language we are informed about the world around us. Humboldt argues that it is *Weltansicht* which enables us to distinguish between the way we, as individuals, perceive and understand the world, and how we formulate our shared conception of the world. Through this, one group of people is claimed to understand the world in a different manner than another group although both belong to the same linguistic community. This is also substantially unproven, while interesting at a philosophical level.

For Humboldt, the notion of *perception* is a dynamic process that informs language. He considered language to be the work of individual minds, and individual creativity has a significant role in language. Humboldt argued that people cultivated language as they use it and that different languages evolve along different lines over time, due to the cumulative influence of the individual in a community in their expression in speech.

3.5 Worldview orienting and a comprehending function

A worldview helps us in comprehending events as meaningful and insightful, and in guiding and orienting people through their lives. The influence of worldviews on how we decode the world is significant, and as humans we tend to take our own worldview as a lens to see and interpret the world we inhabit.

A worldview, then, has an orienting and a comprehending function (Note et al. 2009: 9). Orientation and comprehension are typically seen as related. In order for a worldview to have an orienting function, people perceive the basic beliefs of their worldview as correct. The notion of a worldview is often connected with the notion, or perhaps metaphor, of an orientating map. Maps are used by people as devices for orientation, with some explanatory power, such that we can put forward opinions and visions of the future. A common feature of maps is that they organize, in an accessible representation, elements of the world so we can build a mental model. A worldview is considered by Lieve (2011: 160) to be "a set of rules and representations for the organization of sensory experience that individuals carry in their heads and that are available for transmission independently of their bodily activity in the world".

A worldview, as a cognitive model, reflects the knowledge gained from the experiences of generations of people, and is translated into cognitive patterns and arrangements which ontologically characterize how we experience the world. However, the ongoing interaction with other cultures, and experiences within one's own culture and personal lives, constantly reshapes our worldviews. For Libbrecht (2009: 38), our mental model operates as a frame in which one can place different worldviews, which is able to contain contradictory views of these at the same item, while managing values that seem to conflict. Worldviews emerge as a characteristic feature of the social environment where individuals and groups interact. Interculturally, however, we need to be aware of the basic categories of our own worldview in order to consider and incorporate other perspectives. Worldviews are properties of individual agents. Indeed, Lauer (2009: 114) considers a worldview as belonging to an individual and encompassing all of the beliefs, attitudes, rules of inference and grammar, the values, needs, experiences that the person has had – an individual's worldview is reality for that person.

3.6   Culture and worldview as a signification system

One view of culture by Naugle (2002: 314) is that it acts as a signification system. Eco (1976: 22), for example, suggests that "the whole of culture should be studied as a communicative phenomenon based on signification systems" and that "only by studying it in this way can certain of its fundamental mechanisms be clarified". In this view, semiotics is considered a theory of culture, such that all of the cultural dimensions can be characterized via semiotics. Eco subsumes the entirety of human culture under the discipline of semiotics. He has two propositions, which are that the whole of culture must be studied as a semiotic phenomenon, and that all aspects of culture can be studied as the contents of semiotic activity. Those sign symbols, as a semiotic phenomenon, designate a worldview.

Semiotics owes much to the work of C. S. Peirce (Naugle 2002: 317, Nöth 1990: 41, Pierce 1882a, 1882b, 1897, 1989, n.d.), who established a theory of signs on the notion that all thought and cognition, and indeed human beings themselves, are thoroughly semiotic in their basic nature. Furthermore, and important for this discussion, Peirce adopted a semiotic worldview in which signs are not merely regarded as one class of things among many non-semiotic objects.

> It seems a strange thing, when one comes to ponder over it, that a sign should leave its interpreter to supply a part of its meaning; but the explanation of the phenomenon lies in the fact that the entire universe, – not merely the universe of existents, but all that wider universe, embracing the universe of existents as a part, the universe which we are all accustomed to refer to as "the truth," – that all this universe is perfused with signs, if it is not composed exclusively of signs.
>
> Peirce quote from Nöth (1990: 394).

Hence, for Peirce, semiotics characterizes not only our world but also human beings as sign-making and sign-using creatures and that the comprehension of reality is possible only by semiotic means.

> Without fatiguing the reader by stretching this parallelism too far, it is sufficient to say that there is no element whatever of man's consciousness which has not something corresponding to it in the word; and the reason is obvious. It is that the word or sign which man uses *is* the man himself. For, as the fact that every thought is a sign, taken in conjunction with the fact that life is a train of thought, proves that man is a sign; so, that every thought is an *external* sign, proves that man is an external sign. That is to say, the man and the external sign are identical, in the same sense in which the words *homo* and *man* are identical. Thus my language is the sum total of myself; for the man is the thought.
>
> Peirce quote from Nöth (1990: 54).

Signs are essential to human thought (Naugle 2002: 317–319), cognition, and communication, and central to all aspects of culture. Signs are instruments of reflecting conditions in situations, and they create meaningful worlds in which people live, move, and interact. Signs possess unique cultural power and they determine the meaning in life. It has long been recognized that the semiotic orientation of humans to tell stories forms a symbolic world. Stories establish a context for life. According to this perspective, sign systems lead to knowledge, and in a semiotic epistemology, everything that has meaning is composed of symbolic forms, including artifacts such as language, myth, art, religion, science, and history.

It is important to note that there are, of course, other perspectives on the nature of worldview and culture that differ significantly to the consideration of culture as a semiotic system. One of these views culture as situated cognition (Oyserman 2015: 9). The theory of culture as situated cognition, with its attendant worldview, focuses attention on the impact of social contexts, human artifacts, physical spaces, tasks, and language, and on how people think. It appeals to situations to make cultural mindsets accessible. An accessible cultural mindset (e.g., individual or collectivistic) is predicted to influence affect, behavior, and cognitive processes. These effects reside outside of conscious awareness. Importantly, *situations* evoke expectations about how things will unfold, and may result in a shift toward systematic reasoning. This situated approach highlights the constructive nature of cognition where thinking is for doing. It recognizes that people are sensitive to their immediate environment and use the subset of all their knowledge, that is accessible in the moment, to interpret what emerges in mind from contextual demands. What matters is the situation and what the situation is about. The consequences arising from the situation depend on how it is interpreted.

3.7   Defining worldview as a frame of reference

Worldviews are an important source of meaning, and they function as a frame of reference for communities to understand life events. They enable people to see order in their experience and their lives (Aerts et al. 2011: 138). Worldviews stimulate people's imagination, and act as sources of meaning in life, offering potential for growth and development, and possibilities to be explored. Worldviews may show alternatives realities. For example, religious, socialist, or humanist worldviews will color our attitude to injustice, oppression, violence, and poverty in the world. An examination of worldview as a frame of reference has the potential to expose the conceptual foundations in our thinking, expose hidden assumptions, and reveal intrinsic linguistic structures determining our knowledge.

Riegler (2005: 27) argues for the notion that cognitive activity consists of constructing a worldview out of experience whereby every perception and every action is the result of a construction process. Riegler (2005: 31) defines a worldview as a coherent set of bodies of knowledge concerning all aspects of our world which allows people to construct an image of the world and thereby facilitating an understanding of many elements of their experience. Consequently, a worldview must be considered to be a theory about the world. Aerts et al. (2005: 8–9) define a worldview as a map that people use to orient and explain, and from which they evaluate, act, and put forward predictions and visions of the future. These basic aspects are as follows:

---

(3)   The worldview as system-based frame of reference (based on Aerts et al. 2005: 9)

a.   An ORIENTING model of the world of our implicit collective ontological conceptualisations of the nature of the *physical*, the *social*, and the *ethical* worlds, such that they have an orienting function for human beings.

b.   An EXPLANATION model of the range of epistemologies in order to understand these worlds appropriately.

c.   An EVALUATION model of the way our worldview is able to coherently cover as many elements of our experiences as possible.

d.   An ACTION model of how we act and create in this world, and influence and transform it.

e.   A RATIONAL model of the future that is projected ahead of us, and the criteria for guiding us in our future choices.

According to Aerts et al. (2005: 31), a worldview can be described as a system-based frame of reference in which everything presented to us by our diverse experiences can be placed. Such a system allows us to integrate everything we know about the world and ourselves into a single map that illuminates reality as presented to us within a certain context or society. As people, we integrate experiences every day. To quote Aerts directly: "observations that do not fit into an existing network provide a feeling of 'uneasiness' that needs to be resolved".

3.8 Worldview, imagination, art, artifacts, and lived experience

Imagination is a process that contributes to understanding by enriching it with fresh perspectives which can deepen one's understanding of an event or situation (Aerts 2011: 137). Artifacts such as works of art act instrumentally to facilitate of this process. The relationship of imagination and art is complex, and imagination is needed to both construct and appreciate art.

Worldviews are understood as being directly related to lived experience and behavior (Aerts et al. 2011: 163). People gain knowledge of the world by engaging in it and exploring it. A worldview may also be considered as a kind of master narrative. As reflecting parts of our worldview, language-based artifacts such as folklore, myths and literature from around the world present stories about human reality in the context of universal human meaning. Worldview can be understood as meaning transmitted by these narratives and, as such, are part of the human progression of an individual becoming a developed person (Aerts 2011: 165).

Culture emphasizes meanings embedded in interactions. Regarded as a social construction, culture is a product of meaning-making processes with the power to influence individual and institutional behavior. The diversity of cultures results from the diversity of meaning-making processes in a society. Therefore, worldview, and culture, comprise social representations, mental models, and ordering schemata (Ridgeway 2006) and the environmental conditions that sustain or challenge them. Some elements of worldview are visible and explicit (Figure 3.1), while others tend to be less visible and to be more concealed. Worldview encapsulates much of what is hidden in culture, including a range of attitudes, societal roles, expectations, perceptions, along with deeply held core values and engrained beliefs and assumptions.

As well as acquiring schemata for mentally constructing the environment, understanding the world requires skills for direct perceptual engagement with its constituents, objects, and artifacts, human and non-human, animate and inanimate.

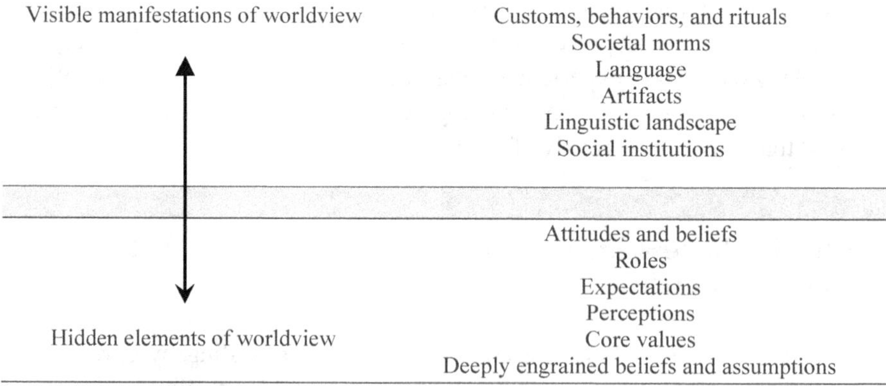

Figure 3.1 Worldview as a meta-context.

3.9 Summary

In summary then, our worldview enables us to perceive and organize our world. Reflected in a worldview is the culturally informed set of beliefs and values shared by members of a community, and which guides their patterns of behavior. The key characteristics are that the worldview is shared by members of a group or community, conveyed from one member to another and affecting our thinking and behavior. A worldview is relatively stable yet quite dynamic, and it functions as a meta-context for us in our engagement with the world.

As part of our worldview, we have a culturally informed mindset, personal world, and a certain perspective. From Underhill (2011), we understand that the cultural mindset is our conception of the world which frames our perception, the individual's place in the world and our social relations. Our personal world is our own perception and conception of the world. A perspective facilitates the way that each person perceives and conceives the world in real time, allowing us to embrace new ideas. The relationship between language and worldview requires us to consider the language system which provides us with access to concepts and knowledge, and enables us to systematize the relationships between these in a worldview model. According to Swidler (1986), culture influences action by shaping a repertoire (a toolkit) of habits and skills from which people construct strategies for action. This sees culture as something with a beneficial utility to be used within society. From this perspective, people do not just live within a culture but use elements of that culture to inform their behavior and decisions. They make use of cultural apparatus, tools, and artifacts, to make sense of their world, while selectively using culture to inform or justify their behavior. People's social existence, behavior, and choices are enabled and constrained by their worldview.

A worldview, then, is a system-based frame of reference that provides us with an orienting model of the world. A worldview allows us to explain and understand our world. Additionally, it allows us to evaluate our worldview against the knowledge of our experiences. A worldview provides us with a model of how to act and create so we might influence and progressively transform our world. In this way, our worldview guides us into the future and gives us criteria for making informed future decisions.

4   The linguistic landscape

4.1 Introduction – the linguistic landscape

In this chapter we examine the linguistic landscape as an environment where language is found on public display as signs of various kinds. Often, these signs or artifacts consist of a mix of visual and textual elements. We therefore look at their linguistic and visual structures within the realm of visual communication and visual semiotics. The functions of the linguistic landscape support cultural identity and provide important identity markers of communities. People reside within this human linguistic landscape in time and space. In this assessment of the linguistic landscape we explore elements of the semiotics of place, along with a case study on linguistic landscape, cultural identity, and language diversity.

4.2 Language on public display in the linguistic landscape

The linguistic landscape is defined by Landry and Bourhis (1997: 23) as "the visibility and salience of languages on public and commercial signs in a given territory or region". This includes the language of street names and place names, public road and traffic signs, office and commercial shop signs, public notice boards, neon advertisements and advertising billboards, topographic information and area maps, emergency guidance and information, political posters, public signs on government buildings, stone inscriptions, and urban graffiti, which combine to form the linguistic landscape of a given territory, region, or urban area. This use of the term has often been found to be not sufficient for capturing the complexities of the linguistic reality that exists in modern societies. Hence the concept has been extended to include texts, images, artifacts, placement in time and space, as well as people. This extended sense of the term encompasses diverse multimodal resources such as graffiti and street art (Rubdy 2015: 22). Our environment contains very many written messages on public display. We find these pieces of language all around us as we traverse our environment. The visibility of language on signs constitutes what has now come to be referred to as the linguistic

Figure 4.1 Raftery the poet – Street art from Temple Bar Dublin.

landscape of a place (Backhaus 2007: 12–15). This use of language on signs of various kinds (including actual information signs or graffiti), in the public area constitute the linguistic landscape. Language on these public signs is a specific type of language use which is distinct from other forms of written and spoken communication.

We start our discussion with an example of some street art found in Dublin. This street art in shown in Figure 4.1. As an artifact in the linguistic landscape, this is a representative instance of how the language lives within the public space. The ideas within the poem found in the street art resonate with people in a living vibrant culture. In this instance, the language is found on the bilingual (Irish and English) street art in a public space in the environment, and consists of a mix of word, phrases, and image displayed in an interesting way.

Figure 4.2 Image of pre-Euro Irish bank note with poem fragment.

In particular in this street art, the poem[3] *'Is Mise Raifteirí'* (I'm Raftery) illustrates how the cultural constituent of artifact is an expression of human culture within the linguistic landscape of Dublin city center. A fragment of the poem was also to be found on the pre-Euro Irish bank note (Figure 4.2), another cultural artifact that uses language in the linguistic landscape.

Research on the linguistic landscape is therefore concerned with the use of language in its written form in public, and it refers to any sign, announcement or street art/graffiti located in a given geographical location. The study of language on signs enables conclusions to be drawn regarding the social community, and various cultural ideals that may exist (Backhaus 2007: 21). Of course, it is essential that the language used on the sign be intelligible to those the message is intended to address, and this requires understanding the viewer or reader who is expected to see the sign and its message. A distinction is made by Gorter (2006: 10) between top-down and bottom-up signs in the linguistic landscape (Table 4.1), while Backhaus (2007: 3) proposes nine analytical categories in which the data in the linguistic landscape might be discussed (1).

---

[3] The language of the poem *'Is Mise Raifteirí'* (I'm Raftery) expresses human kindness and warmth. In his poem, Raftery makes rich use of metaphor, for example, the heart is a container of emotion. An English translation is provided. Photo of the street art by the author.

Table 4.1 Top-down vs. bottom-up public signs.

Category	*Type (based on Gorter 2006: 10)*	
Top-down	1.	Public institution
	2.	Religious
	3.	Governmental
	4.	Municipal-cultural, educational, medical
	5.	Public signs of general interest
	6.	Public announcements
	7.	Signs of street names
Bottom-up	8.	Shop signs
	9.	Private business signs
	10.	Private announcements: wanted ads, sale or rental of items

---

(1) Linguistic landscape analytical categories (From Backhaus 2007: 13)

1. *Languages* contained;
2. *Combination* patterns;
3. *Differences* between official and non-official signs;
4. *Regularities* in geographic distribution;
5. Availability of *translation* or transliteration;
6. *Order* of the languages combined;
7. Visibility of the *multilingual* nature of a sign;
8. Occurrence of linguistic *idiosyncrasies*;
9. Coexistence of *older and newer versions* of a given type of sign.

A sign coding scheme for these linguistic objects found in the linguistic landscape has also been proposed by Gorter (2006: 18) to include elements such as those found in (2).

---

(2) Coding scheme for these linguistic objects (based on Gorter 2006: 18)

1. How language *appears* on the sign,
2. The *location* of the sign,
3. The *size* of the font used,
4. The *number* of languages on the sign,
5. The *order* of languages on multilingual signs,
6. The relative *importance* of languages,
7. Whether a text has been *translated* fully or partially.

Top-down signs are coded according to whether they belong to national or local, and cultural, social, educational, medical, or legal institutions. Bottom-up items are coded according to categories such as professional (legal, medical, consulting), commercial (by category type like food, clothing, furniture etc.) and services organizations, like manpower or real estate agencies. In any event, public displays of language are all around us, displayed on shop windows, signs, posters, official notices, traffic signs, street posters, etc. A question that arises from this observation then is: what constitutes such an object or sign, and what therefore is the unit of analysis?

As we have already indicated, the term "linguistic landscape" refers to the linguistic objects that are found in the public space. The linguistic landscape is a gestalt of physical objects, shops, post offices, kiosks etc., associated with visual elements, specific locations, and written words that make linguistic elements of some kind.

4.3   Signs in the linguistic landscape

Signs in the linguistic landscape take a physical form of one kind or another. The world we live in, and our culture, is full of signs. All that we understand about ourselves and our culture is based on transmitting and interpreting signs. The example of a speed-limit sign is given by Backhaus (2007: 17) as a flat metal disc of a certain standard size and design displaying Arabic numerals that is typically attached to a pole by some roadside. This can function as a sign only when located in the appropriate context, such as by a road side and viewable by people. According to Backhaus, the quality of being a sign is conferred on an object "if and when human beings attach a signification to it that goes beyond its intrinsic physical properties, whether in furtherance of a particular program of activities, or to link different aspects or phases of their activities, to enrich their understanding of their local circumstances or general situation".

Information and knowledge cannot have any independent existence. Information and knowledge must be represented by a system of signs – icons, symbols, and indexes. All signs, whether they are icons or symbols, are also indexes, and must be located in the material world to exist (Scollon and Scollon 2003: 8). C. S. Peirce assumed a three-way interaction between i) a signifying *"representamen"*, ii) a conceptual *"interpretant"*, and iii) a designated *"object"*, which emphasizes the interpretation process and the role that the viewer, hearer, or reader takes in making sense of a given sign. Following Peirce, it is generally agreed that a sign can function semiotically as an index, icon, or as a symbol. The three types of signs – index, icon, and symbol – are not mutually exclusive, as the relationship between the signifier and the signified of a sign can be based on more than one property (Backhaus 2007: 18). Language is the most comprehensive symbolic sign system and it functions by virtue of conventional speech signs.

Index, icon, and symbol are concepts applicable in different ways for information provision on public signs. An index is a sign with a signifier directly connected or pointing to its signified, with a factual relationship between signifier and signified, which can be observed or inferred such as with smoke indicating fire (Backhaus 2007: 17). Some of the characteristic features of indexicality include arrows and various pointing elements to show a direction in which the indicated object is to be found. Language indexes the world. Scollon and Scollon (2003: 12–13) remind us that we use communicative language not only about the world but also in the world, and much of what we understand depends on context, exactly where we are located in the world. One very important aspect of the meaning of language is based on the actual placement of that language in the physical world. The fundamental basis of indexicality is that quality of language that refers to things in the world by pointing to them, or locating itself on or in them, and positions us within that world. Indexicality, the meaning of signs which is based on their material location, is the key to the analysis of any human action. Indexicality then is the property of the context-dependency of signs, especially language, whose aspects of meaning depend on the placement of the sign in the material world. The word "sign" means any material object that indicates or refers to something other than itself. Indexicality has been known to be a universal characteristic of language at least since the work of Charles S. Peirce (Scollon and Scollon 2003: 18).

Iconicity is the second way in which a relationship between signifier and signified can be established, where the signifier is linked to its reference object through resemblance or likeness. Examples include portraits, diagrams, or gestures that imitate. The use of iconic elements on public signs contain informative or directive messages that, through resemblance or likeness, do not rely on a specific language. Maps are an example of iconic elements on public signs which provide geographic information through a graphic representation of a local area. A symbol has an arbitrary link between signifier and signified determined by convention. Symbolic elements on public signs refer to all forms of information provision by means of written language. The symbols on public signs, which use written language, are meant to be viewed and read by any members of the general public who happen to pass by the sign. The symbolic value of a sign may have an important political or socio-psychological background. For example, the underlying aim of the sign and its message may reflect a desire to assert power ("By controlling the languages of the sign, I assert my power over this place") or to assert identity ("My sociocultural membership is through this language"). We typically prefer to write signs in our own language, or in a language with which we wish to be identified, in which case the choice of the language itself is the message (Backhaus 2007: 36). Some signs, of course, are multilingual.

Our purpose here is to focus on all of the ways in which language-based artifacts in the linguistic landscape (signs, images, graphics, texts, photographs, paintings, and all of the other combinations of these and others) are produced as meaningful wholes for visual interpretation. This focus necessarily includes art, and any other discipline which takes as its main objective to understand how we produce meanings through instrumental use of these artifacts in the linguistic landscape.

4.4 The functions of linguistic landscape – supporting cultural identity

The linguistic landscape functions, in one perspective, as an informational marker, and in another perspective as a symbolic marker communicating the power and status of various linguistic communities in a given territory (Gorter 2006: 15). An example of the linguistic landscape functioning as symbolic marker is provided by Hicks (2002: 2–3) in his discussion article where he examines the linguistic landscape situation in Scotland. Hicks makes the not unreasonable point that we can assume that the absence or presence of our own language on public signs impacts on how we feel as a member of a language group within a bilingual setting. Having our own language used on private and public signs directly contributes to the sense that the language of the cultural group has value and status. The presence of the minority language, Scottish Gaelic in Hicks' case, in the linguistic landscape contributes directly to the positive social identity of ethnolinguistic groups, while exclusion of a minority language from signage can convey a message that it is not valued and has little status in society.

Absence of the minority language on public signs may lead activists to use graffiti to add the subordinated language to signs in public spaces, while more radical graffiti campaigns block out or deface signs in the dominant language and replace them with words in the minority language. A humorous and witty example of graffiti on a bilingual (Irish and English) street name in Dublin is shown in Figure 4.3. The sign has some handwritten textual graffiti

Figure 4.3 A typical bilingual sign showing a street name in Dublin.

above and below the English representation of the street name that plays on the pronunciation of "Merrion", as "Jesus, *Mary, and* Joseph".

There is a function to the linguistic landscape that is of some considerable importance to societies in reflecting their native traditions and folklore in place names. Places in the landscape are named so as to provide a focal point for various traditional stories, sagas, and myths that are part of the traditional culture. In this way, place names reflecting cultural content act to give added sense of place and belonging of the in-group to its territory. Such names are important to cultures. Often the name is all that remains of some element of a culture. Such place names help the traditional culture to be transmitted and they help cast a thread back hundreds if not thousands of years (Hicks 2002: 4). A point to bear in mind is how place names[4], and associated place-name signage, reflect not only existing linguistic territory but also past, ancestral territory. From the interest shown in place names, it is clear that people feel that the names on the landscape are identifiable with community, cultural identity, and nation. To take away any of these names and replace them with other names in a different language takes something away from the community, and diminishes a culture. Often, it is only with place names that we can discover anything about this wealth of cultural information. With place names we can get a strong sense of a rich and diverse linguistic heritage. Some examples of this kind of information can be seen in the place names of Gweesalia, in Mayo, and Clifden, in Galway. Gweesalia is an anglicization of the native Irish name *Gaoth Sáile* meaning sea wind, and which refers to the fresh, bracing Atlantic breeze that locals typically experience in this part of the world. Clifden, in turn, is an anglicization of

---

[4] In Ireland, a, rich and informed online source of information on place names is the institution Ordnance Survey Ireland: www.osi.ie/blog/irish-place-names/.

Figure 4.4 Bilingual sign beside Carlingford Lough in Omeath, Co. Louth (in the Irish Republic near the border with Northern Ireland).

the native Irish name *An Clochán* meaning "the stepping-stone". Many Irish place names come from descriptions of rivers and crossings.

A typical information sign is shown in Figure 4.4. This is of a sign found in Omeath[5], beside the slipway to Carlingford Lough. This sign is about 1 meter tall and has both Irish and English information on it, equally represented. Opinions on political events can also find expression on signs in a humorous way. We see an example of this on a sign erected in Omeath (Figure 4.5) which is indicative of the general frustration felt on the island of Ireland with the UK Brexit. Harsher political messages are also found on signs relating to current issues that are important to people. In Figure 4.6, we see a mono-lingual sign calling for direct action by local people in Newry, a city just inside the border within Northern Ireland. This is indicative of the opposition and resistance felt by the majority of people within Northern Ireland against the UK Brexit. We will see that, reflected in the linguistic landscape,

---

[5] Omeath (Irish: *Ó Méith*) is a village in County Louth in Ireland, overlooking Carlingford Lough and close to the Northern Ireland border, in an area with outstanding natural scenic beauty. The village is steeped in Irish history, and is located on the east coast of Ireland. Omeath is roughly mid-way between Dublin and Belfast, close to the County Louth and County Armagh/County Down border. Omeath is approximately 8 km/4 miles from Carlingford town and about 10 km/5 miles from Newry city.

Figure 4.5   A partially bilingual sign in Omeath. (This somewhat humorous sign is indicative of the frustration felt by ordinary people on the island of Ireland with the UK Brexit. The Brexit sign points out to sea towards Britain.)

Figure 4.6   A mono-lingual sign in Newry, near the border within Northern Ireland. (This sign is indicative of the opposition by the majority of people within Northern Ireland against the UK Brexit.)

there is a dissonance in cultural identity between the two communities living in Northern Ireland.

4.5   Identity markers of communities

Within the linguistic landscape, identity markers of communities resonate strongly with different languages utilized that are important to different audiences in the symbolic construction of the public space. In this way, the linguistic landscape gives insights into what Gorter (2006: 11, 17) calls the symbolic structuring of the public space. The public life of a community is shaped by the many actors operating under the influence of various motives. These actors may include any mix of public institutions, associations, commercial firms, community groups, and individuals that are found across the wide strata of society. These actors do not necessarily act with harmony or coherence, but they nonetheless leave their mark on the linguistic landscape.

Linguistic tokens can delineate the geographical and cultural boundaries of neighborhoods. To the extent that linguistic tokens are artifacts of a central or regional agency, they may reflect the overt language policies of a given region, with the concomitant markers of identity, status, and power. These markers of status and power are also reflected in the linguistic tokens employed by business operations and institutions, such as religious establishments, cultural centers, banks, hospitals, and so on. According to Gorter (2006: 39), "linguistic artefacts within a given linguistic landscape, for example signs and advertisements of local businesses, notices posted by individuals and other locally produced tokens, are a manifestation of the covert language policy of a community, and may display the grass roots cultural identity and aspirations of its members".

In the process of sign-making (Kress and van Leeuwen 2006: 21–25), the signifier (the form) and the signified (the meaning) are relatively independent of each other until they are brought together by the sign-maker in a newly made sign. However, meanings belong to culture, and visual language is culturally specific. For Kress and van Leeuwen (2006: 30), the semiotic approach addresses both communication and representation, where:

i.   COMMUNICATION requires participants to make their messages maximally understandable in a certain context. They therefore choose forms of expression which are believed to be maximally transparent to other participants.

ii. REPRESENTATION requires that sign-makers choose forms for the expression of their message, forms which they see as most apt and plausible in the given context.

Roland Barthes (1977: 39), one of the most recognized names in semiotics, distinguished two types of elaboration, one in which the verbal text comes first, so that the image forms an illustration of it, and one in which the image comes first, so that the text forms a more definite and precise restatement of it (Kress and van Leeuwen 2006: 35). In an image–text relation, the verbal text can extend the meaning of the image, or vice versa, as is the case with speech balloons in comics, and memes. In an image–text relation, the verbal text may also elaborate on the image, or vice versa. As a resource for representation, images, like language, display a set of regularities which can be subject to formal description. Kress and van Leeuwen (2006: 37) call this a "grammar" to draw attention to the culturally produced regularity. In a multimodal sign using images and language, the writing may carry one set of meanings and the images carry another.

Two kinds of visual literacy are distinguished by Kress and van Leeuwen (2006: 40) in relation to signs. The first is that in which visual communication has been made subservient to language and where images are to be regarded as unstructured replicas of reality. The second is that in which language exists side by side with forms of visual representation. While both visual and verbal structures can be used to express meanings drawn from a common cultural source, the two modes are not just alternative means of representing the same thing (Kress and van Leeuwen 2006: 93). Many signs in the public space use images with text. As regards the images, we are interested in how they represent the real social world, and how they mean what they mean in virtue of where we find them (Scollon and Scollon 2003: 99). These visual means of communication are expressions of cultural meanings, accessible to characterization and analysis. In this, the realities of the linguistic landscape are brought about by social, cultural and economic factors along with the intensification of linguistic and cultural diversity within communities, and by multiculturalism, the internet and social media (Kress and van Leeuwen 2006: 53). Societies develop explicit ways for utilizing those semiotic resources which they value most highly, and which play an important role in controlling common understandings needed in order to function.

The layout of text and images is seen to follow principles of composition with information value distributed in terms of center vs. periphery or polarized, so that given information is presented on the left with new information on the right, or images of some ideal at the top of a painting with the real at the bottom. Salience may be conveyed through size, foregrounding, color, sharpness of definition, and other features. Another element of composition is framing, with varying degrees of connection of information units. Represented participant systems, modality, and composition all help make up the semiotic landscape of visual images and thus guide and mediate interpretations of our personal experience and social interaction (Scollon and Scollon 2003: 33). In our society, truth is generally associated with naturalism or a high degree of correspondence between what the eye sees and the visual representation of an object.

4.6   The semiotics of discourses in place

The linguistic landscape involves a discourse in an actual physical place, that is socio-culturally motivated, and may be decontextualized, situated, or transgressive (Scollon and Scollon 2003: 161, Backhaus 2007: 48). Within decontextualized we include all the forms of signs, pictures, and texts appearing in multiple contexts but always in the same form. The idea of a situated semiotics includes such common regulatory signs or notices as directions to the train in a transport system or an exit sign. Transgressive refers to signs that violate the conventional semiotics expected in a place. Graffiti and street art are the most prominent instance of this type.

Discourses in places are constrained in several ways. For Scollon and Scollon (2003: 181), there are four factors to consider (3).

---

(3)   The constraining factors to be considered regarding discourses in places

1.   the social *actor*, i.e. the habitus of individual humans,
2.   the interaction *order* in which they conduct their social lives,
3.   the *visual* semiotics – the discourses of images and texts which they encounter,
4.   the *place* semiotics in which all of this happens including all the other signs and their placement or location in time and space in the locality.

Information becomes knowledge when it is concretely interpreted into a cognitive model for use in the social world (Scollon and Scollon 2003: 8). The way that a word, a sentence, a picture, a graph or a gesture can have meaning in semiotic theory is as a sign of some kind: an icon, symbol, or index. As we earlier mentioned, a sign can be an iconic picture of the thing in the world. A sign can also be a completely arbitrary representation of the thing in the world, a symbol. Finally, a sign is an index when it means something because of where and when it is located in the world.

4.7   Case study: Linguistic landscape and cultural identity

In this section, we provide a brief case study of Irish in the linguistic landscape in Ireland generally, but in particular within the north of Ireland. We find evidence for a cultural conflict within the linguistic landscape, where language has been, to some extent, used as an instrument of cultural domination.

To start this discussion, we first contextualize the Irish language and its relation to culture by looking at its language family. Then, via a very brief history of Irish, we examine some cultural issues with Irish today, within the north of Ireland, that amplify the cultural dimension and the problematic issues found there within the linguistic landscape.

Irish Gaelic, or *Gaeilge*, or simply Irish, is a Celtic language and a member of the Indo-European language family. Celtic (from Proto-Celtic) has been attested since the 6th century BC. The position of the Irish language within the Celtic family of languages is indicated in Figure 4.7. The Modern Celtic languages include Welsh, Cornish, Breton, Scots Gaelic, Irish Gaelic, and Manx. Within Modern Irish, there are three distinctive dialect[6] areas, generally called Munster, Connacht, and Ulster or Donegal Irish (Ó Siadhail 1989 [1991]) after the regions in which they are found. The main diagnostic of dialect is the use of synthetic forms in the Munster dialect within the verbal system, with the other dialects preferring analytic constructions with the subject pronoun appearing as a separate morpheme. Together with Scottish Gaelic and Manx, Irish is a member of the Q-Celtic grouping of Insular Celtic.

Very old and early forms of Irish appeared on Ogham[7] (see Figure 4.8), an Early Medieval alphabet used to write the early Irish language (between 1st century BC and 6th century AD), and, later, the Old Irish language

---

[6] For a descriptive account of regional differences of Irish covering the morphological and phonological aspects of the dialects see Ó Siadhail (1989 [1991]). The date of the introduction of the language into Ireland is unknown and many theories have been proposed, for which see Ó Dochartaigh (1992:11ff) for details.

[7] Ogham is pronounced as "O-am" /O:M/.

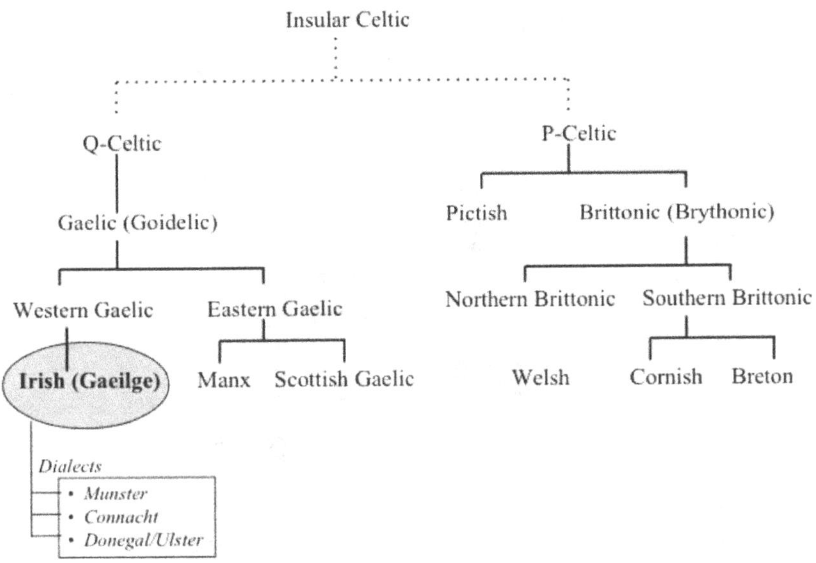

Figure 4.7 The relationship between the Celtic languages (based on MacAulay 1992: 6).

(scholastic Ogham, 6th to 9th centuries). Primitive Irish Ogham inscriptions date from the 4th or 5th century AD. There are roughly 400 surviving orthodox inscriptions on stone monuments throughout Ireland, the majority of which are in southern Munster. Most of the inscriptions consist of personal names. Ogham itself is an Early Medieval form of alphabet or cipher, sometimes known as the Celtic Tree Alphabet. These Ogham stones are one part of our linguistic landscape and Ogham appears in decorative "Celtic" signage in various places (see Figure 4.9).

Irish is a Celtic language within the Indo-European language family. In the syntax of the Irish language, the word order is VSO, with the verb and grammatical subject tightly bound. One characterization of Modern Irish is found in Nolan (2012), using the functionalist-cognitive approach of Role and Reference Grammar (RRG). Language is a rich and complex tool uniquely intended to assist human communication and therefore the forms of language make sense in terms of communicative function.

The Indo-European languages are a language family of several hundred related languages and dialects. The term Indo-European was itself first used in 1813, the name deriving from the geographical extremes of the language family: from Western Europe to North India. There are about 445 living Indo-European languages, with over two thirds of them belonging to the

Figure 4.8 The Ogham alphabet.

Indo-Iranian branch. The most widely spoken Indo-European languages are Spanish, English, Hindustani (Hindi-Urdu), Portuguese, Bengali, Punjabi, and Russian, each with over 100 million speakers, with German, French, Italian, and Persian also having significant numbers. Today, about 46% of the human population speaks an Indo-European language as a first language, and that is by far the highest of any language family. The Indo-European family includes most of the modern languages of Europe. All of the Indo-European languages are descended from a single prehistoric language, called Proto-Indo-European, that was spoken sometime in the Neolithic era. How and when was the Indo-European family discovered? Well, around the period of colonial expansion, in the 16th century, European visitors to the Indian subcontinent began to notice similarities among Indo-Aryan, Iranian, and European languages. In 1786, a British judge, Sir William Jones noted the striking similarities among several of the oldest languages known in his time: Latin, Greek, and Sanskrit, along with Gothic, Celtic, and Persian.

Let us now look a bit at the history of Irish on the island of Ireland[8]. Before 600 AD, we are unclear as to what Irish might have looked like (Doyle 2019). Most of what we know comes from monuments called Ogham stones from the fifth and sixth centuries. These stones are marked with lines and notches (as shown in Figure 4.8) which represent the letters of the Latin alphabet. Mostly, as we have noted, the inscriptions consist of personal names.

---

[8] A relevant read on this topic is Doyle (2019).

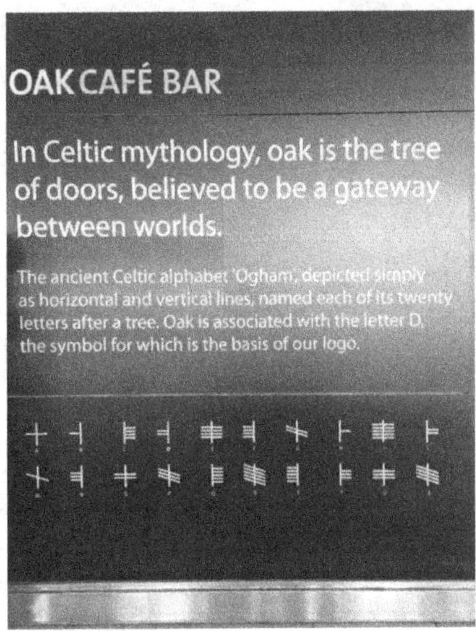

Figure 4.9 A sign as cultural artifact from Dublin Airport.

On the basis of the Ogham stones and some other scraps of evidence, scholars have been able to put together a tentative outline of what is known as Primitive Irish.

The period 600–900 AD is labelled Old Irish. In this era, we find texts written in manuscripts, on the basis of which scholars have been able to reconstruct reasonably completely the language of the time. The period 900–1200 AD is called Middle Irish. Sometimes, the whole period 600–1200 AD is called Medieval Irish. The next phase of Irish, 1200–1600 AD, is referred to as Early Modern Irish. In terms of culture, however, the period 1200–1600 AD in Ireland is part of the medieval era, or the Middle Ages. Modern Irish, sometimes called Late Modern Irish, is regarded as beginning about 1600 AD and extending to the present day.

Languages and their relationship to cultures have always been tricky, even more so when a society has multiple cultures and languages, as is the case within Ireland. The relationship is especially tricky when one of these culture-language pairs is dominant and the community on which it resides seeks to protect its dominance rather than support diversity across culture and language.

An example of this is to be found today in Northern Ireland, that part of the island which resides within the UK (and not the Irish Republic), where there is a level of political tumult, for several reasons to do with parity of esteem between different parts of the community, and cultural and linguistic diversity. One of the reasons for this turbulence has been the status of the Irish language within Northern Ireland.

As we read and hear in the news, a major barrier to progress to the formation of a new governing executive has been around the introduction of an Irish Language Act – called *Acht na Gaeilge* in Irish – that the British government committed to introduce in the St Andrews Agreement back in 2006. However, the largest pro-British unionist party, the Democratic Unionist Party (DUP), have stated they are unconvinced of the need for an act and have, instead, spoken of broadening out the discussion to accommodate Ulster Scots, plus British and Orange (i.e. pro-British unionist) culture, to be included in a "Culture Act".

The push for a standalone Irish Language Act by several Northern Ireland parties was cited by the DUP as the reason that talks with the other (pro-Irish) political parties over government formation broke down. The specific impediment surrounds the introduction of an Irish language Act (*Acht na Gaeilge*) which would give Irish equal status with English, and support a naturally bilingual community in line with typical European norms, in Northern Ireland. Very recently, the Council of Europe supported the promotion of Irish and the rights of Irish speakers in Northern Ireland. What would an Irish Language Act involve? The *Conradh na Gaeilge*[9] organization published information on supporting an Irish Language Act – Acht na Gaeilge, from the discussion document ([Irish Language Act] 2017). This included several information points on official status, services, cost, workable solutions, place names and signage, and other provisions. These are indicated next.

- OFFICIAL STATUS: Recognizing the Irish Language as one of the official languages of Northern Ireland, within the UK. A simple but important measure that would protect the rights of Irish speakers, in a similar manner to those of Welsh and Scots Gaelic.
- SERVICES: Enabling public bodies to provide a baseline service level of interaction with the Irish Language community through Irish. Prioritizing those bodies that have a higher level of interaction with the

---

[9] *Conradh na Gaeilge*, founded in 1893, is an Irish language non-governmental organization with extensive links to the community and a core interest in the protection and the promotion of the Irish language.

public, and requiring commitments such as having official forma and websites in Irish.

- Cost of under £4m per year: The *Conradh na Gaeilge* discussion document explains how a language act would not be expensive, and how the cost reduces over time. It shows that it would be an investment in Northern Ireland.
- Workable solutions: The *Conradh na Gaeilge* discussion document convincingly details a host of practical workable solutions to implementing an effective and reasonably costed Irish Language Act. This discussion document has taken on board International best practice as well as the successful aspects of legislation in Wales, Scotland within the UK, and the Republic of Ireland.
- Place names and Signage: The positive visibility of the Irish language is key to its growth, and to demonstrate that it is part of our shared heritage. To achieve this, an act would legislate for bilingual road signage (these are different from road signs) and official recognition for place names in Irish. Methods were outlined in the discussion document to introduce these in a cost-effective manner.
- Other provisions: The act should provide legislative protections for Irish Medium education. It should create one Central Translation Unit to support public bodies to implement various provisions; increase BBC investment in media in Northern Ireland; create the Office of the Language Commissioners.

The aims of the Council of Europe are to promote human rights, the rule of law and culture across Europe. Part of the Council of Europe's work is to promote language, including minority languages. What is being sought after is legislation which would allow for:

I   The use of Irish in courts, in the Assembly, and for use by state bodies including the police.
II   The appointment of an Irish language commissioner.
III   The establishment of designated *Gaeltacht* areas in Northern Ireland.
IV   The right for education through Irish.
V   Bilingual signage on public buildings and road signage.

The Council of Europe recommended that the UK introduce legislation to protect the Irish language and the rights of Irish speakers in Northern Irish. It also recommended that the UK government create a "political consensus" to ensure this happens. Among the recommendations were that the UK adopt "appropriate legislation protecting and promoting the Irish language and take measures to ensure progress on language rights of Irish Speakers", and that the UK government "should engage in a dialogue to create the political consensus needed for adopting legislation". In its report, the Council of Europe also said the Northern Ireland Executive has a duty to ensure that national and ethnic minorities have access to their rights, including language rights. The recommendations from the Council of Europe have been welcomed by numerous Irish language groups, but not welcomed by the pro-British DUP unionist party.

A report ([CnG-CAJ-UU report] 2019), published jointly by *Conradh na Gaeilge*, the Committee for the Administration of Justice[10] (CAJ) and Ulster University, documents how commitments made by the UK government in relation to the Irish language have been implemented by local government in Northern Ireland. This report contains a framework setting out the actions that can be reasonably expected of local councils in light of their specific remits and roles. This report utilizes the Irish language expertise of *Conradh na Gaeilge* and Ulster University and the human rights law expertise of the CAJ to assess the compliance of local government with international obligations relating to the language. Importantly, the report contains the results of a survey conducted by *Conradh na Gaeilge* and Ulster University to measure compliance with the framework by local government in Northern Ireland. This report notes that local councils in Northern Ireland have a particular responsibility in fulfilling the state's duties to the Irish language community. Councils have authority over matters such as street signage and community development, have a role in cultural and heritage activities, and through their own branding and services in local areas have significant potential to promote the language. The council's duties also include keeping good relations which, when interpreted correctly, should involve local authorities tackling prejudice and promoting understanding across a range of equality grounds.

According to this report, despite the range of treaty-based commitments and some examples of good practice, issues of non-compliance with treaty-based undertakings have regularly been identified by the United Nations (UN) and Council of Europe (CoE) oversight committees tasked with monitoring implementation of the state's obligations. The report provides

---

[10] The CAJ, founded in 1981, is a non-governmental organization promoting and monitoring compliance with international human rights standards.

strong evidence that, in spite of challenges created by non-compliance, the census and school enrolment figures show that the Irish language community has grown substantially in recent years. This has, in part, been driven by the continuous growth of Irish medium schools. Irish-speaking communities are found in each of the new council areas.

However, it is evident that the duties to enhance and protect the development of the Irish language are not being fulfilled in compliance with international obligations. Despite international bodies making clear statements to the contrary, there continue to be charges that the use and promotion of the Irish language has of itself a discriminatory impact, or otherwise interferes with the rights of others. Clearly, as the example of the situation in Northern Ireland indicates, language and culture can be very hot topics indeed across a community[11]. Language is a cultural activity and, at the same time, an instrument for organizing our cultural domains. Sometimes this sense of cultural identity relates to the placement of supportive cultural artifacts within the linguistic landscape rather than the notion of culture itself. It also relates to the support within the linguistic landscape for that cultural identity and language within the community.

Progress on resolving the issue has been made with the intervention of the UK and Irish governments and their joint publication of a framework document ([ND-NA] 2020), called the New Decade, New Approach, in January 2020. All of the parties in Northern Ireland have since agreed to this, thereby paving the way for the return of the Northern Ireland Executive. This governing executive is, happily, now operational. While this document contains many important elements for proper responsible government, it also contains a resolution to the language and cultural identity issue that has been accepted by all sides of the discussion. Specifically, the part of the agreement concerned with language and identity offers a new cultural framework that will include a new Office for Identity and Cultural Expression. This office will aim to promote cultural diversity and inclusion across all identities and cultures, alongside a commissioner to protect and enhance the Irish language and a further commissioner to develop the language, arts and literature associated with the Ulster Scots/Ulster British tradition in Northern Ireland.

In this case study we have focused on the linguistic landscape as a place of conflict, exclusion, and dissent arising from the implementation of certain language policies and politics that do not support diversity, language

---

[11] https://cnag.ie/en/membership/39-english-bearla/get-involved/campaigns/current-campaigns/966-irish-language-act.html.

hierarchies, and the linguistic struggles propagated by these. We conceptualized the linguistic landscape as a site for the propagation of particular ideologies through linguistic/semiotic artifacts, and used as a vehicle for social contestation, with a consequential impact on the local community. In this case study, the Irish language in Northern Ireland has been found to be marginalized in the linguistic landscape. As such, the linguistic landscape while representing discursive and semiotic signage is disputed within the communities there. Clearly, the linguistic landscape acts as a location of identity construction and representation.

Supporting linguistic diversity and cultural equality within the linguistic landscape of Northern Ireland will definitely have its challenges! An article in the *Belfast Telegraph*[12] (27th September 2020) reported on a call for the installation of secret CCTV cameras to be used to stop repeated loyalist attacks on the most damaged Irish language sign in Northern Ireland. Councillors are calling for the installation of CCTV cameras to prevent the attacks and the sectarian vandalism of other dual language boundary signs in the district. The local council has continually replaced the sign. This bilingual sign is located on the edge of Ballyward village, outside Banbridge, and it has been attacked more often than any other Irish language sign in the northern province. Since these signs were first erected in the district in the summer of 2016, pro-British loyalists have carried out a series of sustained attacks, using paint, spray cans, builder's plastering cement, and even a blow torch to deface and destroy the signs. These loyalists have used an angle grinder to cut this bilingual sign in half. They have also repeatedly paint-bombed the sign and even etched out the Irish language part of the sign. The *Belfast Telegraph* reports that one of the Councillors says that:

> "The council has a bilingual signage policy. Whilst some may not like this, the language is part of our shared heritage and should be respected. Defacing or damaging Irish language road signs is nothing but sectarian vandalism and amounts to criminal damage," said Mr Brown. "These signs will be replaced as they are necessary to mark the boundaries of the district. Therefore, those responsible are costing ratepayers hundreds of pounds and should be ashamed of themselves. I think it is time council invested in hidden CCTV at these locations…"

---

[12] https://www.belfasttelegraph.co.uk/sunday-life/news/cctv-call-for-irish-language-sign-attacked-by-loyalists-39562701.html.

Tricky times ahead, no doubt, and a lot of work still to be done. Our focus has highlighted the role of the linguistic landscape as a place where displays of words, images, and public signage, reflect the tensions within the local communities contending for visibility and support for their cultural identity. We can conclude that the linguistic landscape as it is found now is not a true reflection of Northern Ireland's linguistic diversity, and factors such as the relations between dominant and subordinate groups come into play in the construction of the public space in a significant way. In the context of Northern Ireland, the linguistic landscape has become a powerful means of generating the active participation of community. This occurs in the creation of the messages of dissent against the lack of advancement of support for cultural identity, language equality and diversity, and its various manifestations in the linguistic landscape.

5 The nature of cultural artifacts

5.1 Artifacts – features, functions, and intended uses

We are everywhere surrounded by the artifacts of our society and our culture. We interact with our world via artifacts and, in many ways, they enhance the quality of our lives and, in many cases, they often have significant cultural value for us. These artifacts have a function, a purpose, and a utility of some kind. In virtue of their ability to retain a cultural significance, the artifacts we value are important because they have the potential to reveal distinctive features of the human mind. Our judgment about the nature and identity of an artifact is sensitive to the context in which we use the artifact, or indeed to the task at hand.

In this chapter we examine in some detail the nature of artifacts, their features, functions, and intended uses. We provide a definition of an artifact and discuss the existence and identity conditions of artifacts and kinds. We explore the nature of artifacts and the different artifact kinds. The way in which natural objects differ from artifacts is discussed, as is the dual nature of artifacts. A special kind of artifact is examined, that of the social objects, along with the ontology of social reality (Preston 2014). We look at language as a system of signs, and artifacts as markers of a way of life. In addition, we discuss the role of artifacts in culture and cognition, and how we create artifacts.

5.1.1 Defining an artifact

The online *Stanford Encyclopedia of Philosophy* ([Artifact] 2018) defines an artifact as an object that has been intentionally made or produced for a certain purpose. The word "artifact" is restricted to refer to human-made objects which represent a particular culture. An artifact is usually a simple object, such as a tool, utensil, or cultural ornament, that shows evidence of human workmanship and modification, as distinguished from a natural object. Aristotle divided existing things into those that "exist by nature" and those existing "from other causes" (*Physica*, Book II, 192 b 9–18). The things that "exist by nature" include "animals and their parts, … and the plants and the simple bodies (earth, fire, air, water)". Those things existing "from other causes" include "a bed and a coat and anything of that sort, qua receiving these designations, i.e., in so far as they are products of art" (*Physica*, Book II, 192 b 9–18; 1930). Aristotle, in making the distinction between natural objects and artifacts ("artificial products", ibid., 192 b 28), considered artifacts as products of the art of making things. The art of making something involves intentional agency, and an artifact is defined as an object that has been intentionally made for some purpose.

Artifacts are often characterized in terms of functions and goals, and artifact kinds can be identified by sortal descriptions which refer to their intended function (e.g., a "hammer"). An object that has been made for a certain purpose may be termed a functional object. The properties of an artifact can be divided into: 1) those properties relevant to the object's functioning and the significant properties of the same object, and 2) the properties that are incidental and irrelevant to that function. For example, the weight of a hammer is one of its significant features, but its color is incidental and irrelevant. An artifact then can be defined as an object that has been intentionally made for a certain purpose.

A feature of artifacts is that they are physical objects which are spatially and temporally continuous, such that when disassembled and reassembled later are considered to be the same artifact. One important exception to an artifact as a physical object is the social artifact which we will discuss shortly. Artifacts can range from modifications of naturally occurring objects, for example, primitive hand axes constructed by chipping away some flakes from a rock, to highly complex technical objects such as computers and airplanes. Because artifacts come into existence through human creativity and ingenuity along with technical expertise of some kind, artifacts have a technical dimension. That is, artifacts come into being through human activity by being invented and made by humans. In contrast, natural things, are not invented and come into being without human intervention. A person, with some engineering or artistic skill or talent, in virtue of creating an artifact, changes the material world in order to adapt that world to human practical needs. Such a person is an actor in this world, not a spectator. A person with the aforementioned engineering or artistic talent changes the world or environment by creating new kinds of artifacts. The term "artifact" itself, means "made by craft or skill". Artifacts are considered to be things made by humans for supporting them in fulfilling their practical needs and ends. That is, they are objects made by humans for practical purposes.

The world in which we live is a world of artifacts and we live our lives with and through them. It is the world of artifacts that conditions human life. This world of artifacts provides us with the means to adapt the physical environment to our needs and desires, and its influence stretches out much further into the world of social affairs and ideas. Consequently, the world of artifacts is a world fabricated by humans. It is part of the broader human environment created by humans which is populated by artifacts in general. This world of artifacts contains many subclasses of artifacts, including technical, human-made artifacts, works of art, and social artifacts.

A general characterization of works of art is not an easy matter. A traditional way of distinguishing (works of) art artifacts from technical artifacts is by characterizing works of art as objects made for aesthetic reasons with an aesthetic function whereas technical artifacts are objects made for practical reasons. The word "artifact" is used in a wide sense for all objects and phenomena that are of interest to us as potential sources of information about past cultures. All works of art, including musical scores and literary works, are considered artifacts as they have been created by human agents. The condition of artifactuality is often regarded as one of the defining characteristics of works of art. Artifactuality is an essential condition in which a work of art is an artifact of a kind created to be presented to an artworld public. Of course, this condition of artifactuality is plausible only if the concept of artifact is understood in a sense in which intentionally created events, processes, performances, musical and literary works, are regarded as artifacts. Essentially, the condition of artifactuality is equivalent to the requirement that a work of art should have a human creator. Works of "found art" are natural objects creatively assembled and configured in some way by an artist. Such works are genuine artifacts in that they are intentionally put together for aesthetic purposes by a composition consisting of a mix of natural objects and artifacts.

Clearly, within an account of technical artifacts, the notion of making and creating plays a crucial role. Technical artifacts are a kind of physical artifact. However, what does it mean to make a technical artifact? What kind of human activities are involved? With regard to these questions it is interesting to observe that artifacts in general, of which technical artifacts are a subclass, are often characterized by philosophers as creations of the human mind (Thomasson 2007: 52): "It is frequently observed that artifacts and other social and cultural objects are in some sense 'creations of the mind', depending in certain ways on human beliefs or activities." Accordingly, human intentions play a central role in the making of artifacts, while physical activity on its own is not sufficient to make an artifact. A fabricated object may become a piece of art solely through the intention of an artist. Human intentions may be considered to be sufficient for making an artifact out of an object found in nature, as we noted with "found art". Therefore, natural objects may be made into technical artifacts by human intentions alone, by using them intentionally for practical purposes. As well as the example of "found art", we can use a rock as a tool artifact to hammer a nail into a piece of wood!

Artifacts then are characterized as creations of mind and hand. In order to create an artifact, it is necessary to have a creative idea and undertake some physical work to make and shape the actual construction. As far as works of art are concerned, in so far as they are characterized by a certain purpose, this is not of the same kind as the practical purpose of the technical artifacts. For our goals here, we define art as the conscious arrangement and production of some selected mix of shapes, colors, forms, sounds, movements, and possibly other elements, in some configuration, in a way that invokes a sense of beauty, in some medium. The function of a work of art is therefore of an aesthetic nature.

So far, we have discussed fabricated objects including works of art as artifacts. We can label this type of artifact as technical artifacts. We do this to contrast them with a different artifact type, the creation of social or institutional objects. These are of a more abstract nature but may have a physical manifestation. These social objects, of which an organization is a prime example, may be taken to have a practical purpose similar to technical artifacts, but as abstract objects they are different from technical artifacts. If technical artifacts are taken to be physical constructions with a *practical* purpose and function, then that notion contrasts technical artifacts with social or cultural objects and works of art. Technical and social artifacts are generally considered different from works of art that are assessed on aesthetic criteria. What is specific for technical artifacts is that they serve practical purposes as opposed to aesthetic purposes and that they are material objects as opposed to abstract artifacts such as poems, or public signs in the linguistic landscape. Other examples of social artifacts therefore are laws, national borders, marriage, money, organizations, agreements, contracts, and so on. Technical artifacts have a significance and may be evaluated in a perspective concerned with values within their cultural environment. Artifacts serve practical purposes and may encapsulate morally significant values related to safety, privacy, and status.

It is easy to differentiate between technical and social objects. These social objects, as institution artifacts, influence and govern the behavior and cooperation of people. Indeed, social artifacts are based on human design and serve a purpose or function. As they are not material objects, social artifacts are not considered to be technical artifacts. Although social artifacts may involve physical objects or phenomena, they do not perform their social function by virtue of the physical characteristics of these objects or phenomena. The way social artifacts perform their functions is fundamentally different from that of technical artifacts. Social institutions perform their function on the basis of collective acceptance of rules by humans.

The existence and features of artifacts depend on human interests, and for many artifacts their continued existence depends on our thoughts and intentions (Grandy 2007: 18–32). As an artifact, a Swiss Army knife[13] owes its origin to an inventor and the factory where it was assembled, but its properties and functioning are actually independent of the inventor and factory. In ontological terms, many artifacts differ in kind from whatever composes them (Elder 2007: 33–51). For example, when a kitchen chair is broken, then ontologically, that artifact is destroyed, though its constitutive materials still exist. When a kitchen chair has a leg replaced, the artifact continues to exist.

Artifacts, and other objects of social and cultural significance, are creations of the human mind and, as such, depend on human beliefs or activities in virtue of the fact that they are the product of human intentions (Thomasson 2007: 52–73). While natural kinds (trees and rocks) are understood in terms of internal essences, artifacts are thought of holistically in terms of their creator's intention, the artifact's characteristic function, and the social and cultural context of the artifact's creation and use (Bloom 2007: 154). The sort of feature that grounds the reference of an artifact kind is that the artifacts must be the products of successfully executed intentions to create something of the kind. Following from this, the existence of artifacts of that kind entails that there is substantive knowledge of the nature of the artifact kind and that the artifact's existence is not independent of human knowledge of them. Simply, the creation of an artifact requires some human knowledge.

5.1.2   The existence and identity conditions of artifacts and kinds

So far in our discussion we have observed that artifacts are material objects that are made to be used by people in a culture. In contrast, social artifacts constitute a general term for abstract arrangements and constructions that can play an instrumental role in social reality, like an organization, in a society. In our daily lives, artifacts like tables, can openers, vacuum cleaners, cars, and so on, play roles comparable to the roles that are instantiated in events by instances of natural kinds, people, animals, plants, and other natural items.

---

[13] Swiss Army knife: https://en.wikipedia.org/wiki/Swiss_Army_knife (accessed 18 December 2020).

Artifacts are individual concrete objects and are bearers of properties that exist in space and persist through time. As such, they are instances or members of certain kinds of artifact classes. Each artifact must have an identity. The particulars of different kinds possess different existence and identity conditions. We will, in the first instance, use the example of natural objects to illustrate the point. The existence and identity conditions of mountains, for instance, clearly differ from those of birds. This is because mountains are a kind of geological formation, whereas birds are a kind of living organism. The existence and identity conditions of the members of artifact kinds carry reference to the people who make and use artifacts for certain purposes, or to serve certain functions. The artifact we call money, in the sense of currency, is an institutional or social construct and exists only in virtue of people having belief in it. We know, for example, that Monopoly money is not real and we don't believe in it beyond the game, its context of use. An artifact could survive the end of all human life, but no artifact could come into existence without human life existing, since only human beings can create artifacts.

With artifact kinds, such matters of persistence and identity appear to be much more problematic. A chair can easily "morph" into a table, and a table into a chair, and can do so very easily. We can place a coffee cup on a chair, thereby using it as a table. We can also sit on a table and use it as a chair. Indeed, whether this may simply rest "in the eye of the beholder" or, at least, of the user. A table can certainly be used as a chair. Does that make it a chair? If so, has it then ceased to be a table? Moreover, it seems that an artifact of one kind can, with a little ingenuity, often be reconfigured so as to turn it into one of another quite different kind – for instance, a stool might be transformed successively into a table that holds one's coffee cup. Some artifact kinds are defined by reference to their use-case functions that we regard them as serving, or as being able to serve. An example of this instrumental category of artifacts is that of utensils which contains tables, chairs, tents, cooking pots, knives, and hammers, and so on, that are individually configured in a way which makes them suitable for use in a particular way.

5.2 The nature of artifacts and artifact kinds

An interesting observation on the intrinsic nature of artifacts comes from the world of technology, where it is commonly recognized that not all fabricated objects are necessarily considered to be artifacts. The notion of artifact is constrained to apply only to objects that are made in order to serve a particular purpose. Additionally, things that are unintended by-products of a production process are not considered to be true artifacts. In order to count as an artifact, an entity should successfully realize, or at least have the potential of realizing, the purpose that its maker had in mind when making it. If there is a failure in realizing that intention, then an artifact has not been produced, only a bunch of scrap or waste material.

An entity such as water is a natural kind and not an artifact. But under certain circumstances it may be considered an artifact. This is when water comes from bottles, cans, taps, hoses, and coolers. Water can be the result of an intentional process in that it can be filtered, processed, flavored, carbonated, purified, and chlorinated. As an artifact, bottled water is advertised on television and sold in supermarkets. We can conclude that water, subject to contextual conditions, is both a natural kind and also an artifact, having this dual aspect.

5.2.1   Intended features unifying artifacts

What is essential to the existence of an artifact is that it is the intended product of human activity, and that, for an artifact to come into existence, it must be intentionally created with certain intended features. The intended features need not include an intended function. Elder (2014: 33) argues that artifacts are classified into artifactual kinds by way of their possessing intended features that are associated with that kind, by virtue of their significant distinctive features, and that these classification-relevant features may, but need not, include intended function.

It is worth noting that if we take the relevant intended features that unify artifacts, into artifactual kinds, to be functional, we take the risk of excluding works of art. If we make them to be structural or perceptible, we get a diminished view of many functional artifact kinds, which can vary widely in structure. According to Elder, the intended functional features are tied to norms about what the object is to do and how, and by whom, it is to be used to achieve this function. Moreover, as suggested above, the intended structural features of artifacts often serve in part to make the type of object recognizable so that it can invoke the appropriate norms. In other cases, the intended structural features may directly serve to invoke norms. Many of the structural features of clothing, such as a shirt or jacket for example, have nothing to do with the function of covering the body, or retaining warmth, but rather invoke norms of behavior in the wearer. Consider the different norms invoked by the structural and perceptible differences say, between gym and more formal clothes. Schools have long noted the force of these clothing types in affecting the behavior of children and have used this as a supporting argument in favor of children wearing school uniforms. Uniforms, for employees, police officers, medical workers, fire service, and so on, invoke appropriate behaviors from wearers and observers.

Can we make an artifact without changing anything about it? We can, for example, use a stone as a paperweight by placing it in the proper context and intending it to be a paperweight. But then, what do we do about the process by which features acquire functions for which they were not originally adapted or selected. When we use, say, a teapot as a paperweight, have we then made a new sort of artifact (a paperweight, co-located with or replacing the teapot)? We clearly have the intuition that one can make something an artifact, or even a work of art, just by way of our intended action in selection and display, and this seems in line with certain practices in the world of art regarding found art, or movements like *Dada*[14]. For example, one may confer the status of an artifact on an object, like a piece of driftwood, by simply hanging it on a wall. The most famous example of this in the history of art is, of course, by Marcel Duchamp who, in 1917, exhibited ready-made everyday objects, found or purchased, which he declared to be art – Duchamp famously, and very controversially at the time, exhibited the art object called *Fountain*. However, this was simply a reused urinal containing the signature of R. Mutt.

Natural objects which become works of art are made into artifacts without the use of tools and the artifact status is conferred on the object, rather than through fabrication. They thereby gain an aesthetic function. When we walk along the sea-shore, we find natural objects like driftwood. However, we cannot or would not normally consider driftwood as artifact or art. The reason being that, by the sea-shore, the right context is not in place for a piece of driftwood to be recognized as a piece of art, and the intention that it be so recognized as art or artifact will fail given this wrong context. But, once the driftwood is collected with this intention, and perhaps later hung on display on our wall, it can be recognized as an artifact, or art, and the intention that it be regarded as an artifact or art will be successful. This is evidence that artifacts are the resulting product of an intentional activity and we can broaden this to say that artifacts are the result of human intentions and practices.

---

[14] https://en.wikipedia.org/wiki/Dada (accessed 18 December 2020).

5.2.2   What are artifact kinds?

What makes individual artifacts members of their kinds? What is the nature of artifact kinds and how are artifact kinds defined? Artifact kinds are defined with respect to what we call their proper functions. Changes in the perception of an artifact, or the use to which it is put, may result in the artifact becoming something else. Artifacts, just as much as natural objects, can be identified at arbitrary levels of generality, say, as a cup, a hammer, or a clock, or as some item for cooking. What goes into an artifact seems a matter of human ingenuity. Whether an artifact counts as a clock, a hammer, or a cup will be agreed by convention and consensus. The diversity among artifact kinds seems much larger than among natural kinds of things. Thomasson (2007: 52–73) proposes to conceive of artifact kinds as being defined by the features of artifacts that were intended by their creators, emphasizing the intentional rather than causal relations in characterizing artifacts. Interestingly, Thomasson argues that artifacts are better conceived of as objects with certain intended features and not, as objects intentionally made to serve a purpose, via a certain function, and that this provides for a better understanding of the role of artifacts in our daily lives. Beyond functional, structural, and perceptible properties, these intentional features may include features that relate to how created objects are to be regarded, used, and treated. Thomasson claims that these intentional features represent the essential features of members of artifact kinds.

Artifacts and their kinds may be mind-dependent entities, without this necessarily implying that they are fictional or unreal. What this means is that artifacts, as they are the products of intentional human activities, are considered "mind-dependent". The classes of artifacts, as human-made items, do not correspond to natural kinds. Artifacts are the result of intentional production and are characterized in terms that refer to human purposes and activities.

5.2.3   Nature of artifacts – Natural objects differ from artifacts

As we earlier mentioned, artifacts are objects intentionally made to serve a given purpose; natural objects come into being without human intervention. Artifacts have proper functions that they are designed to perform. Often, it is the general term for a kind of artifact, such as hammer, screwdriver, scraper, that just names the proper function of the artifact. The nature of an artifact therefore resides in its proper function of that which it was designed to do and the purpose for which it was produced. Natural objects differ from artifacts (Baker 2008: 3) in at least three ways (1)

(1)   Natural objects differ from artifacts

1)   Artifacts depend ontologically for their existence on human purposes.
2)   Artifacts are intention dependent objects that could not exist in a world without people. In contrast, natural objects would exist regardless of human intentions or practices.
3)   Artifacts have intended proper functions, given to them by humans, within a culture and society with beliefs, desires, and intentions.

5.2.4   Artifacts have a dual nature

Kroes (2002: 287–302, 2012) argues that artifacts have a dual nature. Firstly, they are physical objects, constructions intentionally made by people, that have the potential to perform a particular function, while, secondly, they are intentional objects with a function as a technical artifact that distinguishes them from natural objects. This function has meaning only within a context of intentional human action. The creator of the artifact is concerned with how the created object ought to be in order to attain certain goals, and to function. The artifact acts as an "interface" between the substance and organization of the artifact itself, and the surrounding environment in which it operates. The character of the artifact is such that its goals are realized once set in the surrounding environment. Our world has human agents who intentionally represent the world and act intentionally in it, and whose behavior is motivated by individual reasons. Activities are interpreted in terms of realizations of goals, and functions are attributed to certain objects or activities. How do artifacts fit into this conceptualization of the world? An artifact is an object with a function and a physical structure consciously designed, fabricated, and used by humans to realize its function. That is, an artifact has a physical structure, a function, and a context of intentional human action.

The *context* is necessary. It makes no sense to consider an artifact's function without reference to a context of human action (Figure 5.1). Functional discourse is part of the intentional conceptualization of the world and, in language, it is meaningless to speak about functions without a context of intentional human action. Indeed, a context of human action is necessary to

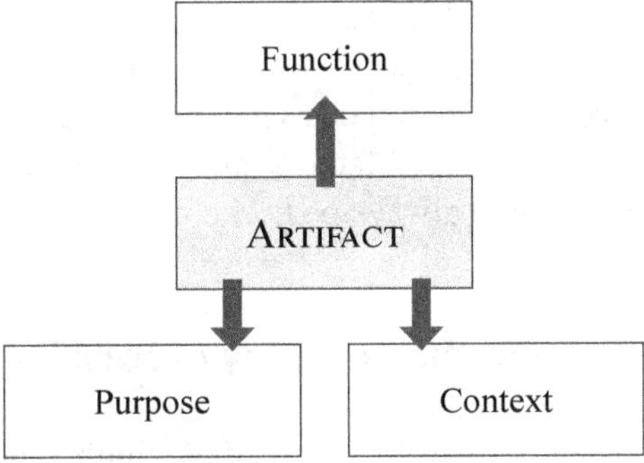

Figure 5.1 Artifact function, purpose, and context relations.

support an artifact's function. Searle (2007) has observed that functions are attributed, in some context of human action, to objects, but they are not intrinsic properties of those objects. We cannot make sense of artifacts without considering their physical structure, or the context of intentional human action in which the artifact is utilized. Simply, without some context of human action, the notion of function has no meaning, and an "artifact" without its function is just some physical object.

What we call art, including music, is about creativity, but it is also the result of shared conventions and a common ground between people who come to inhabit common cultural spaces. As such, creativity is a cultural process. We can link deeper meanings in art to particular times, places, and ideas. As a linguist might document the linguistic resources and structures available to create meaning in linguistic communication, we can also look for the kinds of resources and patterns available for communication in the sounds, images, and worlds of popular music. Individual lexical and grammatical choices in texts can be examined to show the kinds of discourse that they signify. These discourses can be considered as models of the world in context, and include kinds of participants, behaviors, goals, and locations.

These days, we find that much communication is multimodal and communicative interaction can be characterized, along with its values, participants, actions settings, etc., by both linguistic and visual choices. Traditional semiotic approaches address the way that individual signs signify or symbolize. The multimodal approach is concerned with the choices of signs available to communicators and the way that the meaning of individual signs changes when used in combination with others. The signs from which we are able to choose to create combinations do not have fixed meanings, but have "meaning potential" (Halliday 1978). To understand cultural value judgments, it is important to consider the social contexts in which value judgments are made, and, as best we can, the social reasons why some aspects are valued over others. How people interpret artifacts such as media and signs depends on many individual, cultural and contextual factors, and the issue of the contribution of context to meaning should always be borne in mind.

5.3   Social objects and the ontology of social reality

Searle examines the nature of artifacts, and their significance, in the context of the nature of social reality. He remarks that:

> if we look at our social life, it is a remarkable fact that there is a class of entities that have a very important role in our lives, but they only are what they are, because we believe that that is what they are.
>
> …
>
> It looks as if in the case of these institutional phenomena, language doesn't just describe a pre-existing reality, but is partly constitutive of the reality that it describes.
>
> Searle (2007: 16)

In relation to language use, in particular the role of language as a tool, in speech act performatives, Searle (2007: 19) asks: *What is the special role of performatives in the creation of social and institutional reality?* The special nature of a speech act performative is that a large number of institutional facts are brought into existence just by saying you are creating it, provided you have the appropriate authority in the appropriate situation, and the context is correct. We can adjourn a meeting by saying "I adjourn the meeting". With the appropriate authority and context, we can declare war by saying "We declare war", or pronounce somebody husband and wife by saying "I pronounce you husband and wife", thereby creating an institutional reality. In this regard, we distinguish those features of the world that, following Searle, are independent of a human observer from those features that are dependent on an observer. Observer-independent features are those natural kinds that exist in the world independent of us as human observers (such as mountains, rivers, and so on). In contrast to these natural kinds, there are other phenomena in the world whose existence depends on being regarded in a certain way by human agents. These are observer-dependent phenomena and include things such as iPads, tables, and chairs. Many of the most common concepts that we use in engaging with the world (for example, concepts realized as the artifacts cars, tables, chairs, iPads, and houses, and so on) involve the assignment of function to them. Once the notion of function enters the picture, we introduce normativity with respect to establishing, or developing, a standard of behavior. Normativity entails that some action, attitude, or state is justified as one we ought to be in. If we assign an aesthetic function to an artifact, we can say it is an *art object* and, with such an assignment of function, we may consider the artifact to have some artistic and aesthetic value.

A fact about social and collective behavior is the shared intentionality in the form of collective beliefs, desires, and intentions. Searle (2007: 25) notes three steps in this. First, the functions are assigned, the second step involves collective intentionality, and the third step involves consensus on constitutive rules of the form "X counts as Y in context C". People can assign functions to objects, elevating the object into an artifact. They can assign a function of being – a digging tool, or a chair to sit on. Collective intentionality is related to the assignment of function by people. While an entity can be used to perform a function, it may not perform the function in virtue of its physical structure. It can only perform its function in virtue of the collective recognition of the entity in question as having a particular status and a function that comes with the status. Searle calls this an artifact's status function, and defines this as:

> a function that an entity or person performs not in virtue of its physical
> structure alone, but in virtue of the collective imposition on the entity
> as having a certain status, and, with that status, a function that can only
> be performed in virtue of the collective recognition of the status.
>
> Searle (2007: 25)

That is, as Searle says, "X counts as Y". For example, a line of stones, formerly a wall, may count as a boundary. When counting as a boundary, it now has a status that is exercised in virtue of the collective assignment of function in a community. The structure is the collective imposition of a function of the form "this entity X counts as having this status and therefore functions as Y in this context C".

Artifacts such as a hammer or screwdriver have the potential for purposeful action according to the function of the artifact, and have physical characteristics that help us to recognize that purpose. The central property of artifactual kinds may be the function assigned by their individual creator rather than by any group of individuals taking a collective perspective (Thomasson 2007). If we want to reproduce an artifact by making a copy with the same intended function, we must ensure that the new artifact bears the same function that the maker intended for the original artifact. This requires that we have a certain knowledge and understanding of, or can conceptualize, what the original maker intended. Whether the new artifact of the relevant kind succeeds in fulfilling the conditions of application of the corresponding kind, depends on our having the correct knowledge of what the original creator intended to make.

Searle (2009: 9–27) examines the role of language in the creation, constitution, and maintenance of social reality. Intentional attitudes shape, and are shaped by, social institutions. Social factors regulate our attitudes toward interacting with physical artifacts. The intentional attitudes of multiple individuals can be coordinated in order to establish a common ground for planning joint actions and for communication about social facts. According to Searle, for a fact to be of an institutional kind, an institutional artifact, it must be the sort of thing that is collectively accepted as having a status function, where status functions are created and maintained by a class of linguistic representations with a logical structure containing its status function. Entities of institutional reality, institutional artifacts, are "factitive" in structure, the reason being that status functions and deontic powers are brought about by representations of facts about the world and therefore have propositional structure. Searle maintains that the key explanatory unit in social ontology should be institutional facts. Representations of facts about "objects", artifacts, are propositional in structure, where it is the factitive rather than the "object" status of the entities represented that matters for human institutional reality. For Searle, all social reality and all social institutions presuppose language, and he defends the view that the logical form of the creation of the institutional fact is always a DECLARATION, arguing that the theory of speech acts can be applied to institutional analysis. Searle is concerned with the ontology of certain social entities (for example, currency notes, educational institutions, political offices, government, and marriage) and the role that language has in the creation and maintenance of these entities. He calls these social entities "institutional" because they are logically prior to the objects. The object is only institutional if it is created by a certain linguistic operation that results in the institutional fact. This linguistic operation is the DECLARATIVE speech act.

Intentional states and events are those mental states and events that are directed on objects and states of affairs in the world. They include not only intention, but also perception and intentional action, belief, desire, the emotions, and any state that has a directed content. Specifically, intentional states have a propositional content – I can *believe* or *hope* that it is raining. The actual propositional content is that IT IS RAINING. In language, this corresponds to the distinction between the propositional content of the speech act and the type of speech act utilized. The intentional state represents its conditions of satisfaction, which include truth conditions in the case of belief, carrying out conditions for intentions, and fulfilment conditions for desires. The notion of collective intentionality is important for understanding society, and intentionality is not just a property of individual minds. When we engage in some sort of cooperative behavior, such as having a conversation, we are engaging in collective intentionality. Meaningful utterances are those where the speaker intentionally imposes conditions of satisfaction on conditions of satisfaction. This is the essence of speaker meaning. If an utterance is to be meaningful it must have conditions of satisfaction, such as truth or fulfilment conditions. It is the intentional imposition of these semantic conditions of satisfaction that constitutes speaker meaning.

5.4   Language is a system of signs

Language is a system of signs that expresses ideas, where the relation between the signifier and signified is arbitrarily based on convention, and the meaning of the signs can change over time. Peirce wrote that a sign "is something which stands to somebody for something in some respect or capacity" (Zeman 1977: 24). Peirce developed a typology with three kinds of signs: ICONS, which signify by resemblance; INDEXES/INDICES, which signify by causal connections, and SYMBOLS, which signify by convention and must be learned. In Peirce's model, every sign is determined by its object, such that, 1) by characterizing the object, as in an image (we call the sign an ICON); 2) by connection with the object as in smoke generated by fire (we call the sign an INDEX); 3) by interpreting the sign as denoting the object, as with a flag (we call the sign a SYMBOL).

Through language as a system of signs, people find meaning in their everyday lives, in the media they consume, and the messages they receive from marketers and advertisers in contemporary culture. Mostly, these days, the delivery channel or medium for this is digital over the internet. Symbols are things that often have significant historical and cultural meanings in a society. Examples include the Star of David for Jewish people, the shamrock and harp for Irish people, and the Red Flag for socialism. These symbols play important roles in every society (Geertz 1973: 45). We learn the meaning of symbols in a certain culture and the symbol's importance is reinforced by events in that culture. Symbols help us make sense of our world and influence our behavior in many areas, including worldview and status in society. Letters and words in a language are symbols.

As we noted, language is a *social institution*, a human tool, that expresses ideas by using signs, whose meanings are based on convention. In a society, we learn the rules that govern language use. Culture can be seen as a collection of conventions that guide us with respect to what to eat, how to dress, and how to relate to others, in our society. Chandler (2007: 147–148) suggests that there are three basic kinds of conventions (called codes) within a culture: SOCIAL codes (involving language, our bodies, commodities we use, and our behavior), TEXTUAL codes (involving scientific practices, aesthetics, genres, and the mass media), and INTERPRETIVE codes (involving perception, aesthetics, and ideologies). These three types of codes correspond broadly to three key kinds of knowledge required by interpreters of a text, namely knowledge of: 1) the world (social knowledge); 2) the medium and the genre (textual knowledge); 3) the relationship between social and textual codes. According to Chandler, within a culture, social differentiation is observable not only from linguistic codes, but from a host of non-verbal codes. We communicate our social identities through the work we do, the way we talk, the clothes we wear, our hairstyles, our eating preferences, our social environments and possessions, our use of free time, our modes of travelling, and, of course, our artifacts. In all of this, language is a key marker of social *identity*.

5.5   Artifacts as markers of a way of life

To see artifacts as markers of a way of life, and to take an interest in public artifacts, as such, is to take an interest in what they were made for, what norms and practices governed things within a culture and a civilization. Because artifacts can give insights into a way of life, contemporary or long past, they are preserved in museums for us to observe and study. For this reason, anthropologists and archaeologists are not just interested in the actual physical object. Rather, our interest in artifacts resides in what these objects might have been seen as, within a culture and a civilization, and what they were used for within the society in which they were found. More especially, how did these artifacts fit as part of a way of life, and contribute to the construction of cultural identity within the community which created them.

There are several advantages to us in acknowledging the role of intended and recognizable properties in artifactual kinds. One advantage is that it enables us to provide a better account of the classification of artifacts. Another advantage is that it provides a way of understanding the ways in which we experience artifacts. A scientific interest in artifacts helps us to understand the role that human knowledge plays with them. A third advantage is that it can help to understand the aesthetic power of certain works of art. In virtue of their intended structural features, these artifacts invoke the recognition that they are to be treated as members of the kind. By their placement, form, or size, they also intentionally constrain us in following some norms. A prime example of constraining our norms of behavior is to be found in relation to how we treat the various art forms, where we understand art as a special kind of artifact, with an aesthetic function.

Artifacts are inherently meaningful and provide insights into the rules and customs governing their use. Artifacts have significance and are what they are only as part of a certain context. As such, they must be understood against the background of a way of life in the society in which they are found and used. The role of artifacts in our lives helps to bind us into societal models within a community. Artifacts are dependent on societal customs as to how we treat them, and they build in reasons for their functions and behaviors.

5.6   The role of artifacts in culture and cognition

The artifacts in our societies enable the emergence of various kinds of cultural practices which would otherwise not be possible. These artifacts shape the perceptual, cognitive, and social processes that are found within cultural practices. Even artifacts such as clocks and mobile phones, for example, allow for more fine-grained planning and coordination by people than would otherwise be possible. By virtue of their functions, these artifacts provide a foundation for many cultural activities. But some artifacts can only play the roles that they play by virtue of people having common knowledge about them. A fact can function in human reasoning because the representation of the fact is in a propositional form. Facts have priority over objects, by virtue of facts having the quality of designating or expressing the idea of something to be of a certain character. Because of this, facts can function in human reasoning in a way that objects cannot. Artifacts that figure in institutional facts are typically placeholders for patterns of activity. Institutional facts act as a glue to hold subsets of human civilization together, and require collective intentionality amongst people in society for their creation.

Searle (1995) has famously observed how the ontology of some objects derives from their assigned status functions in a social community: money, marriage, and law operate not by virtue of the material properties of currency, wedding rings, or documents, but by anchored and conventionalized social practices. As regards the role of artifacts in culture and cognition (Tylén & McGraw 2014: 135), we employ artifacts across a range of everyday cognitive and cultural practices to achieve many purposes (2). Through stable cultural practices that are nonetheless capable of being manipulated, public properties of artifacts facilitate modes of extended and distributed cognition.

(2)   How we employ artifacts across cognitive and cultural practices

Artifacts:
1) scaffold our memory in society (a kind of collective or institutional memory),
2) modulate cognitive complexity,
3) enable the cognitive division of labor,
4) promote confidence and trust across our society,
5) consolidate a social structure, and
6) support a cultural community.

Human cognition is an emergent property of a system composed of people, knowledge, and objects engaged in a flow of representations. Therefore, cognition must be studied in context, and the study of distributed cognition offers a rich account of the way that people, artifacts, and cultural practices interact, and emerge. A feature of social cognition is the human ability to identify other people's mental states and the function of this ability is to allow us to interpret and predict people's behavior. To the extent that an artifact has a purposeful function, our minds represent it as a tool, whereas the character associated with a status function has a closer association with language. The role of artifacts in cognitive processes is usually characterized by analogy with the use of common tools. Just as a well-crafted tool extends and enhances the capacity of our physical human bodies, so artifacts augment our cognitive powers. For example, in using writing surfaces as "tools for thought", traditionally people have had a varying choice of a wide variety of media, including clay, bark, papyrus, wax tablets, stone, vellum, paper, and, these days, digital tablets such as iPads. All of these artifacts possess qualities that facilitate the recording of images, text, and ideas. The functional properties of durability, transportability, or other such practical aspects favor a particular medium for conveying a particular message. Understanding how these artifacts work as "tools for thought" requires attention to the potential of the artifact. Indeed, many artifacts become "tools for thought" whenever they function well for that purpose – we can easily write on a table napkin, smartphone, or digital tablet to quickly capture ideas and make notes that we might otherwise forget. Populating our environment with artifacts can serve to scaffold memory, significantly expanding the capabilities of our minds, and our collective cultural memory. We all make use of artifacts to accomplish cognitive processes on a daily basis. Cognition plays a role in the world of artifacts (Chazan 2019), and a key question concerns the relationship between artifacts as human-made fabricated material objects in the world and the abstract representation of these objects as concepts in the mind.

5.7   The creation of artifacts

The world we live in today is characterized by the continuous appearance of new kinds of artifacts, be they technical artifacts or works of art/cultural objects (Vega-Encabo and Lawler 2014: 105–124). In most cases, these new artifacts bear strong resemblances to existing ones (i.e., last year's iPhone compared to this year's latest model) and are simply variations of previous artifacts, modified in their material or functional structure. But, often artifacts are new, and do not have precedents of any kind (the original iPad, for example). The creation of a novel artifact involves the appearance of a new kind of artifact that may present a new solution to an old problem or offer a new solution to a new problem.

Two theories capture the dynamics surrounding the creation of artifacts. A functional theory of artifacts gives an account of the nature of artifact kinds and artifacts in terms of the functions they perform, whereas an intentional theory of artifacts is one that reflects on the nature of artifacts in terms of the intentions and concepts of their makers. Functional theories assert that sameness of function is the relevant criterion for membership of an artifact class. Artifactual kinds are primarily functional kinds, and the creation of a new artifact implies the creation of an instance of a functional kind. A description of an artifact then consists in the identification of a proper functional kind to which it belongs, and each new artifact is new in virtue of its function. Correspondingly, if the intentions of the artifact designers are sufficient to assign a function to new artifacts (and to determine kind membership), so are the intentions of users. The creation of a particular artifact is the realization of some human agent's intention, which involves the innovative idea of the kind of thing being created. As the artifacts are the result of intentional creation, several elements characterize the situation within which the emergence of new creations is achievable. These elements (Vega-Encabo & Lawler 2014: 122) have to be considered within an ontology of artifacts (3).

(3)   Elements in an ontology of artifacts

An artifact:
1)   emerges out from the IDEA of what we want to achieve.
2)   is driven by the REQUIREMENTS that must be met.
3)   is not guided by any concept describing the features that characterise what is being produced. Rather, the DISCOVERY is novel and the artifact is new.
4)   is done under conditions of ignorance in relation to the resulting creation.
5)   leverages the KNOWLEDGE, skills, past successes, and experiences of the intentional agents in devising new ways to solve some particular problem.

As regards artifacts, we end this chapter with a quote from Aristotle, and an observation from Givón (2005: 264):

...if a piece of wood is to be split with an axe, the axe must of necessity be hard; and, if hard, it must of necessity be made of bronze or iron. Now exactly in the same way the body, which like the axe is an instrument – for both the body as a whole and its several parts individually have definite operations for which they are made; just in the same way, I say, the body if it is to do its work [function], must of necessity be of such and such character.

Aristotle (*De Partibus Animalium*. Barnes (ed.). 1984: 650)

...the form of all human inventions is chosen for a purpose, be the invention an implement, an institution, or a custom. The forms of human-made artefacts are adaptive, but they are constrained by the purpose for which they were constructed. Aristotle made an analogy between the animate body and man-made implements, and the isomorphism between form and function.

Givón (2005: 264)

Creating an artifact involves realizing our intentions and understanding what goals are achievable. The knowledge (cultural or otherwise) and understanding related to the conceptualization of some artifact emerges in the actual production through which it is discovered.

6   Cultural models and way of life

6.1 Lifestyles and way of life

So far in our study, we have discussed and characterized language and culture, worldview, the linguistic landscape, and artifacts. The concern of this chapter is cultural models and way of life. We will argue that cultural models underpin a way of life of societal community. A way of life and a lifestyle are intrinsically related to cultural models and the knowledge they encapsulate. Various models of the organization of knowledge are examined, including frames, schemata, and scripts, and relate this to cultural knowledge.

A way of life is defined as the habits, customs, and beliefs of a particular person or group of people. It is a style of living that reflects the attitudes of a person or group. What then are individual lifestyles, and a way of life, and how do these relate to cultural models? Within cultural and social frames, people develop individual lifestyles, and a way of life. The notion of lifestyle therefore motivates the individual's active choice of cultural expressions. The individual's choice of lifestyle along with their normal everyday activities is broadly determined by the society and culture in which an individual belongs, and the positions that the individual occupies within that society and culture. However, the beliefs, desires, intentions, worldview, and life goals of people are not fully governed by their social or cultural membership, the reason being that lifestyles are developed and maintained where social and cultural structures intersect with the individual's own actions and choices (Rosengren 1994: 234). People can make lifestyle choices.

6.2 Cultural models

A way of life reflects the cultural models of a society or group. Bennardo and de Munck (2014: 14) consider that an important function of cultural models is to facilitate engagement with the world and thereby allow us to conduct our daily activities naturally, with little cognitive processing cost. For them, cultural models consist of a configuration of default values that typically correlate well with other members of society, such that the behaviors they shape are easily decoded by others. Therefore, cultural models are mental representations shared by members of a culture and function to make sense of communicative behaviors. Cultural models are used to interpret intentions, attitudes, emotions, and social context.

It seems that cultural models are inherently flexible, in that default values may be updated and overridden as required by context. The application of default values leads to automatic responses or interpretations that require little cognitive effort, while value updates and overrides attract a greater cognitive cost. Cultural models, like language, are flexible, fluid, and capable of being used in a variety of different situations and among a variety of different people with slightly different perspectives. A member of a social group will be able to understand the core, default features of a multitude of cultural models while also being able to intentionally adjust and update them as the situation requires. In fact, we do all this all the time, automatically and naturally. Our lives are a flux of cultural models activated in a variety of situational contexts, without our conscious awareness of the cognitive operations involved in instantiating the cultural models. That is, we quite naturally and effortlessly situate cultural models within social contexts, scenarios, and events (Bennardo and de Munck 2014: 15–17). Cultural models are the mental organization and configuration of salient cultural content. Cultural models are not cognitive operations, but may be organized as a semantic network.

Kronenfeld (2008) informs us that the *cultural* element of a cultural model is imagined as if it is objectively real. All cultural models, if they are located in the mind of a single individual, are individual instances of a cultural model. However, the cultural model is assumed to be shared and, because our individual cultural models correlate with those of others, we assume that the cultural model has a collective objective reality. Bennardo and de Munck (2014: 23) discuss theories of culture, comparing the strengths and weaknesses of theories that focus on culture as in the mind (embodied) and theories that focus on culture as an emergent property of the material and socio-structural dimensions of society. They refer to these as *inside (the mind)* and *outside (in the environment)* theories of cultures. An issue is, is the unit of culture the individual or the group? How can culture be both inside the mind and outside in the environment, in the individual, and in the collective? For Kronenfeld (1996, 2008), in his theory of the individual's model of cultural models, the nature of culture is felt to be objectively real. Culture is shared and learned, implying that any unit or definition of culture must include people, since culture inheres in a group as a shared resource, and it is people who learn their culture. By conflating culture with people, the unit of culture is usually thought of as either the individual or some specially constituted group, necessarily entailing a theory of culture as heterogeneous (when the unit of analysis is the individual) or homogeneous (when the unit of analysis is the group). The viewpoint of the individual as the unit of analysis is held by cognitive anthropologists. Bennardo and de Munck (2014: 24) refer to this perspective as the *inside* view of culture. The alternative viewpoint, of the group as the unit of analysis, characterizes a wide variety of different theoretical perspectives, and is referred to as the *outside* view of culture. This shift to "inside the mind" from "outside in the environment" entails that the study of culture moves from observing behavior and its expressions, to determining, as best one can, the cognitive operations that motivate these behaviors.

Of course, there is a significant theoretical downside to moving culture into the mind in that it logically disqualifies artifacts, including buildings, behaviors, movies, and anything else in the environment from being culture. However, notwithstanding this, we might notice that archaeologists, anthropologists, and various forms of scholars of culture have as their object of study not culture, as such, but cultural artifacts that are derived from culture. To study culture in this way, one has to infer what cultural models were being used by the producers of these artifacts. These cultural models and associated schemas now become the object of study, not the actions themselves, and these schemas are subject to psychological constraints and conditions. In particular, our short-term operational memory leads us to chunk information into larger cognitive elements, among them schemas and cultural models (Bennardo and de Munck 2014: 28). However, it would be simply wrong to view culture as purely a mental phenomenon, because it is enabled within the physical world of our environment in a number of ways. For culture to be communicated, and expressed, a communicative medium is required and typically this is language-based in some way, be it through speech, writing, social media, and so on. Without these necessary means of expressing culture, there is no possibility to acquire or develop culture. As a communication system, culture always takes some physical form (usually involving language in some way, as linguistic utterances, texts, movies, gestures, etc.). However, as a system of meaning, it is not necessarily connected with a physical form. For instance, the culturally motivated idea of *humility* has no direct physical counterpart, and it is the mental schema that allows us to distinguish between a humble person and an arrogant, non-humble one. The conventionalized institutionalization of culture occurs in stories, movies, or societal roles.

6.3   Models of the organization of knowledge – frames, schemata, and scripts

Our knowledge is organized via models of various kinds. Artificial intelligence (AI) is an area of computer science that emphasizes the creation of intelligent machines or software that operate like humans in many cognitive respects. Some of the activities that artificial intelligence are designed for involve human speech and language recognition, learning, planning, problem solving, and perception. Research associated with artificial intelligence is highly technical in the formulation of strategies for the organization and management of knowledge, and reasoning for problem solving in specialized areas. AI is an independent field of research and study, but with natural areas of interest with linguistics, cognitive science, and psychology.

One of AI's major scholars, Minsky (1975), first addressed the challenges with the internal organization of the mental representation of knowledge, using frames. His theory about knowledge representation focused on phenomena such as the perception of objects, the perception of places, and comprehension of discourse (Bennardo and de Munck 2014: 51–52). Minsky defined the concept of frame as a data structure for representing a stereotyped situation, like being in a certain kind of room, going to a restaurant, or going to a certain kind of social event such as a birthday party for a child. Each frame contains several kinds of information, including how to use the frame, what is expected to happen next, and how to handle exceptions if these default expectations are not confirmed.

A frame can be considered as a network of nodes and relations. The top levels of a frame are fixed, and represent things that are always true about a situation. The lower levels have many terminal slots that must be filed by specific instances of data. Each terminal can specify conditions that constrain its value, such that its assignment must be to a person, an object of a certain kind, or a value within some range. A frame's terminal slots are typically filled with default assigned values. Collections of frames are linked together into frame systems. As a multi-layered way of organizing knowledge, frames allow one to explain situations in which an individual experiencing a specific object, a place, or an event, not experienced before, to easily retrieve certain features. Similarly, frames with default values help explain why an individual will be surprised to experience non-typical features in objects, places, or events.

As a knowledge concept, a schema is an abstract representation of a generic concept for an object, event, or situation. It consists of a network of interrelationships among the major constituents of the situation represented by the schema. Schemata are the building blocks of cognition. A schema will account for any situation considered to be an instance of the generic concept that it represents (Bennardo and de Munck 2014: 52–53). A schema is a data structure for representing generic concepts stored in memory, and schemata are generated through our experience to reflect the structure of that experience. They are distillations of our experience encoded in terms of the typical instance of what they represent. A schema can be usefully compared to the script of a play, and it already contains all of the reasoning mechanisms required to use the schema.

Schank and Abelson (1975, 1977, and Schank 1975) address the issue of the organization of knowledge, and they argue that people bring to bear two types of knowledge: general and specific. General knowledge enables a person to understand another person's actions simply because they all live in a world which has standard methods of getting things done. With this type of knowledge, they propose several mental organizations called *plans*, *goals*, and *themes*. They define specific knowledge in terms of use:

> We use specific knowledge to interpret and participate in events we have been through many times. Specific detailed knowledge about a situation allows us to do less processing and wondering about frequently experienced events.
>
> Schank and Abelson (1975: 37)

Schank and Abelson (1977) motivate their notion of a script as a basic building block of our everyday understanding. Scripts, based on typical daily routines, are standardized sequences of events that fill in our understanding of frequently recurring experiences. A definition of a script is a stereotyped sequence of events that defines a well-known situation familiar to the individual. One of the classic examples they employ is the "going to the restaurant" script in typical Western settings. In fact, they characterize three different types of scripts: situational, personal, and instrumental. In a situational script, a situation is specified where several participants have roles to follow, and they share an understanding of what is supposed to happen (Schank and Abelson 1975: 61). Personal scripts are typically goal-oriented and have an existence only in the mind of the main actor. Instrumental scripts describe a sequence of actions, as found in situational scripts, but there is only one participant.

The classic "going to the restaurant" script, now famous from being much quoted in cognitive science literature, serves to guide a customer through the interchanges necessary to get a meal at a restaurant, along with the subtasks of getting seated, ordering, paying, and possibly returning an incorrect food order. The classic restaurant script leverages mundane cultural knowledge in its formulation (Quinn & Holland 1987: 31). With respect to scripts, Abelson (1981: 3) foregrounded the notion of an event sequence, which implies the causal chaining of events and results.

A use of the term "cultural script", owing more to linguistic-semantics, is due to Goddard (2009: 68–80), who refers to a technique for articulating culturally specific norms and values, and practices in terms which are clear, precise, and accessible to those inside and outside a culture. Goddard argues that a result is possible once cultural scripts are formulated in what he calls the Natural Semantic Metalanguage (NSM) of semantic primes, a highly constrained mini-language of simple words and grammatical patterns which evidence suggests have equivalents in all languages. The main goal of Goddard's cultural scripts approach is to understand speech practices from the perspective of the speakers themselves. To achieve this requires one to work in a cross-cultural semantics perspective because, to understand speech practices in terms which make sense to the people concerned, one must be able to understand the meanings of the relevant culturally important words – words for local values, social categories, speech alternatives, and so on. Semantic primes can be used as a common code for writing cultural scripts, free from the danger of what Goddard calls "terminological ethnocentrism" and with maximum clarity of resolution of detail.

In many ways, building on the insights of Schank and Abelson, Fillmore advanced a research program known as frame semantics. He understood the frame as representing:

> any system of concepts related in such a way that to understand any one of them you have to understand the whole structure in which it fits; when one of the things in such a structure is introduced into a text, or into a conversation, all of the others are automatically made available.
>
> Fillmore (1982: 111)

The three different organizations of knowledge, into frames, schemata, and scripts, have much in common in that they all represent ways to organize our past experiences in a generic manner within memory. Each individual construction has two layers. The first layer is for the common features of all the experiences represented (I am hungry so I go to a restaurant and eat some food), and the second layer is for features unique to particular instances of those experiences (is it a Thai street food restaurant or a sit-down vegetarian restaurant?). The experiential nature of these mental constructions makes them highly attuned to specific cultural circumstances (Schank and Abelson 1975: 55). Frames, schemata, and scripts all address similar mental phenomena and assign similar properties and characteristics to these phenomena. The script is posited as a sequence of events and, as such, represents a specific type of the more general frame or schema concepts. Johnson-Laird (1983: 10) gives a detailed description of the internal nature and structure of these organizations of knowledge, as mental models: human beings understand the world by constructing working models of it in their minds. As these models are necessarily incomplete, they are simpler than the entities they represent.

After reviewing the contents of schemas and mental models, as well as much of the research associated with them, Brewer (1987: 189) concluded that "in schemas the knowledge structures are old generic information while in mental models the local knowledge structures are constructed at the time of input". Moreover, Brewer (1987: 191–193) suggested that the different concepts actually refer to two different aspects of the mental processing and storing of knowledge. In order to bring clarity to the various overlapping usages of the two terms, he proposes that instantiated schemas are the specific knowledge structures derived from generic knowledge represented in global schemas, while the episodic models are specific knowledge structures constructed to represent new situations from the more specific generic knowledge.

6.4 Cultural knowledge

In their paper on culture and cognition, Quinn and Holland (1987: 7) argue that cultural knowledge, those shared presuppositions about the world, plays a considerable role in human understanding, and that this role must be recognized and incorporated into any successful theory of the organization of human knowledge. Cultural knowledge appears to be organized in sequences of prototypical events or schemas that Quinn and Holland call cultural models and that are themselves hierarchically related to other cultural knowledge. Having pursued the question of what one needs to know in order to function as a member of one's society (Goodenough 1957: 167), cognitive anthropologists arrived at a view of culture as shared knowledge, not just as a set of people's customs, artifacts, and oral traditions, but what they must know in order to act as they do, create the things they make, and interpret their experience in the particular way they do (Quinn & Holland 1987: 16). As such, cultural models are presupposed, widely shared, and taken-for-granted models of the world utilized by the members of a society and they play a significant role in our understanding of the world.

A useful question is: How is the knowledge embodied in cultural models brought to language and to the various, cognitive tasks that require this knowledge? In this regard, Lakoff (1984: 10) makes a useful observation about how cultural and other knowledge is embodied in different types of cognitive models, in his distinction between what he calls propositional models and image-schematic models. Propositional-schemas specify concepts and the relations which hold among them. In turn, Lakoff regards image-schemas as gestalts, just as visual images are, but they are much more schematic than visual imagery, and they may contain kinesthetic information of all kinds. For example, our knowledge of sports grounds includes a trajectory schema while our knowledge about candles includes a long, thin object schema. In this, Lakoff makes clear that image schemata convey knowledge of physical phenomena, such as shape and motion information. The result of a mapping, from physical experience in a source domain to social or psychological experience in some target domain, is that elements, properties, and relations that could not be conceptualized in image-schematic form, without a metaphor, can now be so expressed in the terms provided by the metaphor. Such a result is achieved, for example, by the metaphor of ANGER AS A HOT FLUID IN A CONTAINER, which can be conceptualized as boiling and producing steam, and exerting pressure on its container, which, consequently, can be imagined as ready to explode (Quinn & Holland 1987: 38–40). Metaphorically derived image-schemas, like other image-schemas, are gestalts that make multiple relations more immediately understandable. These gestalts can then be interpreted to arrive at entailments among related elements.

Scientists working with natural language processing within artificial intelligence discovered that language cannot be understood, or properly translated, without reference to a huge amount of knowledge of the world. Somewhat similar to Ryle's (1949) distinction between "knowledge *how*" and "knowledge *that*", cultural knowledge is often productively analyzed into "models *of*" and "models *for*", into representational and operational knowledge. Sometimes these cultural models serve to set goals for action, sometimes to plan, and sometimes to make sense of the actions and goals of others.

One of the most important ways in which people negotiate understanding and accomplish social goals is through language use in interaction (Quinn & Holland 1987: 21–25). How do cultural models, whether invoked to persuade another, or to order one's own inner experience, motivate behavior?

Linguistic forms can deliver an amount of persuasiveness to knowledge by packaging it as cultural wisdom.

Cultural knowledge is typically acquired via advice and occasional correction – it is learned from others, mostly through language. Cultural models frame our understanding of how the world works, including our inferences about what other humans are up to, and motivates and guides our decisions about what actions we will undertake in given situations. The notion that these cultural models with their schematic structures and schemas, systematically organize how experience is understood (Quinn & Holland 1987: 34), has achieved wide acceptance in cognitive science.

Cultural models can be considered as a resource or tool to be used when suitable, and set aside when not. These cultural models guide our way of life and worldview, and help us to live our lives. When we look around us, we find confirmation for our own lives in the beliefs and actions of other people. The cultural models that have some force or significance for us, as individuals, are often the models that are historically dominant. Cultural models organize our understanding. They gain force when they are utilized in understanding oneself and one's life. Lifestyle and way of life, ideas about what is right and what is inevitable are motivated by cultural models of the world.

7   Knowledge and its representation

7.1   The central question – what is knowledge?

In the previous chapter we characterized cultural models and how they encapsulate cultural knowledge, but we did not address the nature of knowledge itself. The major concern of this chapter is *what is knowledge* and *how do we represent it.* We examine the different types of knowledge, the correspondence theory of truth, and the value of knowledge to us as people in our endeavors. We examine the ways in which we acquire knowledge of the various kinds. We discuss the idea of extended knowledge via extended cognition. We follow this with an exploration of knowledge representation in artificial intelligence (AI) and natural language processing. This leads us then to a discussion on knowledge, discourse, and common ground.

The theory of knowledge is known as epistemology, and the characteristic questions of epistemology (Truncellito 2007) are: What is knowledge? And what types of knowledge are there? The goal of epistemology as the theory of knowledge is to clarify what knowledge involves, how it is applied, and to explain its characteristic features (Rescher 2003: 14). We actually know very many things. We know that the earth is round, and you probably know that Dublin is the capital of Ireland. We most likely know that water has the chemical structure with the formula H_2O, consisting of two hydrogen atoms attached to an oxygen atom. We can think of examples which include geographical knowledge of the region in which we live, linguistic knowledge of our favorite languages, the mathematical knowledge that two plus two is equal to four; that pi, or π, is an irrational number with an approximate value of 3.14, along with aesthetic, ethical/moral, and various kinds of scientific knowledge.

We can distinguish, for example, between knowledge of propositions, or propositional knowledge, and know-how, or ability knowledge (Pritchard 2018: 20). A discussion of knowledge needs to recognize some basic linguistic facts about how the verb *know* actually functions in discourse. In particular, it is important to recognize that to *know* has both a propositional and a procedural sense. This contrast is found in the matter *of knowing that something is the case* (that-knowledge) versus the practical knowledge of *knowing how to perform some action* to realize some end result (how-to-knowledge). Rescher (2003: 16) distinguishes three sorts of knowledge in terms of the kind of thing they address: i) knowledge of facts, ii) knowledge by acquaintance with individuals or things, and iii) ability knowledge.

Questions are epistemologically important because of what they reveal of knowledge. What people know is reflected in answers they offer to the questions asked of them. Propositional knowledge is related to the capacity to answer questions. In the case of knowledge-that-p, this means being in a position to correctly and appropriately answer the question: "Is p true or not"? This sort of knowledge can further be classified (1).

(1)   How knowledge is classified (based on Rescher 2003: 16)

i.   By SUBJECT matter (as per mathematical or botanical knowledge).
ii.   By EVIDENTIAL SOURCE (personal observation, reliable reportage, etc.).
iii. By MODE OF JUSTIFICATION (personal experience, scientific investigation, etc.).
iv.   By THE COGNITIVE STATUS of the matters at issue (empirical facts, formal relationships in logic or mathematics).
v.   By MODE OF FORMULATION (verbally, by diagrams, by mathematical symbolism, etc.).

As Rescher indicates, knowing a fact is not something that one does; it is a condition one has come to occupy in relation to information. It is a situational imperative for us as humans to acquire information about the world, to look for and find knowledge, and to make sense of things around us. As humans, our cognitive orientation is a practical need and, correspondingly, we find that cognitive disorientation is stressful. Knowledge is not an activity – mental or otherwise. To know something, then, is not to be engaged in an activity but to have entered into a certain cognitive condition. Therefore, propositional knowledge is a cognitive state.

The oldest and most important epistemological question is *What is knowledge?* Plato wrestled with it in his dialogue, *Theaetetus*, and sought a definition of knowledge, but came to no clear answer and the dialogue ended inconclusively (Lemos 2007: 13). In ordinary language when we say that someone knows something, we can mean different things by *knows*. There are different kinds of knowledge. Somewhat similarly to Rescher, for Lemos (2007: 14), the three most significant kinds of knowledge are: 1) propositional knowledge, 2) acquaintance knowledge, and 3) ability knowledge. Pojman (2001: 10) also identifies three different types of knowledge as:

knowledge by acquaintance, competence/ability knowledge, and descriptive or propositional knowledge.

As it turns out, there are many different kinds of knowledge. The work of cognitive scientists has uncovered the different kinds of knowledge that people use, how this knowledge is mentally organized, and how it is effectively leveraged in problem solving. Knowledge representation attempts to capture an individual's understanding of a given subject. One can examine the different kinds of knowledge there are, such as scientific, moral, or even religious knowledge (Ichikawa & Steup 2017).

7.2   The different types of knowledge

Knowledge by acquaintance is where a person knows something or someone. We have direct experience with the objects and artifacts within the world, with our thoughts, and our sensations. Acquaintance knowledge is distinguished from propositional knowledge. One can have a great deal of propositional knowledge about someone without having knowledge of him/her as an actual acquaintance. When we say, "Aisling knows Tara", we are sometimes using *know* in the propositional sense and sometimes in the acquaintance sense. Of course, one can have acquaintance knowledge of things other than individual people.

In addition to propositional knowledge and acquaintance knowledge, let us consider ability knowledge. When we say, "Aisling knows how to X", we typically mean or imply that Aisling has the ability to X, whatever X represents. Of course, one can have a considerable amount of propositional knowledge about how to do something without having the ability to do it (Lemos 2007: 14–17). Competence knowledge, also called ability knowledge, is where a person knows how to do something requiring a level of skill. This is *know-how* knowledge. This competence knowledge involves an ability to perform a skill and may be done consciously or unconsciously. Ability knowledge, of course, is different from propositional knowledge. I know how to drive my car, for example, but I do not know a set of propositions about how to drive my car. It can be rather difficult to explain how to drive a car, but, notwithstanding this, I do know how to drive my car. Propositional knowledge (or descriptive knowledge) is where a person *knows that p* (where p is some statement or proposition). Propositions have a truth value. They are the objects of propositional knowledge. When we claim to know that p is the case, we are claiming that p is true. Propositional knowledge is knowledge of facts or true propositions. We may think of belief as a relation between a subject and a proposition. If the proposition one believes is true, then one's belief is true and if the proposition one believes is false, then one's belief is false. We may also think of propositional knowledge as a relation between a subject and a true proposition. Propositional knowledge is not the only sort of knowledge. Traditionally, philosophers, who are typically concerned with what is true, have been most interested in the nature of propositional knowledge. They want to know what is true and they want to evaluate and assess their own claims, and those of others, to know the truth. When philosophers ask, for example, about the extent of our knowledge, they are typically concerned with the extent of our propositional knowledge, with the extent of the truths that we know. Whenever we consider a proposition, there are three different attitudes we can take toward it (Lemos 2007: 19–21). First, we can believe it or accept it as true. Second, we can disbelieve it as false or believe its negation. Third, we can withhold belief in it or suspend judgment.

Propositional knowledge is knowledge of a proposition. A proposition is what is asserted by a sentence which says that something is the case (Pritchard 2018: 16–20). When we talk about knowledge, we generally have propositional knowledge in mind, unless explicitly stated otherwise. For possessing knowledge, one needs to have a belief in a relevant proposition, and that belief must be true. So, if you KNOW that Dublin is the capital of Ireland, then you BELIEVE that this is the case, and your belief must be a true belief. To ascribe knowledge to someone is to credit that person with having got things right, and that means that what we regard that person as knowing had better not be false, but true (Pritchard 2018: 17). This knowledge, then, requires belief. However, for most propositions, thinking that they are true does not make them true. Belief aims at the truth, in the sense that when we believe a proposition, we believe it to be true. When what we believe is true, then there is a match between what we think is the case and what actually is the case.

7.3 The correspondence theory of truth

The correspondence theory of truth relates to the nature of truth and is concerned with what makes a proposition or a belief true or false. The theory makes two main claims: 1) a proposition is true if and only if it corresponds to the facts, 2) a proposition is false if and only if it fails to correspond to the facts. Whether a belief is justified, and the degree to which it is justified, is often, if not always, a function of the evidence one has for it. A person's evidence to support a proposition at a certain time might consist of all the information or data they have at that point in time. It is widely accepted that sense perception, memory, introspection, and reason are evidential information sources, as providing information or data that serves as evidence for our beliefs. They provide evidence through such things as memory experiences, sense experiences, introspective experiences, and rational intuitions (Lemos 2007: 29). Such experiences along with our justified beliefs may be thought to constitute our evidence.

The correspondence theory of truth (Pojman 2001: 11) is the theory that truth consists in the relationship between the proposition and the facts, or states of affairs, that confirm the propositions. A belief is true if it asserts a proposition that corresponds to facts. The correspondence theory captures our common-sense intuition that truth depends on something objective (or mind-independent) in the world that makes it true. Beliefs are not made true by mere wishful thinking or imagination, but have an objective basis in reality. Ludwig Wittgenstein said that "A proposition is a picture of reality. A proposition is a model of reality as we imagine it" (Wittgenstein 1922 TLP 4.01). And, as Immanuel Kant observed:

> Though all our knowledge begins with experience, it does not follow that it all arises out of experience. For it may well be that even our empirical knowledge is made up of what we receive through impressions and of what our own faculty of knowledge supplies from itself.
>
> Kant (1781/2008: B1: 41)

Locke's (1690/2014) representational theory of knowledge claims that what we know is caused by the world itself, though some qualities are the products of our perceptual mechanisms affected by the world. These primary qualities, which include motion, size, shape, and number, are the true building blocks of knowledge because these qualities are accurate representatives of the objective features of the world. Secondary qualities are modes of apprehending the primary qualities, and examples include taste, color, smell, and sound. Because the color or taste of the same object can appear differently to different people, or to the same person at different times, secondary qualities are subjective, even though they are caused by the objective primary qualities (Pojman 2001: 19).

Another kind of knowledge is testimonial knowledge. Testimonial knowledge is knowledge that we gain via the testimony of others. In the usual case, this will simply involve someone telling us what they know, but we can also gain this kind of knowledge in other, more indirect ways, such as by reading the testimony of others.

A common distinction that one finds in philosophy is between *a priori* and empirical/*a posteriori* knowledge. The distinction rests upon whether the knowledge in question was gained independently of an investigation of the world through experience and empirical inquiry. If the knowledge in question was gained independently of an investigation, then it is a priori knowledge. Otherwise, if it gained from an investigation then it is empirical/a posteriori knowledge that proceeds from observations or experiences to the deduction of probable causes. Scientific inquiry is widely considered to be a paradigmatic way of acquiring knowledge about the world around us. Pritchard lists five conditions which scientific knowledge had to satisfy. These are:

(2)   Conditions for scientific knowledge (Pritchard 2018: 134)

i.   It is guided by natural law.
ii.   It has to be explanatory by reference to natural law.
iii. It is testable against the empirical world.
iv.   Its conclusions are tentative (i.e. are not necessarily the final word).
v.   It is falsifiable.

There is one other kind of knowledge that we will briefly mention here. This is religious knowledge, and it is the kind of knowledge that often motivates certain cultural models behind an individual's world view. Religious knowledge is knowledge of religious truths, such as truths about the existence and nature of some god. A reason why one might doubt religious knowledge is because one holds that there are no religious truths. It is suggested that religious beliefs lack adequate supporting evidence, such that even if they are true, they do not amount to knowledge. This is known as the evidentialist challenge (Pritchard 2018: 138) to religious knowledge. Clearly, this lack of adequate supporting evidence for a religion's view does not prevent many people from holding these views strongly. Often, however, as an extreme example, terrorists claim that their religious views, and hence the righteousness of their world view, justify their actions against some perceived "unbeliever". We have all read about these kinds of attacks and atrocities, with horror, in our news in recent times.

Another one of the tasks of epistemology is to explain the value of knowledge (Schroeder 2016). While it is obvious that we do value knowledge, it is not obvious why this is the case, nor what the nature of this value is. One way of accounting for the value of knowledge is to observe that if we know a proposition, then we have a true belief in that proposition, and true beliefs are useful, and valuable. In particular, true belief has instrumental value in that it enables us to achieve our goals (Pritchard 2018: 29).

7.4   How do we acquire knowledge?

How do we acquire knowledge? A great deal of our knowledge of the world is acquired via perception, that is, via our sensory faculties, such as our sense of sight, hearing, touch, and so on, and our faculty of memory (Pritchard 2018: 19). Kant, in his *Critique of Pure Reason*, was aware of this as we can see from his two quotes following:

> All our knowledge begins with the senses, proceeds then to the understanding, and ends with reason. There is nothing higher than reason.
>
> Immanuel Kant (1781: 310)

> We have no intuitions except through the senses; thus no other concepts can inhabit the understanding except those which pertain to the disposition and order among these intuitions. These concepts must contain what is universal, and rules. The faculty of rules in abstracto: the learned understanding; in concreto: the common understanding. The common understanding has preference in all cases, where the rules must be abstracted a posteriori from the cases; but where they have their origin a priori, there it does not obtain at all.
>
> Immanuel Kant (1781: 119. A5I /B75)

Locke (1690: bk. 2 ch. 1 sect. 19), in his essay "An Essay Concerning Human Understanding", tells us that "No man's Knowledge here can go beyond his experience." What Locke means is that there are no innate ideas. Instead, all of our ideas, and our knowledge, are derived via our direct experience of the world.

> …If they say that a man is always conscious to himself of thinking, I ask, how they know it? Consciousness is the perception of what passes

in a man's own mind. Can another man perceive that I am conscious of anything, when I perceive it not myself? No man's knowledge here can go beyond his experience…

Locke (1690. bk2 ch1 sect.19)

What we directly experience is only how the world appears to us, and not how it is. On this basis, we can then make inferences to how the world really is.

7.5   Extended knowledge via an extended cognition

In today's digital world, we can gain knowledge through the selective and strategic use of technology via an extended cognition. That is, some uses of technology can act to extend our cognition. For example, we can Google stuff, thereby extending our memory, or use a spreadsheet to extend our calculating abilities! Additionally, when we use technology as an instrument, such as when we use a calculator to work out a large sum or use a spreadsheet to make some calculation, then the cognitive processes involved are very different to the corresponding non-extended cognitive process working out the result in one's head. Indeed, the technology we employ can be a genuine part of our extended cognition. Cognitive extension can be social (i.e., crowd sourcing information over digital media) rather than just technological, in that other people can form part of a joint cognitive process. This is called "socially distributed cognition" by Pritchard (2018: 170). Pritchard also notes that if there is such a thing as extended cognition, then there will also be extended knowledge. That is, knowledge that has been acquired via an extended cognitive process.

The idea that the technology that we use can be a part of our cognitive processes may surprise us, since we tend to think that cognition is the sort of thing that happens in our brains with the assistance of our central nervous systems (Cowart 2017, Wilson & Foglia 2015). But cognitive scientists supporting the idea of extended cognition argue that it is not the case that cognitive processes can only take place within the brain of the subject. If an extended cognitive process, using technology, functions in the same way as a normal, non-extended, cognitive process, then it needs to be considered as a genuine cognitive process, notwithstanding the use of technology. The technology constitutes cognitive augmentation that dramatically enhances our cognitive capacities. Indeed, we now depend on technology to achieve many cognitive tasks, and very often these tasks have great complexity. Extended cognition is when a cognitive process extends beyond the subject to involve an "external" factor, like technology. Not that every use of technology is extended cognition, but only when the way we use technology is analogous to how we employ our non-extended cognitive resources.

7.6 Knowledge representation in AI and natural language processing

Understanding the nature of knowledge is tricky. It becomes particularly acute in the world of artificial intelligence and natural language processing (NLP), for example with intelligent software agents, where a rigorous level of formalism is necessary, and knowledge must be specified precisely, in clear detail, in a form readable by software.

Typically, in the AI world of intelligent software agents, for example, a well-focused domain-specific knowledge is captured. Knowledge representation is used to encode knowledge in the knowledge base of an intelligent system. The purpose of knowledge representation is to express knowledge, typically these days in computer-tractable form, such that it can be used by, for example, the intelligent software agent. A knowledge base is a repository, an ontology, of world knowledge that functions as a core part of a knowledge-based intelligent software agent. It maps computational objects and relationships onto real-world objects and relationships.

There are several different kinds of knowledge and we overview these here. Declarative knowledge describes what is known about concepts, facts, and objects. This includes simple statements that are asserted to be either true or false. This also includes statements that more fully describe some object or concept via its attributes and values. Heuristic knowledge is empirical and represents the knowledge compiled through the experience of solving past problems. It describes a rule-of-thumb that guides the reasoning process. It has been shown that this tacit knowledge is not a vague knowledge but is reflected in a skill-based practice. Experts in a domain have a mastery of sophisticated rule-following procedures in their fields which is shown in performance, their very practice, hence it is a skill that can be passed to others, for example, through apprenticeship (Goranzon and Florin 1990: 14). Meta-knowledge is knowledge about the other kinds of knowledge and how to use them. Knowledge about knowledge is used to pick what is best suited for solving a problem. This type of knowledge enhances problem solving by directing our reasoning processes to the most promising area. Procedural knowledge describes information on how to do something. It is concerned with rules, strategies, agendas, and procedures. Structural knowledge describes our overall mental model of a problem. It is concerned with ordered sets of rules, relations between concepts, and relations between concept and object. Typical of this type of knowledge is our mental model of concepts, sub-concepts, and objects.

A knowledge representation, then, is a set of conventions about how to describe classes of things. The function of any representation scheme is to capture essential features of a problem domain and make that information available to a problem-solving procedure. A knowledge representation typically consists of four component parts: 1) a LEXICON that licenses the symbols allowed in the representation's vocabulary, as a lexical entry; 2) a SEMANTIC COMPONENT that associates a meaning with a description, 3) a STRUCTURAL COMPONENT (grammar) that puts constraints on how the vocabulary symbols can be arranged in a meaningful relationship, 4) a PROCEDURAL COMPONENT that specifies rules for how we can create and modify descriptions, and provides an ability to answer questions concerning these knowledge descriptions.

There are several kinds of knowledge representation schemes including the following. Logical schemes use predicate and propositional calculus and represent knowledge using mathematical symbols with an associated set of inference rules based on precisely defined syntax and semantics. Procedural schemes consist of various IF *condition* THEN *do_something* rules. In procedural schemes, knowledge is represented as a set of instructions to solve some particular problem, and which allows us to easily update a knowledge base. This scheme separates the knowledge base from the inference mechanism. Networked schemes use certain strategies for the representation of knowledge, and involve semantic nets and conceptual graphs. Essentially, these networked schemes use the notion of a graph structure to represent knowledge where the nodes of a graph display objects or concepts in a domain, while the arcs between nodes define relationships between objects, their attributes, and attribute values. Structured schemes consist of scripts and frames. Structured schemes extend networked representations by displaying each node in a graph as a complex data structure. A semantic network, sometimes known as a frame network, is a knowledge base that represents semantic relations between concepts in a network. A semantic network functions as a directed or undirected graph consisting of vertices or nodes, which represent concepts, and edges or arcs, and represent semantic relations between concepts, mapping or connecting semantic fields (Sowa 1987, Chein & Mugnier 2008).

Put simply, a semantic network is defined as a knowledge representation schema that captures knowledge as a graph. As we mentioned, the nodes denote objects or concepts, their properties and corresponding values. The arcs denote relationships between the nodes. Both nodes and arcs are generally labelled. The arcs may have weights that denote a cost factor of some kind. The nodes of semantic nets can represent concepts, objects, events, attribute features, and time. The idea is that concepts are a part of our knowledge about the world. Concepts are related with relationships between them, people perceive concepts and reason with them. Knowing the relationships between concepts therefore informs a person's understanding. Several kinds of relationships are used in semantic nets. These kinds of relationships include:

(3)   Semantic net relationships

i.   Class–Superclass with the IS-A relationship,
ii.   Instance of a class with the IS_AN_INSTANCE_OF relationship.
iii.   Part-Whole reflecting the PART_OF relationship.
iv.   Attribute of an object showing a HAS_A relationship.
v.   Value of an attribute reflecting the VALUE relationship.
vi.   Logical relationships such as *and, or, not*.
vii.   Linguistic relationship such as *prefers, possesses, travels*, etc.

As part of the design of a semantic net, features of an entity can be inherited from a class higher than it in the structure. This is known as feature inheritance. More technically and formally, inheritance is a process by which the information residing within a superclass node is assumed by a class, subclass node, and an instance node.

The typical example of this relates to a car where a CAR is a class of a superclass VEHICLE. Then, CAR inherits all the features of VEHICLE, including its model and brand name. Another example is where a SPARROW is a class of the superclass BIRD. Then, SPARROW inherits appropriate features of superclass BIRD, including that it i) has feathers, ii) has wings, and iii) can fly. Inheritance of features is not mandatory. For example, a chicken is a class of the superclass BIRD. As with the SPARROW, it inherits appropriate features of superclass BIRD, including that it i) has feathers and ii) has wings. Importantly, the chicken cannot fly so it correctly does not inherit the feature "can fly" from the superclass BIRD.

Operating somewhat similar to a semantic net, a conceptual graph (Sowa 1984, 1997, 2008) is a finite, connected, bipartite graph. A conceptual graph is a graph representation for logic, based on the semantic networks of AI and the existential graphs of C.S. Peirce (1882a, 1882b, 1989).

7.7   Knowledge, discourse, and common ground

Generic knowledge serves primarily to construe what are called mental models, that is, subjective event representations involved in the production and comprehension of discourse such as news reports or stories, and more generally to engage in everyday social interaction. A distinction is made by van Dijk (2014: 13–16) between generic, socially shared knowledge, on the one hand, and personal knowledge about specific events, on the other, along with personal generic knowledge about our individual routines or people we know. Culture is often defined in terms of the shared knowledge of its members, the cultural common ground, and of course, knowledge may differ from one society to the next.

A linguistic approach to knowledge will characterize the many ways that old and new knowledge or common ground, is implied, presupposed, signaled. This may be expressed through intonation with special stress on new, focused information. It may be expressed in syntax with definite articles and pronouns expressing known information. We are reminded by van Dijk that discourses are somewhat like icebergs, with only the new information visible and explicitly expressed, while large amounts of known or inferable information remains implicit and invisible. This expressed information may contain evidential marking that refers to the sources of knowledge. As people acquire knowledge largely through language, it is argued that a linguistically oriented approach is needed which details the grammatical aspects of such communication. Additionally, as most of human knowledge is acquired through discourse, language use and discourse are impossible without the activation of massive amounts of knowledge of the world.

8   Context, situation, and common ground

8.1   Context as a central notion within pragmatic analysis

It has long been recognized that context informs pragmatic meaning and assists in the construction and maintenance of common ground. Within a dialogue, context helps to differentiate, for example, between *what is said* vs. *what is meant*. The nature of the contribution of context, therefore, is a central area of research interest within pragmatic analysis. One definition of pragmatics that reflects the importance of context (Auer 2009) is that pragmatics treats the ways in which linguistic utterances become meaningful through their relation to context(s). Discourse is held to be a system of knowledge and beliefs, social practices and socially recognizable identities (Flowerdew 2016: 1), and the term "context", relates to the situations in which discourse is produced. However, it is recognized that context is quite difficult to define. This chapter examines the nature of context, situation, and common ground. We explore context as a central notion within pragmatic analysis. We examine the notion of context of situation as found in the work of Malinowski, Firth, and Wegener, along with the context of situation and the context of culture. We provide an overview of van Dijk's assessment of Malinowski and Firth, and explore context, and its relation to discourse, in the van Dijk approach. We follow this with an exploration of context and mental model theory, following Johnston-Laird, and Givón's approach to the nature of context. We look at common ground as the interface between culture and language in interaction, and the nature of shared knowledge and understanding. We provide a case study on how we meet the challenges of context in linguistic analysis. In this, we mediate knowledge and language through a speech act taking into consideration both situation and context.

Several definitions of context are to be found, and we introduce a few here, pending a larger discussion on context later. Blommaert (2005: 251), for instance, defines context as "the totality of conditions under which discourse is being produced, circulated and interpreted". Baker (2016: 27–48) defines context as "the constraints on a communicative situation that influence language use". In the case of language use, he argues that the most relevant contexts are the social and the linguistic environments. Different features of context are differentiated by Wodak (2016: 321–346), including the extralinguistic social, environmental variables and institutional frames of a specific "context of situation", and the broader socio-political and historical context within the cultural community.

Whatever the difficulties in agreeing on a definition of context and the knowledge that it includes, it is true nonetheless that discourse interlocutors, the speakers and hearers of a conversation, are skilled at understanding which are the relevant features of context to apply to make their utterances contextually relevant and meaningful. People have sets of linguistic, cognitive, social, cultural, and institutional skills and knowledge that they use for retrieving meaning from a discourse.

One approach to the notion of context, described in Flowerdew (2016: 1), is to treat this as the interplay of FIGURE and GROUND, where the FIGURE is the focal point of analysis and the GROUND is the background context. Generally, the focal situation is regarded as the central focus of the participants' attention, while features of the context are not highlighted, but treated as background phenomena. The focal situation and context thus seem to stand in a fundamental FIGURE–GROUND relationship to each other.

An alternative but useful approach is to consider context as a frame which surrounds the focal situation. Framing is the process by which certain features of the situation are made salient, and this places boundaries on the extent of the context applicable. The frame therefore contains a relevant subset of the context, and thereby allows for the interpretation of the situation. According to Goffman (1974: 10–11), frames are basic cognitive constructs which guide our perception of reality:

> I assume that definitions of a situation are built up in accordance with principles of organization which govern events…and our subjective involvement in them; frame is the word I use to refer to such of these basic elements as I am able to identify.
>
> Goffman (1974: 10f)

Interlocutors can change the context with each utterance produced indicating that context is mostly dynamic. The context of everyday conversation may be quite unpredictable, with interlocutors free to switch topic at will. However, the context, for example, to a wedding ceremony is typically much more formal and fixed, at least within its ritual dimensions. Consequently, language is utilized to be aligned with expectations of the context for enabling a successful speech act. Auer (1992: 4) defines contextualization as follows:

> ...contextualization...comprises all activities by participants which make relevant, maintain, revise, cancel...any aspect of context which, in turn, is responsible for the interpretation of an utterance in its particular locus of occurrence.

A socio-cognitive view of context is taken by van Dijk (2008, 2009), with social cognition being concerned with the mental processes involved in how we relate to people in our social world. For van Dijk, the mental models and representations that speakers use to make their utterances appropriate, involve context, culture, and social structure. Context is defined by van Dijk as the cognitive, social, political, cultural, and historical environments of discourse.

The study of language in context is a central area of linguistic pragmatics, and is related to language in use. In this regard, a core role is assigned in communication to context by Grice (1989 [1967]), Recanati (2003, 2010, 2012), and Sperber and Wilson (2005). In their view, utterance interpretation is an inferential process, based on reasoning and context. Utterances may have a literal meaning (*what is said*), but their meaning in actual use will depend upon the context within which they are made (*what is meant*). Discourse interlocutors use (verbal and non-verbal) signs to assist in the determination of *what is meant*, over the *what is said*. All language use is indexical and that the meaning of a word or utterance can only be determined by reference to its context. The inferential process, referred to as implicature, depends upon the conventional meaning of the words used, together with the identity of any references, the cooperative principle and its maxims, the context, linguistic plus cultural and background knowledge, and an appropriate common ground. The role of context is expressed in Grice's cooperative principle.

> Make your conversational contribution such as is required, at the stage at which it occurs, by the accepted purpose or direction of the talk exchange in which you are engaged
>
> Grice (1989 [1967]: 26).

It is worth noting that Chomsky (1965: 31) explicitly excluded context from his model of language, choosing instead to describe language in context as PERFORMANCE, while preferring to focus on individual sentences in isolation, as COMPETENCE. Actual language use [PERFORMANCE] was viewed as "fairly degenerate in quality", because it does not correspond to his idealized model of perfectly formed grammatical sentences [COMPETENCE]. As a counterpart to Chomsky's *linguistic* COMPETENCE, Hymes (1962: 14) introduced a framework for *communicative* competence, as knowledge of grammar, social knowledge, knowledge about how, when, where, and why to appropriately use language in some given context. He elaborates how this framework can be used in the interpretation of utterances, via the use of a linguistic form that identifies a range of meanings, and a context which can support a range of meanings. Then, when a form is used in a context, it constrains the meanings possible to those that the form can signal, and the context eliminates from consideration the meanings possible to the form other than those supported by context.

The importance of context in the interpretation of utterances was argued for by Malinowski. Specifically, Malinowski argued for a consideration of the utterance in terms of the *context of situation*, and the cultural background or *context of culture*.

> A word without linguistic context is a mere figment and stands for nothing by itself, so in the reality of a spoken living tongue, the utterance has no meaning except in the context of situation.
>
> Malinowski (1923: 307)

Although Sapir and Whorf did not use the term *context of culture*, they nevertheless expressed the idea of a language as representing the mental life, or culture, of its speakers. The Sapir–Whorf hypothesis states that because different languages represent reality differently, speakers of different languages will perceive reality differently. This is a strong claim, very controversial and unproven, even today.

While much linguistics in the latter half of the twentieth century was concerned with formal syntax, to the exclusion of other linguistic domains, such as the function of language and the role of context, this was not always the case (Nerlich and Clarke 1996: 298). These formalist models of the twentieth century (Chomsky 1965, Newmeyer 1995), essentially the generative program of Chomsky and his colleagues, known as The Chomskyan Revolution, displaced the earlier, more functionalist models, developed in Europe, between about 1880 and 1930. The formalist models pushed aside the important questions of these earlier theories, relating to the way in which language functions and our understanding of what language is, including how we interact with each other, and use language. Today, however, many of the ideas of the previous functional and contextual approaches (Harris 1993) have re-emerged in contemporary modern functional and cognitive linguistics as active areas of rich scientific endeavor and investigation.

8.2   Context of situation – Malinowski

As it turns out, two rediscovered sources of pragmatic insights into language were from the linguistic anthropology work of Malinowski and the linguistic contextualism and functionalism developed by Firth (Nerlich and Clarke 1996: 294).

Malinowski's linguistic investigation was the first to systematically use the idea of context in a way that was directly linked to the notion of function. In his functional view, a language is regarded as an instrument of communication, used to actively achieve our goals and purposes, and used in speech acts with effects and consequences. The meaning of a sentence is considered to be its function, or set of relations, within a context. Language has many functions and these can only be properly understood by examining the context of the situation in which it is used. What is interesting for us is that Malinowski applied the term *context of situation* in several ways in his linguistic analyses. He used this term to refer to the whole of the communicative circumstances, including in particular, the *speech* situation, as well as, in general, the *sociocultural* context.

8.3   Context of situation – Firth

The linguist J. R. Firth, critically reviewed in Chapman & Routledge (2005), was influenced by the work of Malinowski. Of interest to us here is that Firth's main interests converge on the idea that the study of meaning and context should be central in linguistics. Firth's ideas on meaning and context are core to his conception of language, as he considered the analysis of the meaning of utterances (note, not sentences!) to be the primary goal of linguistics. As utterances occur in real-life contexts, Firth argued that their meaning was informed by the particular situation in which they occurred. He borrowed the phrase context of situation from Malinowski and called his theory the "contextual theory of meaning". Firth also applied the concept of context of situation (Nerlich and Clarke 1996: 363) in motivating his contextual theory of meaning to refer to a scheme based around various general categories. In this, a linguistic text with its various characteristics finds a place and function in relation to other categories such as the *participants*, relevant non-verbal *behavior*, relevant *objects*, and *effect or result*.

This view by Firth of the context of situation importantly allows for the possibility of a sequence of multiple related events within it. To understand an act of speech, one needs to examine the speech event, itself central to a certain context of situation. This context of situation has an internal structure associated with what Firth calls the type of speech function. This is a setting in which a certain act of speech becomes a speech act, assumes an illocutionary force which goes beyond the mere lexical meaning of the words used – that is, it reflects *what is meant* in context, rather than merely "*what is said*".

We can summarize Firth's (1968) contribution to the theory of context as having the following properties for the "context of situation" (1).

(1)   Properties within the "context of situation" (based on van Dijk 2008: 34)

a)   Contexts are embedded in the experiences of the everyday lives of people.
b)   Contexts must be described in abstract, general terms.
c)   Contexts only consist of the relevant aspects of a social situation.
d)   Contexts consist mainly of participants, actions and their consequences.
e)   Contexts feature social aspects of participants and of the societies they belong to, as well as genres and speech functions.
f)   The description of contexts is only given in the social terms of observable and objective acts or events, and not in terms of hidden mental processes.

The context of situation, then, is central to linguistic analysis in order to account for language in its situation of use, rather than as a collection of structural units to be analyzed individually.

8.4   Context and situation – Wegener

Of course, Malinowski or Firth were not the only philosophers or linguists to study the relatedness of language context and situation. Nerlich (1988, 1990) considers the study of language in the nineteenth century by focusing on the writings of three linguists (William Dwight Whitney, Michael Bréal, and Philipp Wegener) across three countries (USA, France, and Germany). As Nerlich (1990: 1) reports, these three linguists brought new insights to the understanding of language change. What is interesting is that despite their different backgrounds and geographies, Whitney, Bréal, and Wegener converge upon the realization that the problems of understanding can only be resolved if linguists stop regarding language as an autonomous entity independent of the users of the language. Instead, these scholars proposed that the focus must be on the *actions*, (advocated by Whitney), the *mind of the language users* (stressed by Bréal), and importantly, on the *situational context* in which people use language (proposed by Wegener).

We are more concerned with Wegener in this discussion, as Wegener studied language as "situated action". Wegener was much admired by both Malinowski and Firth, and a direct influence on their research into language and context. In his study of language as "situated action", Wegener motivated his theory in virtue of his concern with the social construction of language. In this view, language does not live and grow according to fixed internal rules. Instead, because every utterance has to be understood by the hearer, the hearer has to retrieve and construct a relevant meaning, based on the context, situation, and pragmatic common ground. Whether the utterance meaning is successfully retrieved depends on the hearer's expectations, the purpose and goal of the action, and the dialogue schema.

When we take a situational perspective in context, we are able to make some sense of the relatedness of sequences of actions that unfold within a situation. We can better understand the situation because we know in virtue of our experience that certain actions have a certain consequence. In understanding the relatedness of sequences of actions, we first recognize the order of the unfolding events, and we locate the temporal dimension of the situation with potentially some cause and effect, the event participants, and any causality. Implicit in this view is that context and situation can be understood as containing the possibility of multiple events which are structured in some way. This view then is not dissimilar to that of Malinowski or Firth. Nerlich (1990: 129) gives the example that, if somebody says "He is digging"[15] we only understand the description of the action if we understand the purpose

---

[15] We get a sense of this from the poem "Digging", by Seamus Heaney (from *Death of a Naturalist* 2006), in which the poet describes his father digging on their family farm. He admires his father's skill and relationship to the spade in the act of digging turf, but states that he will dig with his pen instead. This fragment demonstrates Heaney's commitment as a poet as he names his pen as his primary and most powerful tool for the use of language.

> …
> Between my finger and my thumb
> The squat pen rests.
> I'll dig with it.

of the activities involved in the action, e.g. stabbing into the earth, lifting the shovel, and so on. The purpose of the action informs the meaning.

According to Nerlich (1990: 129), the recognition and understanding of actions is informed by clarity on the purpose of the activity. In many ways, these ideas resonate with ideas on the retrieval of meaning as expounded within relevance theory. The insights of Wegener inspired many functional linguists in their research into language, and he directly asked questions that, over time, influenced new functionalist approaches to language, such as: What is the function of language, and how do we understand language?

For Wegener, the main function of language is to influence and cause an effect (understanding) within the hearer, and not to simply express thoughts. From this fact, that language can have an effect on a hearer, we motivate the idea that in language it is the function that is primary, not the linguistic *form*. As linguists investigating language understanding, of course, we consider both the speaker and the hearer, and the goal that the speaker desires to achieve with certain utterances. Additionally, if we want to understand how communication works, we have to consider the situation in which dialogue occurs. Speakers can only achieve their goals, desires, and intentions, and a hearer can only understand the speaker if both interlocutors can draw sufficient inferences from context, that complex linguistic, cognitive, and extralinguistic background, to co-construct a viable common ground. For Wegener (1885 [1991]: 66–67; English translation. 1991: 174–175), the purpose and intention of speech emerges in dialogue, with the purpose for the speaker to influence the hearer in some intended way.

Wegener proposed the perceptual context of situation, the context provided by memory, and the general context of culture. He stressed that language is not a fixed system of signs for representing reality, but, instead, that language is continually evolving as a system of signs that utilizes relevant elements of a situation in the continuous dialogue between speaker and hearer. Wegener understood the description of actions in context by drawing inferences from world knowledge, and by having a linguistic frame for the representation of actions (Wegener 1991 [1885]: 161ff) at our disposal. The attributes of the situation for Wegener can be characterized following (2).

> **(2)   The attributes of the situation for Wegener (based on van Dijk 2008: 69).**
>
> The situation
> a)   serves as the basis, environment or background of talk,
> b)   features preceding events, actions and participants/object,
> c)   features properties of recipients,
> d)   is defined by a current event and by previous events still in our conscious foreground.

When the situation does not contain the necessary elements needed by the hearer to retrieve a meaning, then a more comprehensive description and explanation is required within the dialogue. This will be in proportion to the amount of knowledge that is missing from the common ground of the hearer in this situation. Of course, the degree of individual knowledge varies from person to person and the construction of meaning, through the maintenance of common ground, is a linguistic undertaking between speaker and hearer in advancing a dialogue. In Wegener's conception of language as action in context, the unit of analysis is what we now understand as the speech act, with an intentional action having a specific goal. Recognizing that a speaker's prime intention is to bring about a mental act in his interlocutor, there must always be some coordination between speaker and hearer to facilitate understanding (Wegener 1991 [1885]: 58).

Both Malinowski and Firth refer to the situation theory of Wegener, as formulated in his book *Untersuchungen über die Grundfragen des Sprachlebens* (Investigations into the Fundamental Questions of the Life of Language). According to Wegener (1991 [1885]: 21), we become aware of the situation via the environmental conditions, and the presence of the person being addressed, because of our perception. Within a communication, the situation is determined by the conditions of the environment, by the immediately preceding facts and the discourse interlocutor, and not just the words. This is called the perceptual situation (van Dijk 2008: 68). Importantly, a situation has a level of complexity and is defined by what is present, along with any previous events that are still in the foreground of our consciousness, and that may be inferred from what we know already. Wegener calls this the situation of remembering (*Situation der Erinnerung*). Another kind of situation distinguished by Wegener is called the situation of consciousness (*Situation des Bewusstseins*). These are the elements of consciousness, the groups of representations, that are currently under focus, as is the case for the knowledge that interlocutors share. These may override the consciousness of locally preceding events defined by the situation of remembering – for example, when some particular ideology determines a biased interpretation of an event. For this reason, Wegener speaks here of the "prejudices of a period", or a WORLDVIEW[16]. This distinction between two kinds of consciousness or representation might today be formulated in terms of episodic memory and its mental representations of ongoing events, on the one hand, and semantic (or social) memory or shared social beliefs, on the other (van Dijk 2008: 69). Wegener discusses perception, experience, consciousness, memory, remembering and representations, and much of what he calls a situation is actually a mentally represented situation, and not a social environment. He shows that because of our worldviews, the actual perceptions, or memories, of the current situation may become biased. Wegener builds a cognitive interface between social situations and actual language use.

8.5   The context of situation and the context of culture

Moving the discussion from Wegener back to Malinowski, we note that Malinowski extends the notion of context beyond the context of situation into the context of culture, so that the definition of a word consists partly of placing it within its cultural context. This means that language, considered as a lexical and grammatical system, is related to its context of culture; while instances of language in use are related to their context of situation. Both these contexts reside outside of language itself. This is reminiscent of the more recent work of Wittgenstein (2009: 109 §340) when he posits that a word can only be understood from its function in use: "One cannot guess how a word functions. One has to look at its use, and learn from that." With regard to a situation and context, Wittgenstein also theorizes that:

> An intention is embedded in its situation, in human customs and institutions. If the technique of the game of chess did not exist, I could not intend to play a game of chess. In so far as I do intend the construction of a sentence in advance, that is made possible by the fact that I can speak the language in question.
>
> Wittgenstein (2009: 108 §337)

---

[16] We characterized worldview in Chapter 3.

We have seen that Malinowski was the first to use the expression context of situation in the sense of the events unfolding and happening when people speak (Firth 1957a). Following this insight of Malinowski, in the broad functional linguistic perspective, linguists started to take account of the situation to recognize factors like reference to persons, entities, and events within the speaker's attention, as well as other forms of interaction with the environment. The situation functioned to cast into the perceptual spotlight a subset of context, as the situation framed and informed a piece of spoken discourse. Firth saw the possibility of integrating this notion, of the situation as a type of context, into a general theory of language, as all linguistic analysis was a study of meaning, and meaning could be defined operationally as "function in context". To study meaning, it is necessary to treat context *and* situation within linguistic theory.

The notion of culture, which we considered in Chapter 2, as a context for a language, for language considered as a system, was more fully articulated in the work of their contemporaries Sapir and Whorf (Whorf 1950, 1956 [1984]). Though Sapir did not use the expression "context of culture", he considered that language expressed the mental life of its speakers. Based around this idea, he developed a view of the relationship between language and culture, known as the "Sapir–Whorf hypothesis", that language shapes our views of reality. Closely related to this "Sapir–Whorf hypothesis" is the notion of linguistic determinism – the idea that the structure of language determines how we think, and linguistic relativity[17] – that the language we speak influences how we see the world. To date, these have not been conclusively proven to be the case in any strong or weak form.

Malinowski's approach to language analysis was influenced by his theory of culture (Malinowski 1960:vi), which saw theory as an instrument that enabled a researcher to anticipate solutions and explain them. For Malinowski, theory was a core instrument in scientific investigation and the description of linguistic facts. The study of acts of speech, as speech events inside the situational context, is a central part of descriptive linguistics. However, the study of speech acts is a part of pragmatics and discourse analysis. Rather than looking for the universal features of speech acts, Malinowski was looking for the culturally determined illocutionary forces. Malinowski (1960: 5) viewed culture as the context of human behavior and, therefore in his view,

---

[17] For a recent discussion on linguistic relativity the reader is recommended to look at Caleb Everett (2013).

the study of meaning in linguistics is the study of language in the context of culture. For Malinowski, the nature of context and situation was of critical importance:

> The meaning of every single word is to a very high degree dependent on its context…the conception of context must burst the bonds of mere linguistics and be carried over into the analysis of the general conditions under which a language is spoken…the study of any language, spoken by a people who live under conditions different from our own and possess a different culture, must be carried out in conjunction with the study of their culture and their environment.
>
> Malinowski (1923: 306).

In this regard, in relation to the study of meaning and language, Malinowski (Senft 1996: 200f, Nerlich and Clarke 1996: 320) emphasized that "grammar can be studied only in conjunction with meaning, and meaning only in the context of situation". According to Senft (2007: 84), for Malinowski, the meaning of a word lies in its use, and to study meaning one cannot examine isolated words but, instead, we must examine sentences or utterances in their situational context as "…the real understanding of words is always ultimately derived from active experience of those aspects of reality to which the words belong" (Malinowski 1935: 58). Malinowski (1923: 307) argued that an utterance only has meaning in the context of situation and he continually tried to link grammar with the context of situation and with the context of culture (Malinowski 1935b:73). He stated that: "the real linguistic fact is the full utterance within its context of situation" (Malinowski 1935b:11). The linguist and anthropologist Michael Silverstein (1975: 167) agrees with this insight of Malinowski, and he states that the study of grammar cannot in principle be carried on in any serious way until one:

> … tackles the ethnographic description of the canons of use of the messages corresponding to sentences. … This means, …, that if we call the "function" of a sentence the way in which the corresponding message depends on the context of situation, then the determination of the function of the sentence, independent of its propositional value, is a necessary step in any linguistic analysis. Thus, a theory of rules of use, in terms of social variables of the speech situation and dependent message is an integral part of a grammatical description of the abstract sentences underlying them.
>
> Silverstein (1975: 167)

Silverstein also states that the:

> … rules of use depend on ethnographic description, that is, on analysis of cultural behaviour of people in a society. Thus, at one level we can analyze sentences as the embodiment of propositions, or of linguistic meanings more generally; at another level. which is always implied in any grammatical description, we must analyze messages as linguistic behaviour which is part culture…a description of a language by grammar demands description of the rules of use in situations that are structured by, and index, variables of cultures.
>
> Silverstein (1975: 167)

Indeed, Malinowski (1935b, vol. II:7, 1923: 297) characterized his theory of meaning as a theory that insists on the linking up of linguistic analysis with its cultural context, and culture with its linguistic interpretation.

8.6   van Dijk's assessment of Malinowski and Firth

A criticism of Malinowski by van Dijk (2008: 47) is that Malinowski's claim that language use should be studied in context is rather programmatic rather than concrete and as such does not significantly contribute to a theory of context – apart from mentioning speakers and hearers, minimal explanation is given of the nature of contexts. For Malinowski, context is largely the semantic referential context, consisting of entities or persons in the current situation where the awareness of present entities allows utterances to be incomplete, and deictic expressions to be meaningfully derived from the knowledge of this context. Therefore, Malinowski's idea of context is not a significant contribution to the study of the functional nature of language. In van Dijk's assessment, Malinowski's examples are limited to the realm of contextual semantics and do not suggest a pragmatically motivated concept of context.

Malinowski's emphasis on the study of language use as action and social experience provides the background to Firth's contribution to the study of context. Firth sees the study of "speech events" as the main object of study for linguistics (van Dijk 2008: 48) and the context of situation is an important element in his approach to language study. Firth's definition of this context has relevant features of participants: 1) persons and personalities, including (a) the verbal action of the participants and (b) the non-verbal action of the participants; 2) the relevant object; and 3) the effect of the verbal action. Firth accepted that no exhaustive system of contexts of situation has been set up. Indeed, Firth's remarks on context are not sufficiently robust to constitute a theory, even by the standards of the time of his writing – for instance in terms of the sophistication of linguistic theory and description (for critique, see Hasan 1995). Firth's contribution to the theory of context is summarized by van Dijk (2008: 50) as (3):

(3)   Firth's contribution to the theory of context

a)   Contexts are embedded in the experiences of the everyday lives of people.
b)   Contexts must be described in abstract, general terms.
c)   Contexts consist only of the relevant aspects of a social situation.
d)   Contexts consist mainly of participants, actions, and their consequences.
e)   Contexts feature other social aspects of participants and of the societies these are members of, as well as speech functions.
f)   The description of contexts is to be given only in the social terms of observable objective events, and not in terms of (hidden) mental processes.

A conclusion of van Dijk (2008: 51) is that Firth has interesting theoretical ideas about context, and about the need for linguistic theories to be contextual, but that his ideas have not been worked out or related to systematic research on the contextual nature of language use.

8.7   Context and its relation to discourse in the van Dijk approach

Theories of speech acts have formally accounted for some of the properties of speakers and hearers, such as their knowledge, intentions, or beliefs, to formulate appropriateness conditions, but have not further pursued a systematic analysis of such contextual conditions. One important study that examines context in its relation to discourse is van Dijk (2008). According to van Dijk (2008: 9), many studies define contexts in semantic terms, for instance as referents for deictic expressions, or as limited to spatial or temporal orientations of participants. According to van Dijk, both cognitive psychology and artificial intelligence have advanced considerably in discovering the processes and representations involved in discourse production and comprehension to the extent that they have provided insights into the fundamental role of mental models and knowledge in discourse processing and use. However, these models have tended not to have a pragmatic orientation. Rather, these models are, in the main, semantic in nature. Broadly, the whole notion of context and its complex nature is understudied.

As almost anything may become relevant for discourse, a theory of context risks becoming quite large and very unmanageable. However, not everything that can be understood as a knowledge background to discourse is necessarily part of its context. Context draws on, but is not the same as, knowledge of the world. Developing a theory of context means selecting those elements of a communicative situation that are systematically relevant for the discourse. This means that there is a need to examine how situations are defined and determine criteria for what must be included in a theory of context.

Context models are constructs within the minds of the participants of a situation. Context models must inform how participants produce and understand discourse, and enable participants to adapt discourse to the communicative situation as it is relevant to them at each moment of the interaction or communication. Context models provide the element missing in the cognitive theory of mental models of events, and the actual formulation of the discourse. Contexts help define the conditions of appropriateness of discourse. The notion of context is used by van Dijk to indicate that some phenomenon, event, action, or discourse needs to examined in relationship to its environment and surrounding conditions and consequences, in order to describe and explain their occurrence or properties. Indeed, the notion of context is frequently used in order to explain things, whereby one places things in their "proper context".

The study of speech acts (Austin 1962, Grice 1969 [1975], Searle 1969) emphasizes the key role of social action in language use, while also accounting for formal contextual conditions of the appropriateness of utterances (Stalnaker 1999a, Horn and Ward 2004). Otherwise, the nature and role of context has unfortunately been omitted from linguistic accounts because contextual structure has tended to be considered as idiosyncratic and too complex to be systematically characterized.

Epistemology emphasizes that beliefs may vary with social situations, and that what is true in one context, for some people, may not be true in another, so that also knowledge may differ over a context (van Dijk 2008: 27). What then is context? The Cambridge Online Dictionary provides a multipart definition of context (4):

(4)   Cambridge Online Dictionary definition of CONTEXT

a)   context noun (https://dictionary.cambridge.org/dictionary/english/context)
(CAUSE OF EVENT)

b)   the situation within which something exists or happens, and that can help explain it
(LANGUAGE)

c)   the text or speech that comes immediately before and after a particular phrase or piece of text and helps to explain its meaning
(RELATED EVENTS)

d)   the influences and events related to a particular event or situation
(SURROUNDING WORDS)

e)   the text or speech that comes immediately before and after a particular phrase or piece of text and that influence how it is used and what it means

What exactly are context models? Context models are considered by van Dijk to be subjective participant mental constructs related to communicative situations. As such, context models reflect experiences that are unique to a situation participant. As subjective definitions of communicative situations, context models are unique constructs, featuring our experiences of ongoing perceptions, knowledge, perspective, opinions, and emotions about the ongoing communicative situation. Also, context models are a special type of mental model. That is, a *context* model represents the relevant properties of the communicative environment in memory, and controls the processes of discourse. Additionally, a context model is a specific type of *experience* model that is dynamic and controls ongoing perception and interaction, and consist of spatial and temporal settings, participants and their identities, ongoing events, as well as current goals. Contexts, as mental models (van Dijk 2008: 32–33), consist of schemas of shared, culturally based, conventional categories, which allow rapid real-time interpretation of communicative events. Without these cultural schemas and categories, participants would not be able to understand, represent and update complex situations (involving time, place, participants and roles, action, goals and knowledge) in real time.

The fundamental pragmatic function of context models is to enable participants to produce meaningful discourse appropriate to the current communicative situation and to understand the appropriateness of the discourse of others. It seems that contexts are signaled or indexed, rather than fully expressed, and their properties are inferred in different social situations. An assumption is that, in the same communicative situation, previous parts of an ongoing discourse are considered to be part of the discourse context when, for example, what has just been asserted becomes part of the shared knowledge in the common ground of the discourse participants. Contexts only foreground those properties that are discourse-relevant. In other words, a context model reflects facets of the interpretations of the situation of the participants. Context models are described by van Dijk (2008: 35) as egocentric within the individual, defined by a set of parameters that include the spatial and temporal locus of the discourse, of SELF (as speaker or listener), of OTHER interlocutor participants, the ongoing actions with their specific aims and purposes, and the relevant belief set.

Discourse and its properties may signal, index, or express properties of contexts in different ways. A distinction is drawn by van Dijk (2008: 36) between the semantics and pragmatics of indexical or deictic expressions. A description of the reference to elements of the communicative situation, such as present time, speaker, or recipient, is part of a semantic account of discourse and, as such, a part of the situation semantics (Barwise and Perry 1983). Instead, a pragmatic account is about the appropriateness of the use of certain expressions in the current communicative situation.

Contexts are culturally variable, and context models and their categories may define different appropriateness conditions for discourse in different societies. Therefore, context acts as a cognitive structure that is able to manage production and comprehension of discourse. One of the main theses of van Dijk's study, then, is that contexts are a socially based subjective construct of participants mental models, where the properties of such a situation are relevant to the participants. Additionally, for van Dijk, context models are assumed to *control* many aspects of the production and understanding of dialogue. Language users are not just involved in processing discourse, but are simultaneously, in real time, also engaged in dynamically unpacking the meaning and interpreting the communicative situation. However, van Dijk (2009: 10–13) reports that, while it is generally agreed that discourse must be understood in its context, it is unfortunate that context is usually ignored or taken for granted in linguistic modelling and analysis. Models of context are therefore important and they inform our understanding of language use culturally, socially, and across situations.

One of the most significant dimensions of context is that of shared knowledge or common ground (Clark 1996). Successful discourse interaction presupposes that language users build situationally appropriate context models that are relevant and aligned within a shared common ground. This way, language users can appropriately express their knowledge and opinions about

their experiences, by adapting their talk and conduct to the knowledge, interests, beliefs, desires, and intentions, and other properties of the recipient
interlocutor, the hearer. Context models must be applicable to our everyday communicative situations, while also being adaptable to new situations.
Members of a culture learn how to understand their world from their community and environment. In the same way, they learn how to understand
communicative situations, and how to communicate effectively (van Dijk
2009: 20). Context models therefore offer a framework for the theory of
pragmatics which characterizes the language users' ability to adapt their
discourse, in real time, to the communicative situation. Within linguistics,
pragmatics has most systematically studied the relations between context
and language. The study of speech acts focuses on the utterances, going
beyond the syntactic form and semantic meaning by studying illocutionary
meaning. Utterances, in specific situations, are defined as social acts such as
assertions, and declarations (van Dijk 2009: 25). For speech acts to be appropriate they need to satisfy a number of conditions, formulated in terms of the
knowledge, beliefs, desires, intentions, and status of the participants, and are
part of the systematic description of language use. The various speech acts
of assertives, declaratives, imperatives, and interrogatives, amongst others,
have a set of felicity conditions that are informed by context. Givón defines
context, in terms of shared knowledge, as common ground.

Grice formulated maxims as principles of conversation and cooperation,
such as telling the truth, saying no more and no less than necessary, being
relevant, and being clear. These maxims are to do with avoiding ambiguity
or speaking relevantly, and coherently, but with a strong contextual dimension of speaking appropriately. It must be noted that there are no formal
linguistic rules that require utterances to be truthful, or relevant. These are
simply norms of interaction that make it easier for interlocutors to understand each other (van Dijk 2009: 26).

The central idea with context is that meaning depends on context, and
context is formulated in terms of the shared common ground knowledge of
the participants, in the context of a situation (Stalnaker 1999a:98, 1999b;
Clark 1996). In his (2008) study, van Dijk notes that a distinction is made by
Malinowski and Firth, and later Halliday, between the notions of context of
situation and context of *culture*. Context of situation is local, and involves
participants face to face, and within a specific setting. Context of culture is
defined as more global, and involving members of a whole community, as
well as many of their properties, such as their knowledge, norms, and values.
Indeed, as we have seen in our earlier chapter on culture, the relationship
of culture to context is difficult to articulate and Kroeber and Kluckhohn

(1952), two major anthropologists, published a review in which they listed 164 definitions of the term culture, all of which were very different.

8.8   Context and mental model theory

A mental model is a characterization of the thought process within a person. It is a representation of the world in our environment, the relationships between its parts and a person's perception about their own acts and their consequences. Mental models help us to shape behavior and provide an approach for problem solving and doing tasks. A mental model is an internal representation of external reality, and one that plays a major role in our cognition, reasoning, and decision making. Mental models are representations (situation models) of events or situations referred to or spoken about. Johnson-Laird (1983) postulated mental models in order to be able to resolve problems of inference. Johnson-Laird's work on mental models offered a unified theory of the major properties of mind: comprehension, inference, and consciousness. He argued that we understand the world by building inner mental models of the relations among objects and events of interest to us. He used the metaphor of the mind as a model-building device (the MIND AS COMPUTER). A sequence of sentences in a discourse interaction is coherent if the interlocutors are able to construct mental models of the events under discussion, and if they are able to relate the events in such models by relations of temporality or causality. These mental models form the basis of the construction of the semantic representation of the discourse by each participant (van Dijk 2008: 73–75). A criticism of Johnson-Laird's mental model theory in relation to discourse processing is that it does not provide an account of the role of context. We articulate on similar events in different ways in different communicative situations. Context informs the mental models of events and the discourses about events. Therefore, language users need to model both themselves and other aspects of the communicative situation in which they are engaged.

Discourses and mental models are defined by schemata that are often repeated as part of our experiences. Accumulated experiences over common situations lead to abstract model schemas in which the attributes of spatial and temporal settings, events, and participants are stable categories. Our experiences are interpretations of the things that have previously happened to us, and mental models are our cognitive representations. Our personal experiences, and the models that represent them are stored in episodic memory. Much of the work on the schematic organization of memory, in cognitive science, has focused on the structure of knowledge in terms of schemas, and scripts as forms of organization (Schank and Abelson 1977). Scripts play a central role in the comprehension of stories, as comprehension of discourses of specific events and which presupposes some general knowledge about such events.

We have considerable amounts of world knowledge, and we build mental models of events by activating relevant parts of this knowledge, and thus saturate the model with the information implied or presupposed by discourse. The amount of general knowledge activated and included in mental models depends on the context, including setting, our assessment of the knowledge base of the interlocutor, goals, and interests. We may assume that people can only activate fragments of this knowledge in real time while hearing a sentence or utterance. We learn from our personal experiences, and we grow our general knowledge through derivation from mental models using abstraction and generalization. Knowledge, including knowledge of the world, plays a fundamental role in informing context models. As we discussed in Chapter 7, a theory of knowledge needs an explicit typology that differentiates between the different kinds of knowledge including specific, personal, general, abstract, fictional, social, and cultural knowledge. In advancing a discourse, the management of knowledge requires that the interlocutors continually assess the extent of available knowledge to the discourse participants, the common ground. The construction and maintenance of the common ground is informed by context and is a fundamental task of context models. We have discussed the nature of knowledge in the previous chapter.

What are the necessary dimensions of a situation model? A proposal by Zwaan and Radvansky (1998) argues that a situation model is necessarily multidimensional and they specifically focus on five dimensions of a situation: time, space, causation, intentionality, and participant(s). It is suggested by van Dijk (2008: 81), however, that apart from spatial and temporal settings and participants and events (and their relations, such as causation), we need to consider beliefs, desires, and intentions. Intention and causation are not independent categories of events or situations and they become relevant when we want to understand and explain events, the building blocks of comprehension, thereby capturing the nuances of situations. Situation models are necessary to explain issues of reference and coreference, coherence, perspective, reordering effects, problem solving, updating knowledge, and common ground. There is therefore general agreement regarding the theoretical importance of situation models but, of course, less agreement on what constitutes a situational model and the types of information it might contain. Typically, the term *situation model* refers to a discourse representation that captures aspects created by the hearer (Johnson-Laird 1983, van Dijk & Kintsch 1983).

A schema with such categories as time, place, participants in various roles, events, or experiences allows us to activate old models efficiently, and to abstract from models, such as the events occurring in one place, or with one person, or belonging to a more general event. The experiences of our lives are a continuous sequence of happenings that we can recall and relate as more or less separate units (van Dijk 2008: 83–84). Mental models are ideal for the discrete representations and interpretation of these experiences. It is important then that mental models, as context models of ordinary life, contain beliefs, desires, and intentions to motivate actions. While each situation is unique, many are so similar that we need not apply all our mental resources at each moment to understand them, and simply focus attention on what is new and relevant.

Across different cultures, these situations may involve such daily routines (scripts) as getting out of bed in the morning, washing, getting dressed, eating breakfast, going to work, and engaging in various sequences of work routines, checking email, going home, preparing and eating food, and enjoying leisure activities. A routine or script may be cognitively defined as an experience model with a fixed schematic structure and contents: event(s) and goals, participants with their thematic roles, and location.

Script theory posits that human behavior largely falls into patterns of actions, called *scripts*. In script theory, the basic unit of analysis is a *scene*, defined as a sequence of events linked by the effects triggered during the experience of those events. A script is experienced as repeatedly doing the same thing, at various times or at regular intervals. Scripts are abstractions from specific experience models and stored in episodic memory. Since many scripts are shared by people in the same culture, large parts of these generalized experience models are part of our cultural knowledge (Schank and Abelson 1977). It is widely recognized, then, that our experiences form patterns and we group these together according to criteria such as the types of persons and locations involved, and the effect experienced. The scripts inform our behavior in various ways, and many of our everyday communicative experiences are instances of scripts. Our shared cultural knowledge underpins our normal interactions and we behave in certain ways in such situations, and expect others to do similarly, thereby facilitating communication.

Context models then are a special kind of mental model of everyday experience because communicative events form a normal part of our everyday experience. Context models instantiate cultural knowledge of our society and a variety of shared beliefs. They may feature beliefs, opinions, and feelings about an event and its participants. They are dynamic and up-dated during an interaction, and they control verbal interaction and adapt it to its environment. We learn from our experiences, and organize this know-ledge as schemas and categories that define various kinds of communicative event. People have different models of the same communicative event and such differences may lead to negotiations about the shared aspects of their context models, and the construction and maintenance of common ground during an interaction. Context models are the interface between culture, so-ciety, situation, and discourse. These models integrate the social and the cog-nitive properties of communicative events, such as participant roles on the one hand, with participant beliefs, desires, and intentions, along with vari-ous kinds of knowledge. It is suggested by van Dijk (2008:92) that a context model schema would additionally have: location, time, place, participants (SELF, OTHERS); participant thematic roles. Communicative situations may be very complex, but participants reduce this complex information in a few schematically organized categories to apply contextual constraints in dis-course processing. Context models thereby support a coherent theory of rele-vance, and also provide the appropriate basis for the conditions of successful illocution and form the basis of a theory of speech acts. Context models are the cognitive representations that integrate the cultural constraints on com-municative events, and they represent what is relevant for the participants in a communicative situation. Sperber and Wilson (1995: 122) define relevance as follows: "an assumption is relevant in a context if and only if it has some contextual effect in that context".

Knowledge plays a core role in communication and has a central func-tion in context models (van Dijk 2008: 99), as we have indicated. Common cultural knowledge of a society is a core condition for the production and understanding of discourse. For interaction in discourse, participants need to represent, in a context model, their own beliefs, desires, and intentions, as well as their understanding of the beliefs, desires, and intentions of the other participants. Language users need to have beliefs along with an as-sessment of the level of knowledge of the recipients when they represent relevant properties of the communicative situation. They need to model the properties of knowledge relevant to themselves, but also an assessment of what the other interlocutor participants already know. This knowledge model forms a hypothesis about what the recipients know at any moment and will be updated as necessary during a dialogue. Common ground will also be correspondingly updated.

Contemporary research in cognitive science and artificial intelligence works towards making this relation between knowledge and discourse explicit. Yet, it is interesting to note that, while the notion of context as an important element that informs meaning came from the scientific study of human cultures in the years 1890–1920, it is an unfortunate fact that most theories of language simply give token lip-service to the characterization of context. Most context-sensitive studies in linguistics have actually been within functionalist paradigms, such as those proposed by Dik (1981), and Givón (1989, 1995, 2005), where context is examined within a discourse, and cognitive, perspective. We examine the Givón approach next.

8.9   Context in the Givón approach

Givón (2005), in his book *Context as Other Minds*, has explored the relations between language, discourse, mind, and context, and he treats a number of philosophical, cognitive, and linguistic issues to advance a theory of pragmatics. In his inquiry, the notion of context is core. People can be understood because they assume that their interlocutors share their grammar and the lexicon, and more general cultural knowledge, within the current discourse context.

According to Givón (2005: 14), almost every facet of our construction of reality, especially in relation of culture, sociality, and communication, depends upon the pragmatics of context, and framing. Givón (2005: 2) elegantly describes this, alluding in his metaphor to a FIGURE AND GROUND understanding of relevant context:

> A picture is not fully specified until it has been framed, but the frame itself remains outside the picture. A figure only stands out vis-à-vis its ground, but the ground is not part of the figure. A map is useless without its scale and coordinates, i.e. without the point-of-view from which it was drawn; but the point-of-view is outside the map. An expression is only meaningful from a given communicative perspective, but the perspective ("I hereby say to you that…") is not part of the expression.
>
> Givón (2005: 2)

The communicative context is a systematic, online construction of a mental model of the interlocutor's belief and intention states, where the act of framing accounts for the fluidity around our mental constructs. The challenge is to understand how we construct the appropriate frame around the picture (Givón 2005: 18), set the figure in its proper ground, choose a suitable point of view for a description, and take the relevant perspective.

Furthermore, Givón (2005: 59) reminds us that meaning is context-dependent and usage-driven. This context dependence and language in use are important dimensions that need to be taken into consideration. Wittgenstein (*Philosophical Investigations*, 2009 edition) indicates that, for context and for use, respectively:

> A move in chess doesn't consist simply in moving a piece in such-and-such way on the board – nor yet in one's thoughts and feelings as one makes the move; but in the circumstances that we call "playing a game of chess", "solving a chess problem", and so on.
>
> Wittgenstein (2009: 33, 17)

> For a large class of cases – though not for all – in which we employ the word "meaning" it can be defined as thus: the meaning of a word is its use in language.
>
> Wittgenstein (2009: 43, 20)

Several facts are noted by Givón in relation to the effect of context on mental representation, and on the pragmatic nature of mental categories. He observes that context is not an objective entity but rather a mental construct, acting as the construed relevant ground in relation to which tokens of experience achieve stable mental representation as salient figures. This mental representation is due to the classification of tokens of experience into generic categories or types. Givón also observes that interpersonal communication cannot proceed in a meaningful and efficient manner unless we assume that our generic mental categories are shared with those of our interlocutor. Another assumption that we can reasonably make then is, according to Givón, given the facts of language, that conceptual and semantic meaning is represented in the mind as a network of nodes and connections. Yet another assumption is that broadly the same (relevant portions of our) conceptual map of our world is also commonly held by members of the same cultural and speech community. In linguistic terminology, this culturally-shared conceptual map is known as the mental lexicon, while in the cognitive literature, it is known as long-term semantic memory. In fact, three closely interacting systems of mental representation in the human mind (5) are recognized by Givón. As context types, Givón distinguishes between what he calls the "generic lexicon", the "speech situation" and the "current text", associated with semantic memory, working memory, and episodic memory.

(5)   Context types as cognitive representation systems (from Givón 2005: 109)

Cognitive label	**Communicative equivalent**
Permanent semantic memory	The generic lexicon
Episodic memory	The current text
Working memory and/or attention	The current speech situation

Episodic memory contains representations of propositional–declarative information about unique events, states, situations or individuals, or about their concatenations in longer chunks of coherent discourse, including both visual and linguistic input (Givón 2005: 110). Working memory represents what is available for current activation by the attentional system and, as such, partially overlaps with the attentional system. Working memory is a limited storage-and-processing buffer of small capacity and short duration, where material is kept activated for a period of time pending further processing decisions. Content stored in the working memory must receive attentional activation in order to reach longer-term episodic representation. Retrieval of information from longer-term episodic memory requires attentional re-activation, to bring content back into the working memory.

In relation to language, the complexity and abstractness of grammar is due in part to the complexity of its functional interaction with many other language-processing components. It interacts directly with semantic memory (lexicon), with propositional semantics (argument structure), with episodic memory (discourse coherence), with working memory and attention. Grammar is used systematically, during online communication, to activate mental representations of the interlocutor's current states of belief and intention. Across a discourse, the assumption is that the mental representation currently activated in one's mind is also currently activated with the other interlocutor, and that there is a shared context (Givón 2005: 118). The culturally-shared lexicon is coextensive with permanent semantic memory and, during online communication, different nodes in this representational system in the mind of the hearer are activated by the speaker's use of different lexical words. Some of these words have unique referents that are accessible to all members of the relevant social unit. Part of knowing the meaning of the word is knowing that it has a unique referent. In language use, the speaker of English, for example, marks a (nominal) word with a definite determiner ("the") which acts as a grammatical marker, signaling to the hearer that there is no need to search widely for a unique reference. An important feature to do with context is what Givón (2005: 121) calls our presumption of access to other minds, the common ground. Specifically, our mental model of the mind of the interlocutor changes constantly in real time, from one clause to the next during discourse. As speakers provide more information, they constantly reassess what they assume the hearer knows and update their mental model of the hearer's knowledge states. It is stressed by Givón that the mental model we have of the minds of the addressees needs to be constantly updated with what the hearer knows.

Incidentally, as regards its suitability as a theory of context, we can note that Givón has an interesting take on the Sapir–Whorf hypothesis (Whorf 1950, 1956) .

> It turned out to be an influential contextual theory of mind and reality, but one largely empty of methodological constraints or empirical substance.
>
> Givón (2005: 47)

We next address the challenge of grounding the notion of context and we characterize how context might be operationally usable in linguistic analysis and modelling.

8.10 Common ground – the interface between culture and language in interaction

This section is concerned with common ground and the way in which it mediates the multifaceted relationship between context and language in interaction, and communication. We argue that common ground is a complex distributed structured entity at the interface between knowledge, language, and culture, where knowledge includes ontology, representation, reasoning, cultural schemata, cultural metaphors, and cultural conceptualizations. In the dynamic model of common ground, as proposed by Kecskes and Zhang (2009: 332), communication is considered to be a process co-constructed by the communicative participants. Communication is the result of the interplay of intention and attention on a sociocultural background, and formed on the basis of mutual knowledge of the interlocutors, that results in the construction of mutual knowledge in the communication process. What Kecskes and Zhang call core common ground is held to be composed of at least: a) *common sense*, which entails general knowledge about the world, b) *culture sense*, which entails our knowledge about cultural norms, beliefs, and values of human society, a community, a nation, and c) *formal sense* (of the linguistic system) which entails our generalized knowledge about the language system that we use in our social and communicative interactions. Clearly, knowledge of various kinds is of central importance to common ground. Indeed, common ground is best understood as contextually relevant knowledge shared between discourse interlocutors, and it not surprising then that, for many authors, definitions of common ground and context overlap.

In addition to Kecskes and Zhang, common ground has been discussed in the literature by scholars such as Clark and Stalnaker. Stalnaker (1978, 1999ab, 2014) introduced the notion of common ground. Clark's theory of common ground (1996: 93) was developed as part of a theory of language use defined as joint action. Clark (1996: 103) defines common ground as the sum of the joint knowledge and beliefs of participants, and a shared representation that accumulates during the joint activities of participants, and specifies its constituent parts (6).

(6)   Common ground as sum of participants joint knowledge and beliefs (Clark 1996:103)

i.   Initial common ground, comprising the set of background facts, assumptions, and beliefs the participants presupposed when they entered the joint activity.

ii.   The current state of the joint activity, consisting of what the participants presuppose to be the state of the activity at the moment.

iii. Public events so far, which contain a record of the events the participants presuppose have occurred in public leading up to the current state, with

iv.   a communal and personal common ground.

The communal common ground of cultural communities represents commonality with respect to nationality, residence, education, occupation, employment, hobby, language, religion, politics, ethnicity, subculture, cohort, or gender, and their members may share (more or less) knowledge about geography, history, values, jargon, ideologies, know-how, and so on (van Dijk 2008: 109). A personal common ground is based on joint personal experiences, and relationships between people. Personal common ground presupposes cultural common ground. Again, core to all of this modelling and theorizing is the assumption that actors in a discourse have the ability to model their other discourse interlocutors, as well as their mental properties, on the basis of shared cultural and societal knowledge, their common ground.

As we mentioned, for Clark (1996: 15), language use is considered to be a form of *joint action* that is carried out by an ensemble of people acting in coordination with each other. It emerges when speakers and hearers, as participants, perform their individual actions in coordination, in the social units he calls ensembles. Language use, therefore, embodies both individual and social processes. Conversations are all characterized by the free exchange of turns among the two or more participants. As participants in a dialogue, the interlocutors begin with a substantial body of knowledge, beliefs, and suppositions they believe they share. This is called their common ground (Clark 1996: 24), and it may be vast. The more time the interlocutors spend together, the larger their common ground. All that has taken place in conversations they jointly participated in, including the current conversation, is assumed to be in common ground. Without reference to their common ground, it is not possible for the interlocutors to coordinate meaning and understanding. Clark (1996: 23) introduced several working assumptions, which he called propositions on joint action and language use (7).

(7)   Clark's propositions on joint action and language use

a)   People use language for social purposes and activities, and for doing things. Language is an instrument for helping people carry out these social activities. Without this instrumental quality used in social activities, languages would not exist.

b)   Language use is a type of joint action. All language use requires interlocutors as speech agents. In using language, the agents participate in joint actions which require the coordination of individual actions across dialogue.

c)   Language use always involves speaker's meaning and addressee's understanding, and it involves one person expressing something to another person who has the capacity to understand it.

d)   The world's languages have evolved almost entirely in spoken settings, and for most people face-to-face conversation is the commonest setting of language use.

e)   Language use unfolds across many types of discourse as a form of action. Each type is minimally specified by a set of participants, a time, a place, and the actions taken.

f)   The study of language use is both a cognitive and a social science. We can view a joint activity from two perspectives. We can focus on the individual and the participatory actions they are each performing. Or

> we can focus on the pair and the joint action they create as a pair. For a complete picture, we must include both. We cannot discover the properties of language use without the participants engaging in a joint action.

Language use in a discourse is one type of joint activity, and one in which language plays a prominent role. Clark (1996: 49) made a number of general claims about joint activities, relating to participants, activity roles, goals of various kinds, and so on (Table 8.1). When people take part in conversations, they bring with them certain prior knowledge, beliefs, assumptions, and other information. Broadly, the presuppositions of a speaker are the propositions whose truth is taken for granted as part of the background of the conversation. The speaker takes propositions to be the common ground of the participants in the conversation, and this is treated as their common mutual knowledge. As the dialogue progresses, incremental changes are made to common ground. The participants' common ground accumulates in the course of that conversation and this updating of common ground occurs in all joint activities (Clark 1996: 51).

Assertions are the prototypical linguistic actions for incrementing common ground. In fact, Stalnaker (1978: 320) argued, that "the essential effect of an assertion is to change the presuppositions in the conversation by adding the content of what is asserted to what is presupposed. This effect is avoided only if the assertion itself is rejected".

Table 8.1 Clark's general claims about joint activities (Clark 1996: 49).

Participants	*A joint activity is carried out by two or more participants*
Activity roles	The participants in a joint activity assume public roles that help determine their division of labor.
Public goals	The participants in a joint activity try to establish and achieve joint public goals.
Private goals	The participants in a joint activity may try individually to achieve private goals.
Hierarchies	A joint activity ordinarily emerges as a hierarchy of joint actions or joint activities.
Procedures	The participants in a joint activity may exploit both conventional and nonconventional procedures.
Boundaries	A successful joint activity has an entry and exit jointly engineered by the participants
Dynamics	Joint activities may be simultaneous or intermittent, and may expand, contract, or divide in their personnel.

Clark's idea is that the participants in a discourse keep track of a discourse representation consisting, firstly, of a representation of the language used during the discourse and, secondly, the representation of the situation being under discussion (Clark 1996: 65). In all this, a discourse record represents the states and events in the current joint activity and how the joint activity was advanced (Table 8.2).

Table 8.2 Joint activity contributing to common ground.

Total common ground	
Discourse representation	
Discourse record	
Language used	Situational representation

Clark (1996: 68) considers that, heretofore, language use has been studied in two broad traditions that he calls the product tradition and the action tradition. What he calls the product tradition is more commonly known as the formal generative approach due to Noam Chomsky and his colleagues. This tradition grew out of the linguistic study of sentences, words, and speech sounds as the products of language use. In the product tradition, sentences, words, and phonetic segments are treated as linguistic types abstracted away from speakers, times, places, and situational context in which they have been produced to the extent that a major drawback of the product approach is its attitude toward context. Specifically, in this approach, there has been little or no investigation of the context of the language use. These various theories within this approach are exclusively syntactic. In contrast, the action tradition, more functional in nature, emerged from the philosophical and sociological investigation of intentions and social actions. In the action tradition, the focus from the beginning has been on what people do with language. Speakers, listeners, times, places, and the circumstances of utterance are considered. Attention is paid to the communicative acts, from utterances to eye gaze (as occurs in sign languages). Context is generally given some level of prominence. Stalnaker (1999b) defined context in terms of the shared knowledge of communication participants, thus viewing context as a set of knowledge and beliefs.

When people talk, they coordinate on both content and process, as they are performing a joint action (Clark 1996: 102). There is coordination of both *content*, what the participants intend to do, and *processes*, the physical and mental systems they activate in carrying out those intentions. Joint actions require the participants to coordinate on their individual actions but they need to decide what it is they coordinate. According to the principle of joint salience[18], the most salient element with respect to the common ground of the participants motivates the coordination and thereby advances the co-construction of the common ground. Everything we do is grounded in knowledge we have about our surroundings, activities, perceptions, emotions, plans, interests, and everything we do jointly with others is also grounded in this knowledge, in the common ground.

Common ground is important to any account of language use that appeals to context. Unfortunately, most accounts don't actually say what context is, instead relying on intuitions about the circumstances of each utterance. According to Clark (1996: 112), we often categorize people by nationality, profession, hobbies, language, religion, or politics as a basis for inferring what they know, believe, or assume. Common ground based on membership in cultural communities includes facts, beliefs, and assumptions about objects, norms of behavior, conventions, procedures, skills, and even ineffable experiences. This knowledge may be represented in many ways. Also, common ground has to be established with each person we interact with. As we mentioned earlier, Clark distinguishes between a communal common ground, based on two people's mutual belief that one or both are members of a particular community, and on a personal common ground, consisting of joint perceptual experiences and joint actions.

Illocutionary acts come in many types, including, for example, asserting, requesting, ordering, asking, promising, apologizing, thanking, and others. The primary way they differ is in what are called their illocutionary point – their publicly intended perlocutionary effect. For some illocutionary acts, the point is to get hearers to do things; for others, it is to commit the speaker to doing things; and so on. The illocutionary point of an assertion is to get the hearer to form the belief that the speaker is committed to, and is trying to get the hearer to accept that belief. Considered like this, as language in use, we can see that language is primarily an instrument for carrying out broader activities in our daily lives. These joint activities with two or more people, in socially defined roles, carry out individual actions using language as a device by which they coordinate those individual actions (Clark 1996: 399). The study of language use is not easy to characterize and is indeed rather complex.

---

[18] We discuss salience, context, and common ground next in Chapter 9.

Context and common ground are essential and key notions that advance language use in a dialogue. Stalnaker (2014: 11) reports that the most important concept of the pragmatic framework is the concept of common ground, a body of knowledge presumed to be shared by the parties to a discourse. The course of a discourse and the interpretation of utterances are guided by that body of knowledge, and by the way that it evolves in response to what is said. To understand that dynamic process, we need an understanding of knowledge and of the content of utterances in context. The exploration of the notion of context necessitates the development of the notion of context in relation to common ground. Stalnaker's main argument is that common ground and speaker presupposition can, and should, be understood independently of the conventional rules of language, and that the process of accommodation is not the application of a rule, but is the result of rational responses to events that take place during the course of a conversation. Any cooperative joint action will be carried out in a situation in which certain knowledge[19] is taken to be shared by the participants, who will be guided by that body of knowledge.

Accommodation is just the adjustment of what the common ground is taken to be in response to evidence that becomes manifest. The knowledge in common ground is about the subject matter of the discourse. It is also knowledge about the discourse itself, about the attitudes of the discourse interlocutors, knowledge about location, what the participants accept about each other, and agree and disagree on. It is natural to think of a speech context as the situation in which a conversation takes place. This situation has a group of participants who each have certain beliefs, including their beliefs about what the other participants know and believe, and intentions and goals, that may diverge.

Context evolves in the course of a conversational exchange, as a resource that the participants might use to achieve their communicative purposes. They can make what they say or mean depend on features of the context, so long as the relevant knowledge is available to the hearer. The context, since it includes the beliefs, plans, and purposes of the participants, is what a speech act acts upon; it is their illocutionary point to change certain features

---

[19] Knowledge is not the same as information. To acquire knowledge, we first need information. Information is simply data that has been interpreted but knowledge is information that is modelled in order for it to be useful. Knowledge results from the modelling of patterns within a given set of information. Knowledge enables us to draw conclusions in certain contexts. We discussed the nature of knowledge in Chapter 7.

of the context. If communication is to be successful, the contextual know-ledge on which the content of a speech act depends must be knowledge that is available to the hearer. While the concept of common ground is modelled on common knowledge, it is not a factive concept in that false propositions may be presumed to be common knowledge, and false propositions may be part of the common ground either because of error, or by deception.

Common ground is a knowledge state. The idea, according to Stalnaker (2014: 45), is that the knowledge in the presumed common background knowledge is shared by the participants in a conversation. This body of knowledge provides a resource that speakers exploit in determining how to say what they want to say. It identifies the possibilities that the participants seek to distinguish between in their speech, thereby providing a resource for the characterization of speech acts in terms of the way the act is intended to change the context. Context therefore constrains content, since the utterance will be context-dependent, and content may, in turn, affect subsequent context.

A conversation is a cooperative business, and successful communication will depend on agreement about what constitutes the common ground. So, it is normal for successful communication that the common ground of the participants should be broadly the same. Changes in the common ground, like changes in common knowledge and belief, will normally take place in response to what Stalnaker (2014: 55–56) calls a manifest event. That is, something that happens in the environment of the relevant parties that is obviously evident to all. Speech acts themselves will be manifest events, when they are successful. When an utterance is produced, it becomes common ground that it has been produced, and when its meaning enters common ground, it will be manifest that an utterance with a certain meaning has been produced. Following the speaker's utterance, the hearer may accommodate the speaker's belief by changing their belief and updating their common ground. It is reasonable for the hearer to accommodate by changing their beliefs in this way. Stalnaker (2014: 135) reports that an assertion is interpreted as a proposal to change the context by adding information to the prior common ground.

We next address the question of how theories of language might effectively characterize the contextual and cultural connection. One way that functionalist approaches do this is through examining performatives and speech acts, that is, language in interaction within a specific culture.

8.11 Shared knowledge and understanding

Language helps us understand things, and communication through language makes it possible to further develop and share our values. Shared knowledge and understanding, common ground, and values enrich our culture. Common ground emerges through communicative interaction in a discourse where assessments are made of the extent of the shared knowledge between interlocutors, such that the respective common grounds are constructed and maintained as appropriate to the context of a situation in which the discourse unfolds (Nolan 2014). In this view, a speech act meaning must be interpreted in the local context of a given situation. A situation is considered to be a structured entity with certain attributes that serves as a unifying device to link semantics to events through to syntax, and onwards to utterance meaning via common ground.

The types of knowledge characterized in common ground (Table 8.3) relate to the various kinds of knowledge, as we discussed in the previous chapter, and includes such types as declarative, procedural, heuristic, meta, and structural knowledge along a scale from volatile and dynamic to less volatile and less dynamic. The function of any knowledge representation in a culturally specific ontology[20] is to capture essential features of a class of things in a set of domain areas and make that information available as required to describe some particular entity. Common ground in this view acts as a kind of decentralized knowledge system supporting the cognitive activation of a subset of those parts of contextual knowledge relevant to a speech act in a discourse between the interlocutors.

In language and linguistics, we can differentiate between sentence meaning and utterance meaning. Sentence meaning is recognized to be a function of the compositional lexical meaning of the words used in the construction of a sentence, suitably organized in the syntax of a language. Sentence meaning contains the "*what is said*". Utterance meaning is different and reflects the "*what is meant*". Not infrequently, in determining the utterance meaning, the "*what is meant*", linguistic accounts appeal to context as a means of adding meaning to underspecified content in the computation of the meaning of an utterance. However, context remains a loosely defined and underspecified concept and it seems to be difficult to provide a characterization that

---

[20] An ontology contains a set of concepts and categories in a subject area or domain that shows their properties and the relations between them. An ontology deals with questions about what things exist or can be said to exist, and how such entities can be grouped according to similarities and differences. The theory of ontology resides in the philosophical study of the nature of being and existence.

Table 8.3 Structure of common ground.

Structure of common ground	Volatility/Dynamicity
Local dialogue knowledge	More volatile/more dynamic
Language knowledge	
Environment knowledge	
Recent events knowledge	
Historical knowledge	
Common-sense knowledge	
Cultural knowledge	Less volatile/less dynamic

connects with language, linguistics, and culture. We examine some elements of the challenge here.

The context of a given utterance exists before the utterance is delivered, and, operating like a data structure, context is updated following a discourse interaction. A subset of the wider context forms part of the current common ground of a discourse between the interlocutors. Context frames a situation, including its event(s) and the participants of the situation, and it has a central role in knowledge activation across a discourse. We can usefully, then, consider context relative to a discourse situation, speech event, and the entities that participate. Context is activated and constructed in the ongoing interaction as it becomes relevant, and is eventually shared to an appropriate extent by discourse interlocutors in the construction of the discourse common ground. A given context is unique to an interlocutor in a situation and acts as a knowledge repository, with knowledge appropriately represented, that assists in building of the situation model. Therefore, context cannot be separated from the knowledge it organizes. Context has a role in the disambiguation of reference within a situation in order that a hearer may retrieve a felicitous, and discourse-relevant, interpretation of an utterance.

Shared knowledge between discourse interlocutors forms their shared common ground. Context contains a disparate set of knowledge (information and data) which can be modified and updated during the discourse, and as a function of time. It acts as a data structure with information that can be used to characterize a situation and its participating events and entities. Context therefore frames our ontological knowledge of events and things in our world, constituting elements may share some relations. Context includes various kinds of knowledge, some of which are process oriented and dynamic. Others kinds of knowledge are less volatile and can include, for example, concepts, propositions, properties of entities in the world. Specifically, context includes cultural knowledge, general knowledge and shared beliefs, and the general experiential and societal knowledge that arises from the resulting interplay of culture and social community.

Context is what constrains our interpretation of a situation – it guides the determination of relevant meaning from a discourse situation with respect to an utterance. The shared common ground frames a relevant subset of the totality of the knowledge of the interlocutors. People interpret what happens around them and, consequently, build a mental representation that reflects their conceptualization and understanding of a specific situation. This interpretation is constrained by the knowledge about what is seen, by what is called their *"ontological commitment"*. Certainly, different observers of the same situation might have the same or, indeed, a different ontological commitment.

> An ontological commitment refers to a relation between a language and certain objects postulated to be in "existence" by that language. The "existence" referred to need not be "real", but exist only in a universe of discourse. An ontological commitment is an agreement to use the shared vocabulary in a coherent and consistent manner within a specific context. An *ontological commitment* is a decision to adhere to a certain interpretation in a language for some context.
>
> Definition from https://en.wikipedia.org/wiki/
> Ontological_commitment

Between interlocutors, having the same ontological commitment in understanding actions in some situation provides for a shared interpretation of what happens. In this, we can therefore attribute to the agent that performed the action, the same kind of beliefs, desires, and intentions, and knowledge that the observer would have in the same situation.

Context helps with the disambiguation of a situation – the richer the context, the easier it is to disambiguate an utterance in real time. A context can be described as the set of knowledge that can be used to inform the characterization of a situation and its participant entities. Location, identity, activity, and time are aspects of context. Context acts as a set of constraints that influences the behavior of interpretation. Observing and understanding a situation means integrating successive events into a coherent whole, with a series of events perceived as a connected chain of actions with causal links (Nolan 2017). Situation recognition can be viewed as an important stage of context awareness used for facilitating the retrieval of the relevant meaning of context. An utterance, such as "Brian made a pot of black tea", can be viewed as encapsulating a situation with an embedded event that is captured in the syntax of the language of expression, here English. In addition to common ground knowledge, the most constraining factors are the amount of context that is processed with, on the one hand, a shared ontological commitment based on shared context and, on the other hand, a different ontological commitment, based on unshared context.

8.12 Common ground as shared knowledge

Common ground knowledge is context-dependent, and discourse is produced and interpreted under the guidance of our mental context models. In discourse, shared knowledge need not be expressed, and may remain implicit. Once knowledge is communicated to a hearer in a discourse, this knowledge becomes part of the common ground pertaining to that discourse, and can be presupposed in all further communication between the speaker and hearer. Such shared knowledge is the common ground of the speakers and hearers.

The role of knowledge in context models has consequences at all levels of the production and comprehension of discourse (Figure 8.1). The management of knowledge guides the production of speech acts such as assertions, and the same is true for questions, when the speaker assumes the hearer has some knowledge that he wishes to acquire. Many elements of discourse are shaped by the ways that participants represent and manage (mutual) knowledge. Knowledge management strategies for most discourse is based on the shared nature of the knowledge of interlocutors of the same cultural community. However, speech participants may be of different knowledge communities, each with its own criteria or standards for allowing its members to regard certain beliefs as knowledge, so that what may be knowledge for members of one community may be false belief or unknown by members of a different culture (van Dijk 2008: 107). Hearers interpret discourses in terms of the model they construe of the communicative situation.

An important question for us then is: How can we characterize, in a model, the structure of common ground and context, and the representation of actions undertaken by others using observable objects, events, spatial and temporal context, with our ontological knowledge of the world, and using appropriate inferences about beliefs, desires, intentions, and goals? Such representation must be available to language and common ground. We next discuss this in some detail in a case study relating to context, situation, and common ground.

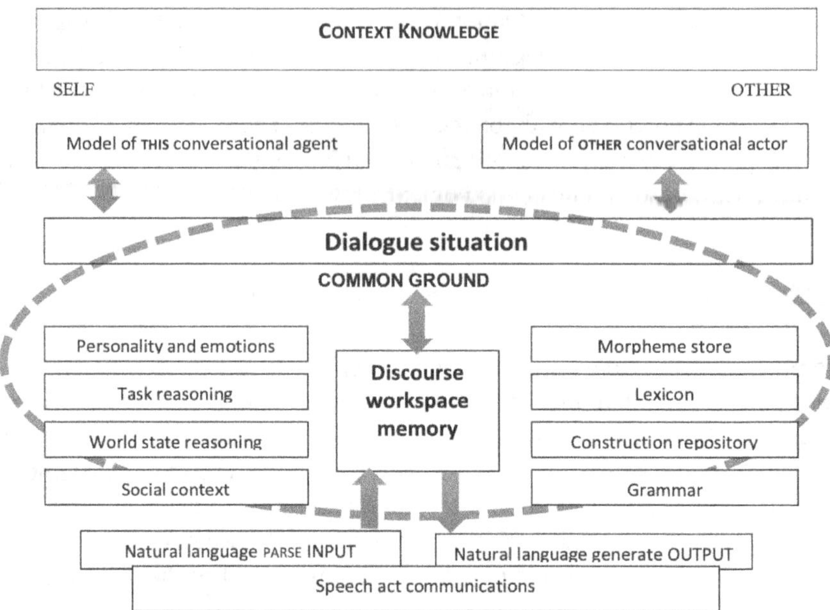

Figure 8.1 Framework for a dynamic common ground.

8.13 Case study: Meeting the challenges of context in linguistic analysis

A key challenge is to ground the notion of context, common ground, and their contents, with the appropriate level of specificity, and to represent it in such a way that it becomes operationally useful in linguistic analysis. Just as we can formalize the semantics and logical structures of natural language, we may formally model some of its context properties, including time, place and participants, in order to interpret deictic expressions, verb tenses, and coreference, among other properties of discourse. In pragmatics, the focus on language use as speech acts formulated appropriateness conditions in terms of situational conditions, such as the beliefs, desires, intentions, and knowledge of the speaker and hearer. It is argued that we need a representation of the communicative situation in which participants participate in the event, that is, a pragmatic situation-oriented context model that includes common ground.

In this section on meeting the challenges of context in linguistic analysis, we describe how we get from participation in a situation to a model of such a situation, how the relevant properties of such a situation are selected, and how this model with its schematic categories operates in discourse. We provide a case study where we contrast the ASSERTIVE speech act of Irish[21] with the DECLARATIVE speech act. In this account, we provide a formalized characterization of these speech acts and their function, where context, along with belief, desire, and intention, are shown to play a significant role. The nature of knowledge and context, and how they inform common ground, is shown within the relationship between knowledge and language. The properties of the situation, context, and common ground all feed into the utterance meaning in a fundamental way. The *what is said* is reflected in the event and its semantics, while the *what is meant* is retrieved via a higher level of abstraction within a situation. Determining the meaning of a speech act in a situation requires us to consider these dimensions as part of the interaction. As we will find, an appropriate context is important as a core satisfaction condition of a felicitous declarative speech act while a common ground is important for assertions. An utterance has a syntactic expression encapsulating an event with a linguistic structure and the utterance type identifies a speech act with an illocutionary force which are both connected in a meaningful way. The meaning of a speech act involves its situational context, content, common ground, and S(peaker)'s[22] communicative intention. Determining the nature and content of utterances is not easy but it turns out that, as people, we are actually good at doing this, given an appropriate shared common ground.

8.13.1 Mediating knowledge and language through a speech act

A conversational dialogue is a form of social behavior that unfolds in the context of a social environment and situation. In such situations and their associated contexts, we create a common ground, determine its scope and parameters. We assess the extent of the interlocutor's knowledge to inform and advance the conversation towards common understanding and a felicitous speech act.

With people we know, we can rely on them having a reasonable set of shared knowledge and, correspondingly, a common ground to facilitate our communication. Communication is successful when H determines, and unpacks in real time, S's intentions from the type of speech act uttered. A linguistic communication is identified initially on the basis of *what is said*, the carrier sentence, together with mutual beliefs in context informing a

---

[21] The functional characterisations of Irish have been reported on in Nolan (2008, 2012, 2013, 2014).

[22] We use S for speaker and H for hearer throughout this case study.

co-constructed common ground. *What is meant* by an utterance is carried in part by *what is said*, the type of speech act uttered, the utterance context, and the contribution of common ground. H can proceed to the identification of the speaker's illocutionary act through determining the speech act via the construction's syntactic pattern – its constructional signature, and through determining the belief, desire, or intention that the speaker is expressing. An act of communication is successfully achieved if H identifies the belief, desire, and intention expressed, in the way that S intends it to be identified. Therefore, to inform someone of something is not only to express a belief in it but also to express one's intention that H believes it. Belief, desire, and intention are interrelated in speech acts and communication. As conversational turns are taken in a dialogue, of course, the role of S and H naturally swap.

We now concentrate on characterizing the syntactic expression of the assertive and declarative speech acts, based on the particular speech act's constructional signature and formalization within a situation such that its meaning as an utterance can be determined. The ASSERTIVE and DECLARATIVE speech act types, as in (8), each have a different function in communication.

(8)   The ASSERTIVE and DECLARATIVE speech act types

a)   ASSERTIVES: Statements of fact that convey information to H which may be true or false.
b)   DECLARATIVES: Establish social facts (e.g., "I hereby declare...") and are themselves causing events.

Common ground (CG) is a dynamic construct consisting of shared knowledge, mutually constructed by the interlocutors (CG.S[23] and CG.H) throughout the communicative process as a dynamic part of the CONTEXT. Kecskes and Zhang (2009) propose an integrated concept of common ground, in which both a core common ground of assumed shared cultural, ontological, and other knowledge, suitably represented, and an emergent common ground, converge to construct a rich background for communication. As a part of the formalization of the assertive and declarative speech acts of Irish, we will present common ground, for both S and H, as specialized knowledge representations relevant to the communication process and the construction

---

[23] We use CG.S and CG.H to stand for CommonGround.Speaker and CommonGround. Hearer, respectively.

of the dynamic common ground. To achieve this, it is necessary to first represent several aspects (9) important to the characterization of the speech act. In addition, following Nolan (2014), we define the cognitive states for an agent and use them to describe the various key dimensions and factors, PRECONDITIONS, AND POSTCONDITIONS. We employ several predicates that are considered to have a reserved meaning (10). Speech act theory informs us of the basis for successful communications, based on the idea that with language you not only make statements, but also perform actions.

---

(9)   Important aspects of speech act characterization

a.   The set of *beliefs* that the agent S has at any given time;
b.   The *goals* that agent S will try to achieve;
c.   The *actions* that agent S performs; and
d.   The *knowledge of the effects* of these actions;
e.   The *environment information/knowledge* the agent S has (which may be incomplete or incorrect).

We indicate a structure and the potential content of common ground in Table 8.2.

---

(10) Cognitive states for an agent in a dialogue (Nolan 2014)

a.   **BELIEVE'** (Agent, P), has the meaning that the agent believes that P is true for the agent, where P is an expression in a human natural language.
b.   **KNOW'** (Agent, P) expresses a state of knowledge of the agent with respect to P.
c.   **WANT'** (Agent, P) means that the agent desires the event or state coded by P to occur.
d.   **INTEND'** (Agent, P) means that the agent intends to do P.

Table 8.4 Context knowledge in common ground.

Structure of common ground	*Contains*	*Volatility/ Dynamicity*
Local dialogue	• Salient events and references within the dialogue chain	volatile/ dynamic
Language	• Knowledge of the linguistic system	
Environment	• Shared knowledge of the entities, actions, and context of the local environment and which may prove relevant to the interlocutors within the dialogue • Meta and structural knowledge • Knowledge structures within our overall mental models • Schemata and frames	
Recent events	• Shared knowledge of the entities, actions in the context of the local environment • Declarative knowledge of concepts and facts	
Historical knowledge	• Shared cultural knowledge of (recent past to far past) historical context and associated entities, actions, and consequences • Declarative knowledge of concepts and facts	
Common sense	• General ontological knowledge about the world, its entities, and events • Heuristic and experiential knowledge • Schemata (Event, Role, Image, and Proposition) • Frames	
Cultural knowledge	• Ways of doing things in our community • Ways of behaving in our society • Common belief sets • Cultural values • Shared perspectives • Schemata and frames • Shared worldview	Non-volatile/ non-dynamic

The appropriate representation of contextual knowledge is an important dimension of this model in motivating the interface between knowledge and language mediated by the speech act. Context has a central role in the determination of the conditions of knowledge activation as well as the limits of knowledge validity. As we have already noted, it is activated, and constructed, in the ongoing interaction as it becomes relevant, and is eventually shared by discourse interlocutors in the construction of the discourse common ground. Context includes a multitude of different kinds of knowledge, including cultural, general and shared communal beliefs of a community, and the general experience that arises from the interplay of culture and social community. Contextual knowledge may also include location and environment. We have already discussed the different kinds of knowledge in Chapter 7. In an ontology, the function of any knowledge representation is to capture essential features of a class of things in a domain area and make that information available as required to describe some particular thing.

8.13.2 The situation and context of a speech act

In this case study, we claim that a speech act must be interpreted in the local context of a given situation, where a situation is considered a structured entity that serves as a unifying device to link semantics to events through to syntax, and through to utterance meaning.

In this account, we argue for a certain structure of a situation with specific components including the schematic structure of a situation (11). These components include the constructional signature (based on Nolan 2017), illocutionary force, initial context at the time of the speech act utterance and containing the initial common ground of the speaker S and hearer H along with the preconditions that exist, the speech act proposition, the belief, desire, and intention (BDI) cognitive states of the speaker, and the post-context *"as it is"* after the utterance of the speech act. The events and arguments of the situation remain represented, of course, as befits the speech act.

Depending directly on the situation and context framing the utterance, the situational preconditions constrain what can be in the proposition for a specific illocutionary force. As well, certain preconditions hold for the successful performance of an illocutionary act. We can consider these preconditions as ranging over the cognitive state of the agent, with respect to belief, desire, and intention. These conditions may additionally have a degree of strength.

---

(11) Constructional schema[24] to support speech act meaning resolution

SITUATION	*this*.SIT
SIGNATURE	
	Utterance syntactic pattern
ILLOCFORCE	IL
INITIAL CONTEXT	
	(CommonGround)
	InitialCG.S
	InitialCG.H
	Precondition(s)
Event(s)	$< v_1 (\dots v_n) \dots >$
Verbal arguments	$< ARG_1, (ARG_2, \dots, ARG_n) \dots >$
Event participants	$< ARG_1, (ARG_2, \dots, ARG_n) \dots >$
PROPOSITION	Prop
Location.time	(time)
Location.space	(place – may be unspecified)
PROPOSITION	Prop
PROPOSITION	Prop
BELIEF	B
DESIRE	D
INTENTION	I
POST CONTEXT	
	Postconditions
	PostCG.S
	PostCG.H

8.13.3 The assertive speech act of Irish

We now examine the assertive speech act as found in modern Irish. We explore the expression of the speech act and its intended meaning. We appeal to belief, desire, and intention as component parts of the speech act. In the determination of uttered meaning, we additionally appeal to a logical form based on the logical structures of Role and Reference Grammar (RRG) (Nolan 2012), along with a predicate calculus type notation to encode belief, desire, intention, and obligation, based on (10), and (11). This assists with the formalization of the situation, context, common ground, and the speech act, as a logical form.

According to Stalnaker:

---

[24] The linking of constructions, considered as grammatical objects, into functional models of grammar is discussed in detail in Nolan and Diedrichsen (2013).

…First, assertions have content; an act of assertion is, among other things, the expression of a proposition – something that represents the world as being a certain way. Second, assertions are made in a context – a situation that includes a speaker with certain beliefs and intentions, and some people with their own beliefs and intentions to whom the assertion is addressed. Third, sometimes the content of the assertion is dependent on the context in which it is made, for example, on who is speaking or when the act of assertion takes place. Fourth, acts of assertion affect, and are intended to affect, the context, in particular the attitudes of the participants in the situation; how the assertion affects the context will depend on its content

Stalnaker (1978: 78–95)

We will now examine the role of the situation of the utterance, context, and common ground pertaining to the interlocutors of the speech act. An ASSERTIVE commits S to a proposition being true such that, in uttering the assertive, S asserts that proposition if S expresses a) the belief that the proposition holds, and b) the intention that H believes that proposition. An assertive is satisfied simply if its proposition is *true* at the moment the utterance is made. We can imagine a context where there is a room with a door that is open. Someone closes the door and it happens to be a person called Lorcán. When S relays this fact to H, as part of an ongoing dialogue, an assertion is made. In the Irish data example, therefore, the assertion *Dhún Lorcán an doras* "Lorcán closed the door" is satisfied in this context of the utterance where it is *true* that the door is, in fact, closed by Lorcán. The assertive form (12) uses a syntactic construction with a lexical verb and has an actor and undergoer.

(12) Assertive utterance

a. *Dhún   Lorcán an doras*
    Close:v.PST Lorcán DET door:N
    Lorcán closed the door.
    [**do'** (Lorcán) **close'** (Lorcán, door) ∧ **be'** [door, **closed'**]]
b. Constructional signature: [v.TNS NP NP]

We next discuss the formalization of these assertive speech acts of Irish. Of course, we make the assumption, central to this discussion of assertives, that the Gricean Cooperative Principle (Grice 1969, 1989) and its associated maxims apply (13). The speech act formalization concerns the objective conditions of satisfaction for the speech act and its utterance meaning. Assertives, being claims of fact, are either true or false.

---

(13) Gricean Cooperative Principle

1) The maxim of quality   Speakers' contributions should be true.
2) The maxim of quantity   Speakers' contributions should be only as informative as the situation requires and speakers should refrain from saying either too little or too much.
3) The maxim of relevance   Contributions should relate to the purpose of the exchange.
4) The maxim of manner   Contributions should avoid obscurity and ambiguity and be clear, orderly, and succinct.

In arriving at an understanding of the assertive utterance meaning, we will appeal to the idea of a context of some situation, specific to S and H, at the moment of utterance. We will also appeal to the idea that S is motivated by a set of beliefs, desires, and intentions which influences his discourse behavior towards H. S will additionally make an assessment of the extent of the common ground shared with H and accordingly, through the discourse, construct the common ground and maintain it appropriately. Both S and H each have a common ground (which we label as CG.S and CG.H respectively) and we assume that some but not all of this overlaps with knowledge of various kinds.

In (14), we provide a formalization of the assertive speech act example (12) indicated earlier. In this formalization we define the speech act construction and identify the Situation (SIT), Context (CONT), CommonGround. Speaker (CG.S), CommonGround.Hearer (CG.H), Preconditions (PRECON), Proposition, (PROP), Belief (B), Desire, (D), Intention (I) states, and Postconditions (POSTCON) resulting from the utterance of the assertive speech act.

Furthermore, we identify the situation with a label *this*.SIT and the context as C, while common ground for S and H is denoted as CG.S and CG.H respectively. The relevant contents of common ground for S and H are explicitly identified.

While the initial CG.H does not indicate content at this point, for CG.S we show this as containing two logical structures: 1) [**exist'** (door)] and 2) [**be'** [door, **open'**]]. These act as the precondition for S in making the assertive utterance. The actor and undergoer are indicated within the various logical structures, along with the B, D, and I states. For B, we use a predicate **BEL'** (LS), for D, we use a predicate **WANT'** (LS) and for I, we use a predicate

INTEND' (LS). Reading these, S BELieves the door is closed. S desires (= **WANTS'**) that H BELieve the door is closed. S therefore intends that H BELieve the door is closed as a consequence of the assertive speech act, and that the closing action was undertaken by Lorcán.

The resulting postcondition is that H BELieves the window is closed. The proposition of the assertive is that the door is closed.

(14) Assertive – Formalization of utterance form

SITUATION	*this*.SIT
Loc.TIME	time
Loc.SPACE	location
SIGNATURE	V.$_{TNS}$ NP NP
ILLOCFORCE	ASSERTIVE
INITIAL Context	C 1. **Is_A** (DOOR, thing): Ontology: DOOR IS_A thing (that may be open | closed) 2. **Is_A** (LORCÁN, person): Ontology: LORCÁN IS_A person 3. **Is_A** (CLOSE:V, event): Ontology CLOSE IS_A event process
InitialCG.S	CG.S 1. **[exist'** (door)] ∧ 2. **[be'** [door, **open'**]]
InitialCG.H	CG.H 1. __
PRECON	1. **[exist'** (door)] ∧ 2. **[be'** [door, **open'**]]
PROP	**[do'** (Lorcán) **close'** (Lorcán, door) ∧ **be'** [door, **closed'**]]
BELIEF	**Bel'** (S, **[do'** (Lorcán) **close'** (Lorcán, door) ∧ **be'** [door, **closed'**]])
DESIRE	**Want'** (S, **[do'** (Lorcán) **close'** (Lorcán, door) ∧ **be'** [door, **closed'**]])
INTENTION	**Intend'** (S, Bel'(H, **[do'** (Lorcán) **close'** (Lorcán, door) ∧ **be'** [door, **closed'**]])
Post Context	**Bel'** (H, **[do'** (Lorcán) **close'** (Lorcán, door) ∧ **be'** [door, **closed'**]])
POSTCON	**Bel'** (H, **[do'** (Lorcán) **close'** (Lorcán, door) ∧ **be'** [door, **closed'**]])
PostCG.S	CG.S 1. **[exist'** (door)] ∧ 2. **[be'** [door, **closed'**]]
PostCG.H	CG.H 1. **[exist'** (door)] ∧ 2. **[be'** [door, **closed'**]]

Next, we provide in (15) a partial sketch of how the various dimensions needed to derive utterance meaning link together, based on our formalization of the assertive speech act in (12). In *this* situation, we have an utterance UTT_1 containing an expression (in Irish) with a constructional signature of $[\text{v.}_{\text{TNS}}\text{ NP NP}]$, signaling an illocutionary force of assertive. This utterance is represented formally as:

$$\text{UTT}_1: [\textbf{do'}\,(\text{s},\,\textbf{say'}\,(\text{s},\,\text{EXPRESSION}_1))\ \&\ \text{CAUSE}\,(\textbf{hear'}\,(\text{h, SA}))]$$

to indicate that the EXPRESSION_1 is the carrier of the *what is said* and which feeds into the speech utterance in the *what is meant* meaning derivation. H is caused to hear the speech act (SA) uttered by S. We represent the utterance UTT_1 and the expression $\textbf{EXPRESSION}_1$ as a logical structure in the style of RRG. We represent the expression embedded in the utterance as:

$$\textbf{EXPRESSION}_1: [\textbf{do'}\,(\text{ARG}_1)\ \textbf{close}_3\textbf{'}\,(\text{ARG}_1,\,\text{ARG}_2)\ \wedge\ \textbf{be'}\,[\text{ARG}_2,\,\textbf{pred'}]]$$

Encoded in the expression is a closing event with the various arguments represented with subscripts which can then be identified from the ontology available in the initial context. At the event level, a simple[25] verbal predication is found in a sentence with a single clause containing a single verb and its arguments that denote a single event and the participants of that event (16). We code an initial context of the situation showing a basic ontology, and we show the initial common ground of S and H. The clause encodes an event which unfolds within a particular time envelope. We schematically identify the semantics as a logical form where the influence of the situation, context, and common ground feeds into the utterance meaning. The "*what is said*" is reflected in the event and its semantics, while the assertion is derived at a higher level of abstraction, as the pragmatic utterance level.

Subscript indexing is used to relate elements across the model to indicate the relatedness and linking between components of knowledge and context. The same subscript denotation method is applied to *arg1*, *arg2*, etc. within the example, for the event participant/verbal arguments. The contribution of the lexicon and the language grammar are all important in communication. Representing meaning in communication therefore necessarily includes the recognition of belief, desire, and intentions in the type of situation, the associated illocutionary force, cultural conventions, various kinds of knowledge,

---

[25] Complex predications and complex events within a situation are reported on in Nolan (2017).

with common ground. Arriving at the meaning of a speech act in the situation requires us to consider the interaction of all these dimensions.

In linguistic interaction, compositionality is a property of structures that combine information conveyed through different linguistic as well as non-linguistic means of communication. The meaning of its utterance is informed by its context. Retrieving an appropriate meaning from a speech act is a dynamic process co-constructed in discourse, and arises from the agent's intention to express views and attitudes.

(15) Linking from speech act to meaning in the situation

SITUATION	*this*.SIT_a
Location.time	time
Location.space	location
SIGNATURE	V._TNS NP NP
ILLOCFORCE	ASSERTIVE
INITIAL	C
Context	1. **Is_A** (DOOR, thing): Ontology: DOOR IS_A thing: $< \text{ARG}_1>$ 2. **Is_A** (LORCÁN, person): Ontology: LORCÁN IS_A person: $< \text{ARG}_2>$ 3. **Is_A** (CLOSE:V, event): Ontology CLOSE IS_A event process: $<\textbf{V}_3>$
Initial CG	CG.S 1. $[\textbf{exist}'(\text{door})] \wedge$ 2. $[\textbf{be}'[\text{door}, \textbf{open}']]$ CG.H 1. ___
Speaker	S
Hearer	H
Speech act	UTT_1: $[\textbf{do}'(\text{s}, \textbf{say}'(\text{s}, \text{EXPRESSION}_1)) \& \text{CAUSE} (\textbf{hear}'(\text{H}, \text{SA}))]$
Event(s)	EXPRESSION_1: $[\textbf{do}'(\text{ARG}_1) \textbf{close}_3'(\text{ARG}_1, \text{ARG}_2) \wedge \textbf{be}'[\text{ARG}_2, \textbf{pred}']]$ $<\textbf{V}_3>$: *dún* "close": $[\textbf{do}'(\text{x}_1) \textbf{close}'(\text{x}_1, \text{Y}_2) \wedge \textbf{be}'[\text{Y}_2, \textbf{closed}']]$
Arguments	$< \text{ARG}_1, \text{ARG}_2 >$

Semantics	$<$*this*.SIT_a
	 $< \text{CG.S}$
	  $< \text{CG.H}$
	   $<[\textbf{do}'(\text{s}, \textbf{say}'(\text{s}, \text{UTT}_1)) \& \text{CAUSE} (\textbf{hear}'(\text{H}, \text{SA}))] >>>>$
	
	Nuclear juncture: Single nucleus, with all ARGS within the single
	 NUC

8.13.4 The declarative speech act of Irish

A function of the declarative is that it establishes social facts during its performance and, consequently, is a causing event in itself. A declarative is satisfied if (i) its proposition becomes TRUE for the first time *at the moment that it is said*, and (ii) while S is saying it, S INTENDS for *that particular* condition to occur and KNOWS how to make it occur.

Proper context is important for the felicitous use of the declarative speech act, as we see with the examples in (16). A contextual condition about the ability, authority, know-how is included to ensure that, at each moment, S is able to ensure the completion of the declarative and thereby ensure the occurrence of the appropriate condition.

This helps eliminate instances where S has the intention, but is not in the right social or conventional position of authority to make the declarative succeed. We will examine the declarative in the context of a wedding ceremony. Here, the appropriate context that must be in place for a valid wedding ceremony to occur, is identified in (17). Crucially, the context must be both correct and appropriate.

---

(16)

    a.   "I hereby SENTENCE you to X."
    b.   "I now PRONOUNCE you to be married."
    c.   "You are under ARREST."
    d.   "I now DECLARE this ship launched."

---

(17) The correct and appropriate context for wedding ceremony DECLARATIVE

    a.   The SETTING is a strict part of the context.
    b.   The PARTICIPANTS all play important and necessary ROLES in the event.
    c.   The priest or minister, S, is vested with AUTHORITY by the state to perform the wedding as a legal event.
    d.   The people getting married are WILLING PARTICIPANTS who both give free consent.

Some other constraints apply as preconditions, of course, as the participants in the wedding ceremony must also be adult and not already legally married.

Example (18) gives one version of this, for a Christian religious ceremony using Irish as the official language. In this, the setting [CONTEXT LOCATION] is a strict part of the context and the participants [SITUATION PARTICIPANTS] all play important and necessary roles in the event [SITUATION EVENT]. The priest or minister, S, as agent of the activity, is vested with authority by the state to perform the wedding as a legal event. The people getting married are willing participants, denoted as H1 and H2 respectively, that give consent. The declarative speech acts are fundamentally culturally informed and cause an event in themselves – the marriage of the two participants.

(18)

a. **AN DEARBHÚ:** *Labhraíonn an sagart leis an phobal. I bhfianaise Dé agus os comhair an phobail seo thug H1.name agus H2.name a gcead agus a móideanna pósta dá chéile. D'fhógair siad a bpósadh trí shnaidhmeadh lámh, agus trí fháinne a thabhairt agus a ghlacadh. Mar sin de, in ainm Dé, fógraím gur lánúin phósta iad.*

b. **THE DECLARATION: The priest addresses the people.** In the presence of God, and before this congregation, H1.*name* and H2.*name* have given their consent and made their marriage vows to each other. They have declared their marriage by the joining of hands and by the giving and receiving of a ring. Therefore, in the name of God, I pronounce that they are husband and wife.

c.   I   *bhfianaise Dé agus os comhair an phobail*   *seo*
In (the) presence (of) God, and before   DET congregation this
In (the) presence (of) God, and before this congregation

thug   H1.*NAME agus* H2.*NAME a*   *gcead*   *agus*
Give:V.PST   H1.*NAME* AND   H2.*NAME* their permission and

a   *móideanna pósta*   *dá chéile.*
their vows   marriage to each other.

H1.*NAME* and H2.*NAME* have given their consent and made their marriage vows to each other.

D'fhógair siad a bpósadh trí   shnaidhmeadh láma,
Declare:V.PST 3PL   their marriage:VN by (the) joining:VN (of) hands
They have declared their marriage by the joining of hands

agus trí   fháinne a   thabhairt agus a   ghlacadh.

and through ring   PRT give:VN and PRT receive:VN.
and by the giving and receiving of a ring.

> *Mar sin de, in   ainm   Dé,*
> Therefore   in (the) name (of) God
> Therefore in the name of God
> *fógraím*   *gur   lánúin phósta   iad.*
>
> pronounce:V.PRS+1SG that couple married 3PL.ACC.
> I pronounce that they are married.

Such performatives have the effect they do because societies endow them with a particular authority and power.

We provide a formalized representation of the declarative for the wedding in (19) that illustrates the important contribution of context to its successful realization. In fact, the context is of critical importance. Conversely, common ground does not have the same importance here with the declarative, as it did with the assertive example seen earlier.

The initial context c has an ontology where *wedding* is known as an event process.

(19) Formalization of DECLARATIVE speech act

Situation	*this* SIT
IllocForce	Declarative
Initial	c
Context	ONTOLOGY: *wedding* IS_A event PROCESS
	ACTOR of speech act has appropriate AUTHORITY
	UNDERGOER(s) (Person_1 & Person_2) are WILLING PARTICIPANTS
	LOCATION of speech act event is an appropriate location
	TIME of speech act is appropriate for the event denoted
InitialCG.S	CG.s _
InitialCG.H	CG.h _
PRECON	**NOT** (**BE'** (PERSON_1, MARRIED)): Person_1 is_NOT MARRIED
	NOT (**BE'** (PERSON_2, MARRIED)): Person_2 is_NOT MARRIED
	WANT' (**marry'** (Person_1, Person_2))
	: Person_1 & Person_2 **WANT** TO MARRY EACH OTHER
	Speech act ACTOR has appropriate AUTHORITY to marry people
Prop	Person_1 and Person_2 **WANT** to marry each other
B	
D	
I	

Post	BE′ (**marry′** (Person_1, Person_2))
CONTEXT	: Person_1 and Person_2 ARE MARRIED to each other
Postcon	BE′ (**marry′** (Person_1, Person_2))
	: Person_1 and Person_2 ARE MARRIED to each other
PostCG.S	CG.s
PostCG.H	CG.h

The actor of the speech act has the appropriate authority to conduct the ceremony. The undergoers, the two people who intend to get married (Person_1 and Person_2) are willing adult participants. Finally, the location of wedding ceremony is in an appropriate and legitimate location. The time scheduled for the wedding ceremony is appropriate for the event denoted.

The initial common ground for S and H (CG.s and CG.h) are underspecified. The contextual preconditions (PRECON), which act as the *felicity conditions* for the performatives are, however, important and necessary for the wedding ceremony to be successful.

Four representative preconditions are specified: 1) Person_1 is not married, 2) Person_2 is not married, 3) Person_1 and Person_2 want to marry each other at this place and time, and 4) the priest or minister who will conduct the ceremony, and utter the appropriate speech, has the legal authority to marry people.

We represent these preconditions as:

NOT (BE' (PERSON_1, MARRIED)): Person_1 is_NOT MARRIED

NOT (BE' (PERSON_2, MARRIED)): Person_2 is_NOT MARRIED

WANT' (**marry'** (Person_1, Person_2)):

Person_1 & Person_2 WANT TO MARRY EACH OTHER

Speech act ACTOR has appropriate AUTHORITY to marry people

We leave the belief, desire, and intention variables (BDI) unspecified for clarity in the example. The post context (POSTCON) is that, after the successful ceremony when the performative was realized, the two people are married to each other. We represent this as:

BE' (**marry'** (Person_1, Person_2)): Person_1 and Person_2 ARE MAR-
RIED to each other

The activated parts of relevant context and common ground include local
dialogue, where salient events and references within the dialogue relate to
the nature of the frame of the wedding and associated participant roles. Language and knowledge of the linguistic system, includes knowledge of Irish,
as the officiating language of the ceremony. Environment, encapsulating
various kinds of knowledge, relates to the wedding frame and its schema.
Knowledge of recent events contains knowledge of concepts and facts to do
with weddings. Similarly, historical knowledge has shared cultural knowledge of weddings. Common sense has general ontological knowledge about
the world, its events and participants as they relate to weddings. Cultural
knowledge captures an individual's sense of the ways of doing things in their
community, ways of behaving in our society, common belief sets, cultural
values, the perspectives they share, and worldview. What is activated here is
a wedding frame and associated schema, a set of scripts for people behaviors
at a wedding, a belief in marriage, and a value system supporting marriage
in that society.

8.13.5 Discussion

In this analysis, we have characterized the ASSERTIVE and DECLARATIVE
speech acts of Irish. We have argued that, in order to characterize the utterance meaning of each, a consideration of the situation, its context and common ground is necessary. This occurs dynamically and naturally between the
human interlocutors in a dialogue.

We have proposed a model of utterance meaning for both the ASSERTIVE
and DECLARATIVE speech acts of Irish. This required a formal specification
of the knowledge needs that feed into the meaning summation (see Figure
8.2) of the particular utterance speech act. The meaningful unpacking of the
meaning of a speech act depends on the situation in which the dialogue utterance occurs and the context of that situation. The context and the situational
frame contribute to the felicitous speech act.

An ASSERTIVE speech act utterance declares some fact that can resolve
to a truth condition, where the situational context informs common ground
and the speech act interpretation. This may include, for example, the contextual assignment of values to any indexical elements and variables in the
logical structure of the utterance. The meaningful unpacking of the meaning
of a speech act interaction involves consideration of S's beliefs, desires, and

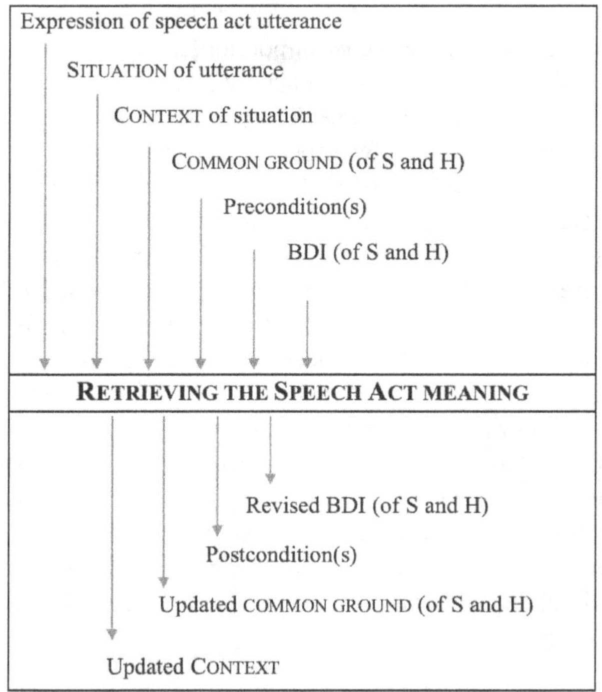

Figure 8.2 Computing speech act meaning from multiple information sources.

intentions, and the requirements posed by the preconditions in context. The beliefs and desires motivate the sets of intentions of S.

In contrast, for the DECLARATIVE speech act utterance, we have seen that context, common ground, belief, desire, and intention are all important. Context contributes to felicity conditions required for its satisfaction. These felicity conditions must be in place and the contextual criteria must be satisfied for the declarative speech act to achieve its purpose. The declarative speech act actor must have a certain appropriate authority for their words to have the appropriate illocutionary force. Indeed, part of the felicity conditions for marrying people concerns the institutional status of the speaker. The declarative speech act is a performative utterance in which *saying is doing* and, as such, is successful if its felicity conditions are fulfilled. We therefore view the declarative speech acts as context-changing social actions.

The development of a formal model of how the discourse meaning (of the ASSERTIVE VS. DECLARATIVE speech act) is composed from linguistic and non-linguistic components requires a formalization of the speech act that takes into consideration its situation of occurrence and context, common ground, the belief, desire, and intention of S and H and their respective common grounds along with several other important factors.

In retrieving the meaning of speech acts, we must consider the context and common ground of the utterance. These inform the conditions under which we would affirm that the given speech act had been satisfied. Context and common ground, belief, desire, and intention are important dimensions of this. Intentions are a matter of what an agent really wants to achieve and reflect the agent's preferences, based on its beliefs and desires. Utterance meaning is therefore highly context-sensitive and determined following a summation of information that is arrived at through different routes. We have outlined what these might be in our speech act formalizations.

In a discourse situation, successful and felicitous utterance meaning needs to be sensitive to information from a variety of different sources and the dimensions of the situation, as we have demonstrated here. Sentence meaning is determined from the syntactic structure of the expression but, beyond that, the resolution of felicitous utterance meaning itself is determined from the situation of use and its actual contextual environment, common ground with its shared cultural knowledge, general knowledge, and local context-specific knowledge.

9 Salience, context, and common ground

9.1 Introduction – The nature of salience

Salience correlates with attention and memory access, and plays a role in information packaging of utterances in a dialogue. The information status of the discourse referents in turn corelates with accessibility and salience. Information packaging operates as a speaker strategy to guide the hearer's flow of attention in discourse. Salience also has a special significance in a consideration of the dynamics of the construction and maintenance of common ground, and the management of knowledge and information flow in the advancement of a dialogue between two interlocutors. In this chapter we examine the notion of salience, the factors which give rise to it, and its relationship to context and common ground. Discourse between the interlocutors is represented by them in individual mental models, and salience is understood as a cognitive attribute of the respective mental model, such that parts of the mental model are ranked according to their salience status.

To set the scene for our discussion and to guide our lines of inquiry, we can pose some questions. The discussion following in this chapter will shed some light on these. The questions are:

1. Why is it that when we are in a dialogue with someone, certain entities, more so than other elements of knowledge, come into our awareness while commanding our attention for a period of time, and becomes salient?
2. What role does salience play, with attention and prominence, in establishing common ground?

We have already discussed common ground in Chapter 8. We have seen that Kecskes and Zhang (2009: 331) understand common ground as the convergence of the mental representations of shared knowledge, memory we can activate, shared knowledge we can retrieve and reason with, and knowledge that we can create in the communicative process. They emphasize that "common ground is a dynamic construct that is mutually constructed by interlocutors throughout the communicative process".

We know it is the case that some knowledge or information becomes more readily available in cognition than other elements of knowledge. That is, some entity or piece of knowledge becomes salient. The entity that is salient, be it a situation, event, nominal referent entity, time, or location, or something from context, can change very quickly and be replaced with a different entity that comes to our attention. What is salient can fade from attention unless reactivated with, for example, some prominence cue; salience is generally viewed as gradient. Salience can occur for a speaker and a hearer, and when this convergence between speaker and hearer salience occurs with respect to the same "thing", the entity, the "thing", enters common ground. With the convergence of salience in the communicative process, the co-construction of common ground is established. The occurrence of salience foregrounds entities of various kinds as candidates for inclusion into common ground.

But, what exactly is salience?

Salience, a term found in various domains such as linguistics, psychology, and cognitive systems within artificial intelligence, is used to characterize the state of being prominent. In the linguistic sense treated here, and which is our concern, salience means that certain things come to be in the foreground of our attention. As such, salience is a cognitive property of mental entities that are referred to within a discourse, and a high degree of salience is associated with the focus of our attention. Salience relates to the attentional state assigned to a discourse entity. One of the functions of linguistic utterances is the signaling of salience and attentional states (Chiarcos 2009: 22). Defining a ranking order of attention over the elements within a specific mental model, salience is considered a graded notion (Chiarcos 2009: 20). In turn, if several mental models exist in parallel, there will also be multiple dimensions of salience, one for each mental model. In discourse, hearer salience indicates the givenness of an entity, and speaker salience underlies the speaker's attempts to influence this status. Salience is defined by Chiarcos et al. as:

> ...the degree of relative prominence of a unit of information, at a specific point in time, in comparison to the other units of information.
>
> Chiarcos et al. (2011: 9)

We know that people use information that is most accessible to them. The conditions necessary for salience to occur are described by Jaszczolt and Allan (2011: 1) as relating to information accessibility in memory in virtue of factors such as frequency of use, the knowledge state of an individual, and familiarity. Jaszczolt and Allan (2011: 3) understand salience as:

(i)   triggered by the recognition of the primary intended meaning;
(ii) caused by the frequent occurrence of a lexical item;
(iii) a probable construal for the particular context.

Some scholars seek to constrain the scope of salience to, for example, entries in the lexicon, as in the graded salient hypothesis of Giora (2003). Other scholars (Jaszczolt and Allan 2011) consider that salience is primarily related to context, in a salience-based contextualism. We review both of these theories, but, overall, tend to agree with the view that the breadth of what can be salient is to be drawn from the full context, as driven by the need of a successful discourse between interlocutors.

Continual access to context is essential for the establishment, and evolving maintenance, of common ground in the sense of Kecskes and Zhang (2009).

> While attention (through salience, which is the cause for interlocutors' egocentrism) explains why emergent property unfolds, intention (through relevance, which is expressed in cooperation) explains why presumed shared knowledge is needed. Based on this, common ground is perceived as an effort to converge the mental representation of shared knowledge present as memory that we can activate, shared knowledge that we can seek, and rapport, as well as knowledge that we can create in the communicative process. The socio-cognitive approach emphasizes that *common ground is a dynamic construct that is mutually constructed by interlocutors throughout the communicative process.*
>
> Kecskes and Zhang (2009: 331)

In the sections that follow, we examine the factors that contribute to the phenomena we know as salience, such as attention, prominence, frequency and entrenchment, expectation, information status and packaging, and the role that context plays with salience. This chapter is organized as follows: in section 9.2 we examine the factors that contribute to the state of salience. We follow in section 9.3 with a review of Giora's graded salience hypothesis, context and relevance theory, and salience-based contextualism as found in the theory of default semantics with its default meanings. In section 9.4, we discuss mental models, situation, and discourse. In section 9.5 we have a concluding discussion. Clearly, these various factors, prominence, attention, accessibility, and gradience, etc. are important to salience, and we consider these next.

9.2   Frequency, accessibility, attention, and prominence

The notion of accessibility is used to characterize the ease with which the mental representation of some potential referent can be activated in, or retrieved from, memory. Accessibility depends on 1) salience, 2) selective attention and 3) situational context. In discourse (Falk 2014: 3), some parts of discourse are activated and accessible in memory more so than others, signaling their relevance in discourse planning and processing. Salience can be both backward-looking, and forward-looking. We will come to forward-looking salience shortly. In backward-looking salience, for example, the choice of referring expression forms, such as personal pronouns, proper names, or definite noun phrases, is motivated by a hierarchy of accessibility[26] (Ariel 1990, 2001, 2013). A pronoun is classified as marking the status of high accessibility, and the choice would be made on the basis of a hierarchical ranking of the possible discourse antecedents. The more salient the antecedent, then the more accessible and easier for the hearer to retrieve from memory, and to establish the correct backward relation. We examine forward-looking salience in section 9.2.2, in our discussion on attention.

9.2.1   Frequency

When we repeat something frequently, we tend to do it more effortlessly and more gracefully, as according to the saying: "practice makes perfect". Repetition of a behavior solidifies it into something that can be done automatically, without thinking (for example, swimming, riding a bike, or speaking our language). That is to say, speaking our language is a usage behavior that is sensitive to frequency (Divjak 2019: 15). The influence of frequency on

---

[26] There are several accessibility theories which attempt to characterize the ways in which the accessibility of entities motivates the realization of referring expressions:

- the Givenness Hierarchy (Chafe 1976; Givón 1992);
- the Accessibility Theory (Ariel 1991, 2000);
- the Centering Theory and the local coherence of discourse (Grosz and Sidner 1986; Grosz et al., 1995; Włodarczyk & Włodarczyk 2006);
- the concept of semantic default (Jaszczolt 2005).

linguistic systems challenges the strict partition between knowledge of language structure and language use, suggesting instead a dynamic model of grammar in which linguistic structure is grounded in language use.

All language units arise from, and are shaped by, usage events through general cognitive abilities. Of course, cognitive abilities are not specific to language, but include cognitive capacities such as perception, attention, memory, categorization, and imagination. Included also are pragmatic and interactional principles as well as functional principles, such as iconicity and economy (Divjak 2019: 20). Frequency has the effects it has because our memory is sensitive to how items are presented over time. While the memory capacity of the brain is remarkable, it is a fact that our brains cannot effectively store and recall lots of information in a short period of time. However, the human brain is very good at storing information regularly encountered.

Certain kinds of knowledge, such as skills and habits, are classed as memories, and a memory is now considered an emergent feature of many different parts of the brain firing in a certain way. Frequency effects are therefore effects of memory, and memory is affected by how items are presented over time. As it turns out, the closest linguistic counterpart of a timeframe is a contextual frame. Contextual frames are available at all levels of linguistic analysis. They conjoin to form chunks that form the clauses and sentences that make up the language that capture our experiences. As memory is context-dependent, the occurrence of a context helps us to retrieve memories, including linguistic memories.

Indeed, because language is used for human social interaction and has a role in our social life, the evolution of language cannot be understood outside a social and cultural context. The nature of language emerges from its role in social and cultural interaction. Over time, humans have developed a conventional system to facilitate communication, and this system is to a large extent arbitrary but entrenched in a speech community. As a consequence of this, the effects of frequency have a corresponding resonance within our memory store. Since memory is affected by how items are presented over time, the course of linguistic elements over time is a consideration of some importance. In this operationalization of salience, we rely on the contextual frame (Divjak 2019: 212). Contextual frames influence the way in which words are organized in a sentence.

Our individual experiences are encoded in our memory, and frequency and attention play a role in the process (Divjak 2019: 219). Importantly, the concept of entrenchment captures how repeated encounters of a linguistic pattern, its usage frequency, strengthens its representation in memory. In fact, our human brain is a memory structure that stores our individual experiences in a way that represents, within our mental models, the way the world is organized, remembering sequences of events and their nested relationships, and making predictions based on those memories. This prediction system, based on memory, is foundational to our intelligence, perception, creativity, and awareness, and we have the capacity to predict the future by analogy to the remembered past. In this regard, representations and a representational capacity[27] are necessary for cognition because "the mind must relate to the world and the world does not fit inside a brain" (Edelman 2008: 17). Memories are represented in an associative fashion, for example, through context frames, and the criteria for memory encoding are salience, emotional value, surprise, and novelty.

9.2.2   Attention with salience

A process associated with salience is the allocation of attention. In a discourse, the attention of the hearer is guided by the speaker to establish a salient profile of foregrounded and backgrounded information in their discourse model (Falk 2014: 4). Foregrounding serves to indicate the salience of discourse parts in relation to upcoming discourse, to support the forward-looking salience of parts of the mental model. Here, speakers convey the importance of an entity in the mental model to the hearer relative to the continuing discourse that is to follow, such that a referent becomes expected to play a role despite the fact that it is not recoverable or predicted from previous discourse. As we mentioned earlier, backward-looking salience relates to the continuity of referents throughout discourse (Givón 1983, 2001), and it enhances the predictability that a referent was continued from previous discourse, making the referent recoverable from previous mention. Importantly, with respect to models, backward-looking salience is common to both the speaker's and the hearer's discourse model (Chiarcos 2009), whereas forward-looking salience is exclusive only to the speaker's mental model.

Attention is related to memory and it modulates the uptake of information. The effects of attention on language are captured with salience. Attention is also a central component of how information is processed. It explains how certain aspects of the information stream are selected while others are suppressed to optimize performance. A situation is complex, multidimensional,

---

[27] Edelman (2008) proposes a computational theory of the mind, and views computation as the formally constrained manipulation of representations. See also: https://en.wikipedia.org/wiki/Computational_theory_of_mind.

and dynamic. In real life, in a situation, linguistic and non-linguistic information interact and influence attention (Divjak 2019: 214). The situation encompasses the speaker-internal relation between the message and the encoding, the relation between the interlocutors, and the relation between the speakers and the larger social group(s) they belong to. Language directs attention and activates memory representations. Elements of a situation that are made salient by means of overt or covert cueing tend to occupy more prominent syntactic positions and, all other things being equal, can tilt the choice of construction in favor of the non-default one.

We pay attention to stimuli that are good predictors of important events. Stimuli with a high associative strength that have a higher predictive value than all other stimuli present will receive our attention (Divjak 2019: 196). Attention can be directed to those stimuli, and a speaker has strategies in their use of language to increase or decrease the salience of an item in order to guide the hearer's attention (Divjak 2019: 25). Attention can be attracted by stimulus properties (such as loudness or brightness), by an actor's goals, or by stimuli that signal situations or events of significance.

Attention is deployed during perception of a situation. Each new situation is unique, and language typically offers multiple ways to construe the situation linguistically (Beckner[28] et al. 2009: 3–5). To capture a complex situation in words, speakers need to selectively attend to the different components of that situation. Aspects of a situation assist in the capture of attention and guide the choice between competing grammatical encodings, while prioritizing the changing of the information flow during language processing. Our experience of reality unfolds across a number of domains simultaneously; there is perception across the visual, auditory, and tactile domains; there are motor events, and mental processes such as emotions. We cannot attend in equal measure to all input channels to our experience. Instead, we concentrate on a small number of areas, and give these our attention. According to Langacker (1987: 115), in virtue of this focus of attention, inputs from those areas are perceived as being more prominent or salient. The cognitive ability of focusing attention is active in a number of operations that are relevant from a linguistic point of view. Langacker's notion of "construal" covers the relationship between the speaker and hearer and the situation represented, and embodies the role that attention plays in language.

---

[28] Beckner et al. (2009) view language as a complex adaptive system shaped by its communicative functions.

Construal reflects the user's ability to adjust the focus of attention by altering the mental imagery representing a situation. These differences can be rather obvious, as when we contrast (1a) with (1b).

(1) a. Belfast lies to the north of Dublin.
     b. Dublin lies to the south of Belfast.

This can be even more subtle, as when comparing (2a) with (2b):

(2) a. Tara sent a book to Lorcán.
     b. Tara sent Lorcán a book.

The notion of "profiling" refers to the effect that construal has. Profiling captures the fact that, for any linguistic act, some entity, the figure, stands out in profile against a (back)ground. The contrast between figure and ground plays a prominent role in cognitive grammar. The figure within a situation stands out against the ground and receives prominence as a pivotal entity around which the situation is organized, and for which the situation provides the background. Langacker (1987: 120–2) notes that the figure/ground organization is not predetermined for a given scene, and it is possible to structure the scene around different figures (Divjak 2019: 198). Different aspects of the expression, content, situation, and context can have different degrees of salience. Languages have means to increase or decrease the salience of the parts of an expression, its reference, or context. The speaker employs this system in formulating an expression while the hearer, largely on the basis of such formulations, allocates their attention in a particular way over the entities. Talmy's (1995, 2000) notions of "windowing" and "gapping" reflect instances of selective attention. Given a referent scene, for example, a motion event with a conceivable initial, medial, and final image-schematic organization, three options are available to discourse participants: windowing of all features, windowing two and gapping one, or windowing one and gapping two. It would appear to be the case that linguistic attention is gradient and organized hierarchically (Divjak 2019: 199). Attention is more focused on the overall meaning of a sentence than on the meanings of its individual words and still more on the contextual import of that sentence's meaning than on the literal meaning of the sentence (Talmy 2007: 266).

The first step in transitioning from viewing a panorama or scene to talking about it involves the creation of a conceptual message. That is, determining *who did what to whom*. Attention can result from the speaker's own goals and expectations, or from the properties of the actual referent (Divjak 2019:

201). Speakers of English automatically focus attention on syntactic placement, because word order is the primary means of determining grammatical relations. A referent's salience might predict its position in a sentence, with the most salient referents occupying the most prominent sentential positions. In English, the most salient referent is put in sentence-initial position, which determines the structural organization of the sentence.

Salience detection via cues is considered a key attentional mechanism, as it enables us to focus our perceptual and cognitive resources on the most relevant subset of the available data. Humans have difficulty paying attention to more than one item simultaneously, and we have the challenge of continuously prioritizing and integrating different bottom-up and top-down influences. It is not clear where the boundary between the bottom-up and top-down effects reside in language. Lexical semantic restrictions, such as a verb's selectional preferences, are regarded as projecting bottom-up effects. Cues play a role in the high-level apprehension of a situation, which in turn affects lower (lexical-syntactic) levels of linguistic processing. Cognitive activation can be achieved by conscious selection, in which a concept enters working memory for processing, or via spreading activation where the activation of one concept triggers the activation of others. Then, salient means loaded into working memory (Divjak 2019: 210), and at the center of someone's attention. According to Giora (2003: 15), salience captures that which is foremost on one's mind. The meaning of a word is considered salient if it is coded in the mental lexicon. Still, the degree of salience of a given word meaning cannot be viewed as a permanent, defining characteristic, but rather as a function of a number of factors, such as frequency, conventionality, familiarity, and prototypicality. The more frequent, conventional, familiar, or prototypical a given word meaning is, the greater degree of salience it holds. Giora's graded salience hypothesis revolves around the assumptions that i) the salient meaning of a word is always activated and cannot be bypassed, and ii) the salient meaning is always activated first, before less salient meanings.

9.2.3 Expectation, surprise, and prediction

During language processing, knowledge about situations, events, and their typical participants is exploited to narrow down predictions for upcoming input. Across the different views on salience, expectation plays a key role. Information that confirms the expectations facilitates processing, while a deviation from expectations increases processing costs (Divjak 2019: 210). Speakers and hearers create context-based expectations about upcoming linguistic input at different levels. Different types of information are drawn upon at syntactic, lexical, semantic, and pragmatic levels of representation at each point in processing to reach an interim evaluation and build expectations at all levels. The flow of information goes in both directions, with the utterances encountered as input-activating representations, triggering expectations for new syntactic structures, event knowledge, and scenarios. We have expectations generated by current context, we have expectations generated by exposure to many contexts over time or we experience a complete lack of context-generated expectations via novelty. One thing that can confound expectation is surprise or novelty. Surprise often accompanies novelty (Divjak 2019: 211). Top-down effects are salient, "cognitively accessible" in the discourse or situation and therefore in current working memory. A part of the operationalization of salience is to consider the degree to which an item is expected given a specific context. This is known as the quality of "surprisal". The surprisal of a word is equivalent to the difference between the probability of possible utterances before and after encountering that word. Surprisal can account for behavioral correlates of cognitive load during comprehension. The underlying idea with surprise is that the cognitive load is proportional to the amount of information conveyed by the input (its surprisal) given the preceding context, and that the speakers' production choices tend to keep the amount of information constant. Processing of surprise requires extra cognitive processing and this has a cognitive processing cost.

We use prediction as means of access to our world knowledge such that we can later use this knowledge to make accurate predictions. In language, for example, it helps to know the grammar of a language if we want to predict the next word in a sentence. Indeed, one way to learn about grammar is to look for the best way to predict the next word in the sentence and to adjust our predictions for future responses according to previously encountered patterns (Divjak 2019: 219). We can use prediction to discover the grammar of a language, and use the grammar itself in future prediction tasks.

9.2.4   Information status

It is generally accepted that salience has to do with attention and memory access, and that salience plays a role in the information packaging of discourse referents. Consequently, the information status of the discourse referents correlates with accessibility and salience. Information packaging serves as a speaker strategy to guide the hearer's flow of attention in discourse (Chiarcos 2009: 29). Attention is a key mechanism for controlling this kind of mental activity. Information packaging builds on concepts of cognitive states, attentional states, and accessibility in memory, along with focusing operations, in the manipulation of these states.

The speaker's focus of attention can be expressed via careful use of grammatical roles to promote entities to the hearer's focus of attention. In turn, referring expressions used by the speaker reflect the assumed attentional states of the hearer. Word order preferences complement grammatical roles and referring expressions in guiding attention. For discourse referents, referential choice, grammatical roles, and word order all play a role where salient precedes non-salient (Falk 2014: 2), such that pronominal > nominal subject > object > oblique. A discourse unit already mentioned in earlier discourse is *given* when it can be inferred from the common ground of the speaker and the hearer. A discourse unit is *new* if it has not been mentioned in previous discourse. Additionally, *topic* and *focus* are two distinctions that are also important to the status of information. The topic (theme) of an utterance is what is being talked about, and the focus (comment, rheme) is what is being said about the topic. Topic allows known information to be fronted, whereas focus introduces new information that is now foregrounded. The focus introduces new contrastive or alternative information in relation to previous discourse.

The focus of attention is defined as a mechanism which selects a subset of information for immediate processing (Chiarcos 2009: 31). The focus of attention is often characterized using the metaphor of a "spotlight on a stage". Like a spotlight, the focus of attention never highlights the whole picture, but only parts of it at a time. As with a play in a theatre, the action unfolds across many situations involving disparate actors, scenes, events, and locations. The spotlight draws attention to one or other as it flits across the scene. The external real world and our internal world are too complex to be realized, understood, or described as a unitary whole. Instead, we use mental representations to highlight a selection of important characteristics, such that a situation is represented with a sufficient level of detail that is sparse enough to be held in memory, but which can be communicated as needed. To understand the whole situation requires that information from previously attended dimensions be appropriately combined within the representation of the situation. Complex memory representations result from the current focus of attention, building on the sequence of prior attention shifts.

9.2.5   Attention control in discourse

Across a dialogue, a speaker needs to ensure that the hearer's focus of attention moves in the intended direction. Without proper guidance by the speaker, through the choice of utterance formulation, the hearer cannot obtain the mental representation of the discourse that the speaker intends that the hearer construct. Both hearer and speaker possess independent attentional states, reflecting the particular individuals, and in order to control the flow of attention, the speaker must be mindful of the hearer's attentional states. The flow of attention in discourse requires an assessment of both the speaker's perspective, and the hearer's perspective. As such, the speaker needs to construct mental models for both his own perspective on discourse and the assumed perspective of the hearer. These are the speaker (SELF) model and hearer (OTHER) models (Chiarcos 2009: 31). In attention control in discourse, to indicate an attention state, a speaker can refer to the attentional state of a particular referent, according to his conception of the hearer model, in order to produce a coherent utterance for the hearer. In the process of attention guidance, known as foregrounding, a speaker may indicate the attentional state of a referent in the speaker model, and thus indicate to the hearer that they need to adjust their focus of attention.

To guide the hearer's focus of attention in order to bring a referent to the foreground, specific types of referring expressions, such as demonstratives, can be used by the speaker. Elements from our short-term memory are more accessible than elements from long-term memory. However, short-term memory has a limited storage capacity, and its contents fade from it if they have not been recently accessed. Attentional states are arranged on a scale along a continuum of cognitive states (Chiarcos 2009: 53) ranging from (in)accessible in memory to being in focal attention. The status of accessibility is characterized by Levelt (1989: 145, chapter 4) as follows:

i.   Inaccessible: The discourse record informs the speaker that the hearer cannot find or infer the entity. The speaker encodes an inaccessible referent as indefinite. It is not in common ground or in the discourse model; it is also not inferable (see (ii) below) from entities in these shared knowledge structures. These referents are "brand new".

ii. Accessible: Though the referent is not in the discourse model or in common ground, the discourse record makes it seem likely to the speaker that the addressee can infer the referent. The speaker will make definite reference. In using a definite description, a speaker tells a hearer that a referent can be uniquely identified, either in their common ground, or in their shared discourse knowledge, or by inference from what is currently in focus.

iii. In the discourse model: The entity is in the discourse model, but it is not in the hearer's current focus. The speaker will express this by making a definite reference.

iv. In-focus: When a speaker considers a referent to be in the hearer's focus, reference is made via "pro-forms".

Chiarcos (2009: 32) argues for a graded notion of attentiveness, where there are i) entities in the current focus of attention, ii) entities in short-term memory, but not in the focus of attention, and iii) entities outside short-term memory. Entities are organized dynamically such that higher-ranked entities are associated with the focus of attention and realized by reduced referring expressions such as pronouns that are frequently used. Referents at the lower end of the hierarchy are represented by more complex, nominal descriptions. The form of the referring expression has a processing cost for the referent to be assessed in the mind of the hearer. Pronouns encode more highly activated referents than nominal descriptions and proper names. Simply, the less frequently used that a referent is in discourse, then more elaborate expressions will be needed to point to it. The complexity of the referring expression and the degree of accessibility to the hearer are therefore in a direct, iconic relationship, and differences in the salience of discourse referents are reflected in corresponding differences in the markedness of referring expressions. Referring expressions indicate attentional states of the hearer, and differ in their potential to access more or less "accessible" or "activated" referents. We already mentioned that the topic of an utterance is the component of a sentence that this sentence is construed about, while the focus refers to the part of the sentence which contains information about the topic (Chiarcos 2009: 51). The topic of a sentence tends to be realized as a grammatical subject. Givenness means that the topic has to be known to the hearer. Aboutness means that the topic is the referent that a particular utterance is construed about. The discourse function of grammatical roles supports the signaling of salience, and foregrounding and backgrounding operations modify the discourse prominence of a referent. The subject, then, is a privileged grammatical role that serves as an indicator of a high degree of salience. The subject is foregrounded and it enters the hearer's focus of attention. The subject becomes salient within the present flow of information. Givenness and topicality also have a signaling function.

9.2.6 Prominence

Interlocutors activate the most salient information in their field of attention in the construction of utterances (by the speaker) and their subsequent comprehension (by the hearer). For Falk (2014: 6), salience represents a cognitive real-time evaluation of discourse-relevant information. Salience refers to the relative prominence of an element of some kind, such that the more important it is, the more accessible it is. Prominence helps identify an event or element that stands out from the context (Falk 2014: 6). Prominence is linked to a relation between a foregrounded element in a situation and the context of its occurrence. A special status with respect to prominence has been attributed to the initial elements in utterances because of their role in establishing a foundation for new structures in the mental model (Gernsbacher 1990, 1997). First-mentioned elements are good candidates for being salient by creating expectations about being mentioned again in the continuing discourse. The prominence of first positions in sentences, and the role they play, are associated with information flow (Firbas 1971) in the *given-before-new* ordering of information packaging to provide high accessibility for both speaker and listener to discourse elements.

With respect to forward-looking salience, the first elements in discourse segments have a high prominence status (Falk 2014: 12) and are likely to be retained in the discourse model as they encode information that is important for the upcoming discourse. Less accessible information is generally found towards the end of the sentence. For Givón (2001: 250), prominence cues generate processing advantages in that: "More prominent and more distinct coding attracts more attention. Information that attracts more attention is memorized, stored and retrieved more efficiently." Efficient processing in discourse structure building is mediated between actual attention allocation, memory processes, and the effort to construct a discourse model. It has been suggested that backward-looking salience is associated with low processing costs while forward-looking salience generates higher processing costs (Almor 1999, Ariel 1990) thereby requiring more explicit coding. Falk (2014: 14) gives evidence in support of this view from a study undertaken by Benatar & Clifton (2014) on reading time which indicates that backward-looking salience of discourse referents yields a lower processing effort and shorter reading times than forward-looking salience.

Prominence cues, such as word order, syntactic role and position, noun phrase form and definiteness, syntactic constructions, and morphosyntactic marking, all contribute to the perception and production of salience in discourse. Word order may be employed as a means to make a part of discourse stand out from its context. Additionally, for example, noun phrases with attributes are more prominent than noun phrases without attributes (Falk 2014: 8). Syntactic roles and their effects on discourse processing are also important in virtue of their prominence. For example, as privileged syntactic arguments, subjects code preferred referents for what the discourse is about. Subjects are more likely to be continued throughout discourse segments by high accessibility markers such as pronouns and are more predictable. Subjects are more accessible and more prominent than other syntactic roles. Hearers show a bias to prefer subjects as antecedents of pronouns. Semantic factors, such as thematic roles and argument structure, can interact with syntactic cues in shaping backward- and forward-looking discourse relations.

9.3   Context, salience, relevance, and default meanings

9.3.1 Giora's graded salience hypothesis

For Giora (2003: 15), stored information is considered more prominent than unstored information, such as novel information or information inferable from context. Salience then refers to the degree of entrenchment of meanings in our mental lexicon. This is reflected in Giora's graded salience hypothesis. Giora's (2002, see also Givoni & Giora 2018) graded salience hypothesis is a theory in which the activation and semantic retrieval of salient meanings is considered to occur inside the mental lexicon, during the language comprehension process. A word's meanings are salient if they are encoded in the mental lexicon, and the degree of salience of a given word meaning is not permanent, but rather is a function of factors, such as frequency, conventionality, familiarity, and prototypicality. The more frequent, conventional, familiar, or prototypical a given word meaning is, the greater its degree of salience. The graded salience hypothesis primarily assumes that a salient meaning in the mental lexicon is always activated before any less salient meanings. In the view of the graded salience hypothesis, context has a non-primary role. Even though context can facilitate activation of a word meaning, it cannot inhibit the process of the more salient meaning activation within the mental lexicon. According to the graded salience hypothesis, default interpretations are salience-based.

The graded salience hypothesis presumes two distinct mechanisms: one that is bottom-up and sensitive to domain-specific linguistic information, and another which is top-down that is sensitive to both linguistic and extra-linguistic contextual knowledge. The graded salience hypothesis assumes that lexical access is ordered, with more salient meanings, due to conventionality, frequency, familiarity, or prototypicality, accessed faster and activated before less salient ones. Coded meanings would be accessed in real time, regardless of contextual information or intent, while coded meanings of low salience may not reach a noticeable level of activation in a context biased toward the more salient meaning of the word (Giora 2003: 23). Contextual information may also affect comprehension immediately and a highly predictive context may deliver meanings very early on. The graded salience hypothesis does not always predict slower contextual effects, and it does not assume that activation of a whole linguistic unit should be accomplished before contextual information comes into play. Instead, context and linguistic effects are considered to operate in parallel, with contextual information availing meanings in its own right, and impacting only the final product of the linguistic process.

According to the graded salience hypothesis (Giora, 1997, 1999), for information to be salient and foremost on one's mind it needs to be stored and coded in the mental lexicon. As mentioned earlier, stored information is superior to unstored information such as novel information or information inferable from context. While salient information is highly accessible, non-salient information requires strong contextual information to become as accessible as salient information. Prototypicality assists in the retrieval process. The more prototypical the meaning, the quicker it is to retrieve. It is reasonable to assume that a meaning that is either frequent, conventional, or prototypical is likely to be more familiar to an individual. According to Giora (2003: 29–30), frequency establishes the strength of association between the components of the collocation that accounts for its salience while familiarity aids the retrieval process. The more familiar the meaning, the quicker it can be retrieved. Conventionality may be viewed as:

> … a relation among a linguistic regularity, a situation of use, and a population that has implicitly agreed to conform to that regularity in that situation out of preference for general uniformity, rather than because there is some obvious and compelling reason to conform to that regularity instead of some other.
>
> Nunberg et al. (1994: 492n)

For Giora (2003: 31), in her graded salience hypothesis, salience is a graded notion. The main claim of the graded salience hypothesis is that salient meanings, via the lexicon, are processed automatically irrespective of contextual information and strength of bias. Although context effects may be fast, they run in parallel and do not initially interact with lexical processes. The lexicon is considered to be hierarchically structured. Giora gives the example of the concept BANK. Even though the various meanings of the word bank may be listed, one (the "institutional" sense of bank) may be more salient, while the other (the "riverside" sense of bank) may be less salient. In turn, the most salient meaning of the word *cool* is not "a bit cold", but "great, excellent". The most salient meaning of a specific word, expression or utterance is the most conventional, frequent, familiar, or prototypical interpretation. Salience is based on the prior experience of an individual in a social and cultural community. According to Kecskes (2004: 309), two important claims of the graded salience hypothesis are:

i.   Salient meanings of lexical units are privileged meanings stored in the mind of individuals at a given time in a given speech community.
ii. Context operates independently in the first phase of processing. It may be highly predictive, but it does not interact with lexical access and only becomes effective post-lexically.

Giora's (2003: 41) graded salience hypothesis emphasizes the role that encoded meanings play in the comprehension process. According to the graded salience hypothesis, salient meanings are processed initially before less salient meanings are activated. As such, processing an utterance involves activation of its literal meaning in the first instance. The meaning of a word or an expression is considered salient if it can be retrieved directly from the lexicon. Giora's graded salience hypothesis therefore makes a core distinction between salient (stored) information and non-salient (unstored, inferred) information. Inferred information that has become grammaticized may form part of the lexical meanings of a word or phrase, and may therefore be processed automatically when it is encountered. The graded salience hypothesis does not advocate any integrated view of the mental lexicon as containing just one type of entry. Instead, the lexicon is understood to contain specific entries for individual word meanings alongside underspecified meanings and senses, with the view that word meanings may be distributed across a semantic network where each word is an assemblage of semantic features such that subsets of these features participate in the meanings of other related words.

> The criterion or threshold a meaning has to reach to be considered salient is related only to its accessibility in memory due to such factors as frequency of use or experiential familiarity.
>
> Giora (2003: 33)

> "salience in spite of context": Privileged meanings, meanings foremost
> on our mind, affect comprehension and production primarily, regard-
> less of context and literality. Access of salient meanings is hard to pre-
> vent, even when context is highly supportive of the less or non-salient
> meaning, irrespective of whether they are literal or nonliteral.
>
> Giora (2003: 103)

Some contextual effects are intra-lexical and operate inside the mental lexicon itself (Giora 2003: 35). A prior occurrence of a word semantically related to an immediately following word may affect ease of processing of that
word. This kind of facilitation is referred to as priming. Priming contributes to the spreading of activation across related meanings in the lexicon.
While agreeing that contextual information does affect interpretations, Giora
(2011) writes that there is difference of opinions as to whether context governs initial lexical processes so that only contextually compatible meanings
are accessed, or whether inappropriate meanings are initially available regardless of context (Jaszczolt and Allan 2011: 5). Giora argues that, starting
with graded salience on the lexical level, interlocutors proceed to the interpretation of larger units, enriching them automatically or through inference
according to information provided by context.

The contextual effects assumed by the graded salience hypothesis occur
when a compelling context informs processes on the basis of previous
knowledge and expectations regarding the progression of the dialogue. Context facilitates word recognition: words may be recognized earlier in context than out of context (Giora 2003: 36–37). The contextual mechanisms
assumed by the graded salience hypothesis allow for the anticipation of on-
coming meanings and concepts rather than the specific words that have been
selected to represent them. Jaszczolt (2011: 17) argues that salience, under
Giora's account, is not contextual salience but relates to the storage of meanings in the mental lexicon. Jaszczolt calls this "pre-contextual salience". The
properties of Giora's salient meanings situates them between a direct access
view and a modular view. In a direct access view, a constraining context
interacts with lexical processes early on and enables an interpretation to be
achieved. This constraint-based view assumes a single mechanism that is
sensitive to both linguistic and non-linguistic information. In this direct access view, context can be responsible for activating the relevant sense of an
ambiguous word to the extent that the lexical salience does not play a part.
In a modular view, ambiguous words cause the activation of all associated
meanings, and contextually inappropriate meanings become blocked during
subsequent processing.

9.3.2   Relevance theory, context, and salience

What about relevance theory, context, and salience? Is relevance the same as salience, and can relevant information be salient information? An important characteristic of relevance theory is that it places emphasis on the role that context and contextual information play in contributing to the understanding of utterances. Relevance theory especially focuses on accessible contexts, such that the immediate context affects the relevance of incoming utterances by decreasing their processing load. It has been observed by Sperber and Wilson (1995: 260) that human cognition inclines to the maximization of relevance. Utterances therefore raise expectations of their relevance. Relevance may be assessed in terms of cognitive effects and processing effort, where the greater the processing effort required, the less relevant the input will be to the individual at that time. However, when a greater amount of positive cognitive effects are achieved by processing an input, then the greater the relevance of the input to the hearer.

In relevance theory, the sentence is seen to interact as needed with the context (Jaszczolt 2016: 12), and consequently, the relevance-theoretic view is that all enrichment[29] is context-driven, and the interpretation of the utterance, arrived at by the hearer with the help of the principles of effectiveness and economy, is the object of study (Jaszczolt 2016: 51). According to relevance theory, information is relevant to the extent that it incurs contextual effects at a reasonably small cost (Giora 2003: 40). Relevant information cost-effectively modifies the hearer's cognitive environment, and, importantly, salient information need not be relevant. Sperber and Wilson emphasize the role that relevance has in language comprehension, where participants' utterances are constrained by relevance in the communicative context.

Relevance theory claims that human attention and processing resources are attracted to information that seems relevant in a given context (Wilson and Matsui 2012: 201). This is expressed as the Cognitive Principle of Relevance: Human cognition tends to be geared to the maximization of relevance. Relevance, then, is defined in terms of cognitive effects and processing effort: a) the greater the cognitive effects, the greater the relevance; and b) the smaller the effort needed to achieve those effects, the greater the

---

[29] The term "enrichment" is used to refer to the process whereby the content conveyed by an utterance comes to include a variety of elements which are contextually implied but not part of the literal meaning of the utterance. It is often the case that many expressions, whose meaning varies according to context, actually have one central meaning and may be enriched at the pragmatic level by context-dependent assumptions, that is, via conversational implicatures.

relevance. Cognitive effects are achieved when new information interacts with existing contextual assumptions in one of three ways: a) strengthening an existing assumption; b) contradicting and eliminating an existing assumption; and c) combining with an existing assumption to yield contextual implications. Processing effort is affected by the form in which the information is presented, the accessibility of the context, and hearer expectations.

According to relevance theory, hearers can identify the intended interpretation of an utterance because utterances raise certain expectations. It is suggested in Wilson and Matsui (2012: 192) that the hearers should, in interpreting an utterance, accept the first candidate referent that leads to an overall interpretation which is true, informative and evidenced. On this view, reference is assigned to the most salient (= accessible) candidate. If the resulting interpretation is pragmatically unacceptable, the set of saliencies are reordered, until an acceptable interpretation is found, using to the following rule of accommodation for comparative salience:

> If at time t something is said that requires, if it is to be acceptable, that x be more salient than y; and if, just before t, x is no more salient than y; then – ceteris paribus and within certain limits – at t, x becomes more salient than y.
>
> Lewis (1979/1983: 242)

Linguists working within relevance theory focus, then, on the end result of the utterance interpretation, where an intention is fulfilled when it leads to communication. According to relevance theory, the linguistically encoded meaning is a starting point for inferring the speaker's meaning. When the most probable meaning is activated, context helps to determine whether that is the relevant meaning or not. Linguistic decoding, a bottom-up process, requires the selection of appropriate contextual information, a top-down process, to support inferential processes. Relevance and salience are not the same, although often it is the case that what is salient can also be relevant. Salience explains the ranking, and foregrounding, of objects or information, which may arise from direct awareness of the world, context, or knowledge in the common ground of the speaker and the hearer.

9.3.3   Salience-based contextualism

The theory of Default Semantics (Jaszczolt 2015: 193) is a contextualist model of discourse interpretation that conforms to principles of pragmatic compositionality and allows for formalization. It emphasizes the *context* in which an action, utterance, or expression occurs, and argues that, with some major significance, the action, utterance, or expression can only be understood relative to that context. The speaker's intention is recognized by the hearer who applies truth conditions to the conceptual representation of the utterance. Its objective is to model utterance meaning as intended by the speaker and recovered by the hearer. Default Semantics (henceforth "DS") Theory identifies sources of information about meaning and the types of processes that interact to produce a representation of utterance meaning called a merger representation. The interaction obeys the principles of pragmatic compositionality and allows for formalization. In DS (Jaszczolt 2016: 1), compositionality is predicated of a representation that puts together information from various sources, arrived at through various processes. The DS theory of linguistic interaction is a theory of acts of communication that concerns the meaning intended by the speaker and recovered by the addressee, in a way that can be formalized.

In contrast to the lexical, context-free salience of Giora's "graded salience", the theory of DS argues instead for default interpretations of utterances (Jaszczolt and Allan 2011: 5), where the defaults are defined as salient, frequent, and automatic meanings ascribed to the speaker by the hearer. These are understood as defaults for the interlocutors and for the context, rather than interpretations based on strict linguistic-units. In DS, there are cognitive defaults as well as defaults of a social, cultural, or general world-knowledge nature, such that in a specific context and for the specific interlocutors, some interpretations occur automatically, subconsciously, and effortlessly. Jaszczolt (2011: 11) argues that, when we claim that context contributes to utterance meaning, it is necessary to indicate, as best we can, how much context, and what context, is involved. That is, it is necessary to address the issue of how much context is allowed in the mental representation, the way in which this contextual information is included, and at what stages in utterance processing it is visible to processing. In a view she calls salience-based contextualism, Jaszczolt proposes using context-driven salience as the main criterion for identifying meaning, arguing that salience is what linguistic interaction is built on. Via salience, we can control the way that information is conveyed, building upon the discourse situation with the history of previous experience, with generalizations and abstractions over this experience, as well as anticipation of conversational goals.

For Jaszczolt (2016: 7), a necessary phase in the recognition of information from context is to argue that meaning depends on the syntactic form of the sentence but to allow for the context-sensitivity of this syntactic form, acknowledging that the main communicated message is the proposition that one ought to be concerned with. The logical form pertaining to this proposition has little or no resemblance to the logical form of the uttered sentence. DS involves an assortment of information sources about meaning, and has devised a system of meaning construction to produce a representation that combines information from all those channels of meaning (Jaszczolt 2016: 31). The lexicon, grammar, recognition of intentions, goals, situation types, social and cultural conventions, general and scientific knowledge are all important in communication. They are equally important for representing meaning in communication. The resulting representation into which the various identified sources contribute on an equal footing is what she calls the "merger representation".

Merger representations are the DS equivalents of logical forms, evaluated for truth conditions, and constructed through processes that allow a formal treatment. In DS then, Jaszczolt advances a communicative-interaction-based theory of meaning in investigating not the language system and its relation to context but also the context of the interaction itself with all its means of conveying information. In DS, significance is given by Jaszczolt (2016: 78–83) to the following sources of information: i) world knowledge, ii) word meaning and sentence structure, iii) situation of discourse, iv) properties of the human inferential system, and v) stereotypes and presumptions about society and culture. World knowledge provides information from physical laws and facts. Word meaning and sentence structure delivers the output of the syntactic processing of the sentence. Situation of discourse is the context of utterance. The human inferential system stands for the properties of mental states that allow us to recover default meanings, which are automatic interpretations available in some contexts. Knowledge of our society and culture facilitates the automatic retrieval of information, side-stepping the need for an inferential process. A mapping is identified within DS between the sources of information and the processes that are active in producing a merger representation. The resulting merged representation contains information about the primary meaning as intended by the speaker and recovered by the hearer.

In DS, this semantic representation of a conceptual unit relates to the main speech act and is called a merger representation, rather than a logical form. World knowledge and stereotypes and presumptions about society and culture are associated with automatic, default interpretations called jointly social, cultural, and world-knowledge defaults, but they can also trigger a process of pragmatic inference. Default and inferential interpretations operate on a unit that is sufficient for the current situation of discourse, ranging from a morpheme to the entire discourse.

In this salience-based contextualism, Jaszczolt (2016: 49) writes that a theory of word meaning has to acknowledge the fact of the contextual variation and should leverage the fact that language users are guided by past experiences of their discourse. They have the memory of the use of a word which guides them in the word selection for the present situation. Language is considered by Jaszczolt to be: i) a sociocultural phenomenon, formed and renewed in use; and ii) a cognitive phenomenon constrained by the structure and operations of the brain. Language users co-construct the meaning as conversation unfolds, and words and structures come with salient, automatically retrieved meanings.

The aim of DS is to articulate a formal paradigm of how discourse meaning is composed from linguistic and non-linguistic components. The DS objective (Jaszczolt 2016: 77) is to model utterance meaning as intended by the speaker and recovered by the hearer. DS focuses on identifying a unit worthy of a semantic analysis, followed by identifying the sources of information that provide the hearer with this unit, and the processes that uncover the intended information or co-construct the semantic content in the interaction. Default interpretations are seen as sometimes enabled by context while at other times they emerge without the influence of context. In other words, default interpretations can be context-free or context-dependent. Default meanings are arrived at quickly and without effort. Jaszczolt defines the term "default" to mean the interpretation that is arrived at automatically, as opposed to information that is consciously inferred. The defaults of DS are defined as being from:

> … the perspective of the agent engaged in the process of interpretation and are meanings arrived at by the agent automatically, be it independently of the context or not, idiosyncratically or in agreement with other agents, because of a word that is used, a phrase, or an entire sentence or a series of sentences.
>
> Jaszczolt (2011: 15)

Jaszczolt acknowledges that utterance interpretation proceeds incrementally, but that it is still prudent to adopt a view of meaning assignment in which the default base, and the inferential base, differ across contexts. Specifically, Jaszczolt (2011: 25) argues that utterance processing is incremental and proceeds through manipulation of the meaning of the uttered words or phrases. Default interpretations of utterances are best understood as defaults for the interlocutors and for the context rather than rigid linguistic unit-based interpretations. They are best defined as salient, frequent, and automatic meanings ascribed to the speaker by the hearer.

9.4   Mental model, situation, and discourse

The ongoing discourse between the interlocutors is represented in a mental model (Johnson-Laird 1980, 1983). A mental model is a dynamically maintained representation in episodic memory, whereby some parts of the representation are more active than others during discourse processing (Falk 2014: 3). We know that dialogue is dynamic by its very nature. Over its duration, discourse interlocutors quickly construct a model covering a complex network of both forward (cataphoric) and backward (anaphoric) relations, between successive discourse components and referring expressions. Salience is understood as a cognitive attribute of the mental model, such that parts of the mental model are ranked according to their salience status. Several referents can be salient but with varying degrees of activation, or attention allocation, in memory. For example, various dimensions of a situation, such as time and location, undergo continuous real-time tracking. Indeed, the salience of the whole situation and its dimensions are necessarily considered in discourse processing. In a dialogue, the situational context has a role to play in determining the interpretation of discourse. Salience encodes a privileged unit for processing in a mental operation, such as memory retrieval, during discourse.

Salience, then, is a dynamic property within a mental model (Chiarcos 2009: 136) that characterizes the attentional state of a given mental representation relative to the attentional states of other mental representations within the model. It produces an ordered ranking over the representations in the model. Chiarcos describes a discourse model as a mental model encompassing discourse-relevant knowledge. A proposition is a complex construct that consists of a set of referents, with a predicate that defines the thematic relations between them. Both discourse referents and propositions are discourse entities.

All processing within mental models takes place in our working memory and is driven by our attention, during the discourse flow of attention. Mental models are used to explain how data from many sources are blended into consistent mental representations that underpin the diverse linguistic utterances. The flow of attention serves a central function in directing the management of the mental models, and it is the key mechanism in the update processes of the hearer's discourse model. The directing of the flow of attention by a speaker is essential in seeking to influence and guide the hearer's focus of attention along the lines intended. To achieve this, the speaker needs to operate on a model of the hearer's discourse model. The speaker can plan a sequence of attention shifts in order to guide the hearer's focus of attention, using a mental representation of the hearer's attentional states. According to Chiarcos (2009: 149), in order to control the flow of attention in discourse, the speaker needs to maintain a speaker model (SELF) and a model of the hearer (OTHER). The speaker (SELF) model incorporates information from previous discourse, as well as the speaker's own knowledge, plans, goals and intentions for subsequent discourse, and other relevant information. The speaker's model of the hearer (OTHER) is a model that a speaker constructs as an approximation of the hearer's current mental discourse model. The speaker constructs the hearer model from assumptions about the state of mind of the hearer and the previous discourse. Speaker salience is salience within the speaker (SELF) model. That is, the current attentional state a referent entity achieves from the perspective of a speaker. Correspondingly, hearer salience is salience within the hearer (OTHER) model. That is, the speaker's assessment of the current attentional state that a referent entity has in the hearer's discourse model, as maintained by the speaker.

Chiarcos (2009: 44) proposes a framework based on the interplay of salience, attention, and attention control. This Mental Salience Framework adopts a production perspective on information packaging, and is compatible with both speaker-oriented (cataphoric, forward-looking) and hearer-oriented (anaphoric, backward-looking) conceptions of salience, as a speaker needs to model both perspectives. The speaker's perspective includes that which the speaker wants to bring to the attention of the hearer and, as such, is forward-looking. The speaker's own discourse model (SELF) includes information about the previous discourse as well as intentions, goals, and plans a speaker has about the discourse to follow. We have already described how the speaker also employs another model, the speaker's approximation of the hearer's (OTHER) discourse model, in order to keep utterances appropriate for the hearer. The hearer's perspective reflects the state of the hearer's current awareness and is predominantly backward-looking.

9.5 Discussion

Salience is an important notion that has a special significance for us in helping to advance the construction and maintenance of common ground, along with the management of knowledge and information flow in discourse. We started this chapter with the observation that some knowledge comes to our attention in cognition more so, and more quickly, than other pieces of knowledge, and that understanding salience goes some way to explaining how this happens. We can have speaker salience and hearer salience and, with the convergence of salience between these two interlocutors, the co-construction of common ground is established. Information that is noticed has a much higher chance of being encoded and being available for retrieval than information that was not attended to.

Prominence, attention, frequency, familiarity, prototypicality, and expectation all play a role in motivating the privileged status of a potential meaning that may eventually emerge as the most likely possible meaning, the salient element. The term "salience" is employed to describe a state of prominence, whereby certain "things" are in the foreground of our attention. Salience, then, is a cognitive property of mental entities that are referred to within a discourse, and a high degree of salience is associated with the focus of attention. One of the functions of an utterance in a discourse is the signaling of salience.

Salience is a considered a graded notion, and defines a ranking order of attention over elements within a specific mental model. In discourse, hearer salience indicates the givenness of an entity, and speaker salience underlies the speaker's attempts to influence this status within the hearer. As we have seen, frequency, prominence, attention, accessibility, and gradience are the factors which are important to understanding salience. The discourse between the interlocutors is represented in a mental model and salience is understood as a cognitive attribute of the mental model, such that parts of the mental model are ranked according to their salience status. A mental model is a dynamically maintained representation in episodic memory, whereby some parts of the representation are more active in memory than others during discourse processing. Our individual experiences are therefore encoded in memory, and our human brain is a memory system that stores experiences in a way that reflects the actual structure of the world, along with sequences of events and nested relationships. We make predictions based on these memories. Memories are encoded in an associative manner, via context frames. Associated with salience is the allocation of attention; and salience detection, via cues, is a key attentional mechanism. Salience correlates with attention and memory access, and plays a role in information packaging of utterances in a dialogue. The information status of the discourse referents in turn correlates with accessibility and salience. Information packaging operates as a speaker strategy to guide the hearer's flow of attention in discourse.

Information selection is essential as memory is subject to processing and capacity constraints. Attention influences the perception, description, and selective focusing on some aspects of a situation, event, or scene. Salience refers to the relative prominence of an element of some kind, such that the more important it is, then the more accessible it is. Prominence helps identify an entity to stand out from context. This perception affects linguistic choices, and salient elements of a scene receive more prominent linguistic encoding. Attention determines the selection of linguistic elements. Speakers need to select the entities they want to communicate and choose between competing words and syntactic constructions. The prominence potential of a constituent is built on its information-structural status, its syntactic status as argument, predicate, or modifier, and its word class. Such marking helps us identify and access shared knowledge for inclusion into common ground. Interlocutors activate the most salient information in their field of attention in the construction of utterances (by the speaker) and their subsequent comprehension (by the hearer).

Salience relates to context. Language is used for human social interaction and has a central role in our social life, in a cultural context. The nature of language emerges from its role in social and cultural interaction. We considered three theories that take a position on the relation of salience to context. In the first of these, Giora, in her graded salience hypothesis, considers that stored information is more prominent than unstored information, such as information inferred from context, and salience refers to the degree of entrenchment of meanings in our mental lexicon. Giora considers salience as a graded notion, and her graded salience hypothesis holds that salient meanings, via the lexicon, are processed automatically irrespective of contextual information. Giora's model takes a lexical, context-free view of salience. Secondly, we looked at relevance theory, a theory that places emphasis on the role that context and contextual information play in contributing to understanding the utterances. Importantly, we noted that what is relevant is not always the same as that which is salient, although often it is the case that what is salient can also be relevant. Our interest in relevance theory resides in its focus on contexts that are accessible, whereby the immediate context has an effect on the relevance of incoming utterances by decreasing their processing load. Thirdly, we summarized aspects of the DS, a theory that gives a strong role to context and salience, and which argues for salient, frequent, and automatic default interpretations of utterances. In this salience-based contextualism of DS, it is argued that one needs to acknowledge contextual variation and the fact that language users are guided by past experiences of their dialogue. They have memory of a word's meaning which guides them in the word selection for the current situation. Salience, with the contribution of context, is important to the creation and management of common ground. Indeed, Kecskes and Zhang (2009: 350) argue that, in their socio-cognitive approach, common ground is identified as a set of knowledge that is salient and pertinent to the current situation. As they (2009: 351) observe, "the processes in which we activate and create shared information are driven by relevance to the intention and realized with salience to attention". Information and context commonly known to the interlocutors becomes a part of common ground in the current conversation if it is salient, or relevant, for both the interlocutors.

10 Culture and language in interaction

10.1 The elements of the Irish cultural narrative

Culture is a collectively held, distributed, pragmatic system within a society and it operates as an interlinked system of concepts, structures, and relations that groups of people use to organize their knowledge and interpret their worlds – including their behavior, relationships, and their personalities, apparent beliefs, and values. Within this view, culture is considered a mix of components that individuals dynamically deploy according to their communicative needs. This chapter is concerned with culture and language in interaction, and elements of the Irish cultural narrative. We look at language in culture, art, and artifact. We focus on an empirical analysis and characterization of elements of the cultural narrative. In this, we are concerned with the multifaceted relationship between culture and language in interaction, and communication, and how culture informs language usage. We posit that common ground mediates this relationship. We examine the application of language in the service of culture and, using authentic data (art, artifact, linguistic landscape, and language), we present two empirical case studies, addressing different facets of culture as a systemic model whose dimensions encompass culture, worldview, common ground, and language.

In the first case study we look at Bloomsday as evidence of cultural systematicity, and the conceptualization of the cultural schema for the celebration of the Joycean Bloomsday in Dublin, as a language-related ritual, and its connection with the linguistic landscape. In the second case study we characterize the pragmatics of Irish tea culture through the pragmatic strategy of a ritualized sequence set of offers and refusals, and the pragmeme as a situated speech act. The interplay between common ground, context, and cultural conceptualizations informs the realization of Bloomsday. Context and common ground are also important in the common social ritual of tea drinking in an Irish frame of reference where different cultural conceptualizations are activated. Additionally, we see how practs and pragmemes have utility in the characterization of the situated speech acts of "offer and refusal". Various strategies for understatement and avoidance of directness are to be found in the responses in question–answer speech acts.

We apply a functional-cognitive approach, sensitive to cultural issues, to characterize the Irish cultural connection with language and argue that culture is systemic, knowledge is distributed, and common ground mediates this relationship between culture, context, knowledge, and language. As we have discussed in Chapter 7, the nature of knowledge relates not just to intellectual knowledge, but also to knowledge of how to behave in a given situation, knowledge of the consequences of behaving differently in that situation, embodied, tacit, and non-verbal knowledge, knowledge of typical emotional modalities in speech or action and the consequences of these for people, knowledge of the behavioral and conceptual implications of situations and roles. Our knowledge is informed by our lived experience, since culture is primarily learned via engagement in the communities rather than explicitly taught.

We have seen that one of the ways that functionalist approaches to language characterize the cultural connection is through examining performatives and speech acts, that is, language in interaction and use in the context of a situation, where cultural and contextual knowledge inform speech act meaning across a discourse. A speech act is an utterance that may have a performative function in language and communication within a cultural community. Performativity then is the capacity of language, speech, and communication not simply to communicate, but rather to act to "do" an action that, in its utterance in the correct context, has a significant societal change. These performatives have prerequisites. These words must be used in a certain way in a specific context within our culture, to become socially-changing actions. Speech acts are fundamentally cultural and we see this in our case study on the Irish tea drinking ritual. Performatives have the effect they do because societies endow them with a certain power. In any culture, the range of speech acts that are used are governed by general principles through which all members of the culture recognize that a speech act of a certain kind has taken place.

10.2 Language in culture, art, and artifact

Language, language fragments, and individual words are very frequently used in the visual arts.

There are several ways in which words or text are used in visual art by artists, and we explore these here. Words can be used explicitly when they are included in, or on, the visual artwork (Dixon Hunt et al. 2010). This mix of language with visual art is not new by any means.

Firstly, we are all familiar with this explicit use of words within medieval art where the words assume a core prominent position. In particular, medieval illuminated manuscripts are a key example of an art form that relies on the cohesive interdependence of graphics and language where words and image contribute equally to the overall reading. One excellent example of this is the *Book of Kells*[30], with its folio 292r, containing artwork with the text that opens the Gospel of John. Secondly, in visual art forms, the use of explicit words are easily recognized, widely accepted and generally understood in virtue of the contribution they make. Indeed, as a contemporary example of this use of words, we can consider pop art, as with the painting[31] *Masterpiece* by the American artist Roy Lichtenstein where the text "Why, Brad darling, this painting is a masterpiece! My, soon you'll have all of New York clamouring for your work!' appears in a large speech bubble in the painting, completely in context. As well as visual art, this is also to be found with modern cartoons, and memes (Diedrichsen 2020), where words are used as a visual semiotic linguistic device that has a cohesive interdependence with the images displayed. Thirdly, a word or words can also appear implicitly within a supplementary role, collaborative with the visual form, when they are added to supplement the visual component of a work in some way. The artist's intention is important here and it seems that, by the design of the artist, implicit words are more elusive.

Some useful examples of this are found in the artworks of the pop artist Robert Ballagh. In the painting[32] called *My Studio*, we have a fragment of a painting by Delacroix incorporated in the main painting. The image of the Eugène Delacroix painting *Liberty Leading the People* is shown (embedded in the painting as a postcard image) to ground the reference for the viewer.

The painting is a pop art version of Delacroix's *Liberty at the Barricades*. The studio setting is symbolized by the inclusion of various art materials. There are several interesting uses of symbols and text in this painting. The newspaper mentioned in this painting as supplementary text is the *Irish Independent* and the name of the city of Derry alludes to the struggles for freedom and civil rights that gave rise to major civil conflict there in 1969 and leading to the subsequent declaration of Free Derry. While the central image of the painting is that of *Liberty Leading the People*, it is presented

---

[30] Image from https://digitalcollections.tcd.ie/home/#folder_id=14&pidtopage=MS58_292r&entry_point=585 (accessed 20 December 2020).

[31] Image from https://en.wikipedia.org/wiki/Masterpiece_(Roy_Lichtenstein) (accessed 20 December 2020).

[32] *My Studio, 1969*. Image from www.robertballagh.com/paintings.php (1976–1981) (accessed 20 December 2020).

in a contemporary Irish context. The flag in the painting is not the French tricolor but, instead, is the "Starry Plough" flag of the Irish Socialist movement. The Starry Plough flag was originally used in 1914 by the Irish Citizen Army, a socialist Irish republican movement of that time, and was afterward adopted as the emblem of the Irish Labour movement. The use of the flag here signals that this represents the struggle of a people for basic rights under an oppressive regime. In a different but thematically related the painting[33] *Liberty on the Barricades after Delacroix*, the artist renders a pop art version of the Delacroix work *Liberty Leading the People* but, in this rendering, the French tricolor is replaced by the red flag of Socialism. Here, we can speculate that the artist's intention is that visual works with the included words in their supplementary role require the viewer of the art to formulate *in their own words, for themselves*, what is depicted, notwithstanding the level of abstraction (or not) in the art work. The supplementary use of language with the artwork is also found in the careful naming of the artworks by the artist to guide the interpretation of the art.

In instances with implicit usages, the language component supplements the visual to complete any underspecified communication such that the viewer, through a series of cognitive operations, retrieves a meaning from the work. We argue that these cognitive operations work to deliver maximum meaning with the least cognitive processing cost. Words may intentionally have a high degree of cohesive interdependence such that it is difficult to discern between explicit and implicit usage. In this category of word use within the art, the use of language with the visual component is deeply connected as a direct element of the artists' strategy for communication within the overall art work. If we reflect for a moment about this use of language with art, we can recognize that we are actually quite used to words added to art, albeit in a variety of ways (for example, as found in the art of Basquiat and Lichtenstein,).

Fourthly, as we have mentioned, the titles of paintings are usually created by the artist with the intention of guiding the receptive viewer in the

---

[33] The *Liberty on the Barricades after Delacroix* image, from www.robertballagh.com/paintings.php (1959–1970) (accessed 20 December 2020), is based on the painting of *Liberty Leading the People* by Eugène Delacroix commemorating the July 1830 Revolution which deposed King Charles X of France. The figure of Liberty is a symbol of the French Republic. In the painting, a woman personifying the concept of Liberty leads the people forward over a barricade while holding the blue, white, and red tricolour flag of the French Revolution, which remains France's national flag.

experience of the visual image, that is, in cognitively retrieving a meaning from the work. We find this strategic use of language, for example, in the titles given to paintings and art objects, and on the captions of the work on the gallery wall, or in art books and catalogues. We can safely assume that paintings depend on this use of words to complement the human instinct to search for meaning in communicative works and that title is considered as having appropriate relevance to aid the art work's interpretation. The text guides the viewer's flow of thought through interpretation of the work, along with the viewing of the brush strokes, structural geometry and application of color. In the absence of a title to a work. We typically question whether a visual work of art is incomplete. In recognition of this, artists seem to need to title a work as "Untitled".

Many artistic works rely on words, and the felicitous application of language. Examples include maps, poetry, illuminated manuscripts, art, book design, advertising, film and video, contemporary memes, and modern websites are modes of communication that rely on words and images. These visual–textual modes of communication are typically so interwoven that often the words seem to be fused as a component graphical image as well as having a linguistic connotation. We can refer to these works as having a cohesive interdependence, with unified graphics and text, as a complex verbal-visual sign. Again, we repeat that word and image, or text and object, are important mediators of meaning when used by the artist to guide the cognitive retrieval of a relevant meaning within the viewer.

How does the viewer retrieve a relevant meaning? The conjunction of word and image engages our human cognitive capacity to map different elements and semantic networks of meaning onto each other. The word plus image, or more correctly, language plus image, guides the cognitive operations behind the retrieval of a relevant meaning. They function to create a vector for the viewer for retrieval of an unexpected, perhaps novel, but relevant meaning. Central to this retrieval of meaning is the cultural common ground of the art creator and the art viewer. Like the characteristic grace notes in a music performance, the use of language becomes an important grace-note guiding us forward in the retrieval of meaning. As such, the conjunction of word and image has the significant potential to capture the meaningful values within a culture. The cognitive operations that retrieve a meaning from the work of art are reminiscent of those characterized in relevance theory, within the field of linguistic pragmatics. As we have mentioned previously, relevance theory is a framework for the study of cognition, proposed primarily in order to provide a psychologically realistic account of communication.

Pragmatics is the study of how linguistic properties and their associated contextual factors interact in the interpretation of utterances. It examines language in use in communication. A sentence of a language can be considered as an abstract object with various morphosyntactic and semantic properties that are organized according to the grammar of the language. We have already had a discussion of relevance theory in Chapter 8, in relation to salience and context, and we revisit some of the important ideas and principles here. Relevance theory considers that the actual act of communicating raises in the intended hearer particular expectations of relevance which are enough to guide the hearer towards the speaker's meaning (Noveck and Sperber 2004). In relevance theory, relevance is defined as a property of inputs to cognitive processes. This includes external stimuli, which can be perceived and processed, and mental representations, which can be stored, recalled, or used within inferences. An input, then, is relevant to a hearer when it connects with the hearer's background knowledge, for example, knowledge in common ground, to yield new cognitive effects. Cognitive effects, then, are adjustments that update the individual's set of assumptions resulting from the processing of an input in a context of previously held assumptions. To be more relevant and more worth processing, an input should yield greater cognitive effects while involving a smaller processing effort. In support of these ideas, relevance theory develops two general principles about the role of relevance in cognition and in communication.

The role of relevance in cognition and in communication functions according to what is called a cognitive principle of relevance where cognition by people is oriented to the achievement of maximum relevance, and a related communicative principle of relevance whereby every act of communication is assumed to convey a presumption of its own optimum relevance. This role of relevance in cognition and in communication facilitates the emergent common ground. According to relevance theory, the presumption of optimal relevance conveyed by every utterance is precise enough to ground a specific comprehension heuristic. This relevance theory comprehension heuristic, a presumption of optimal relevance considers that, once uttered, the utterance is relevant enough to be worth processing, and that it is the most relevant one compatible with communicator's abilities and preferences. Additionally, related to this, is a relevance-guided comprehension heuristic such that a path of least effort is followed in constructing an interpretation of the utterance (and thereby resolving ambiguities and referential indeterminacies), and which operation stops when one's expectations of relevance are satisfied. Relevance theorists (convincingly) argue that this approach has good explanatory power because it captures the idea that, in interpreting an utterance, the hearer automatically aims at optimal relevance.

Context and salience also play a significant role in the retrieval of meaning in communication. Indeed, Peleg et al. (2004: 172–186), assume that more salient meanings are accessed faster, and that context also affects comprehension online. They hold that:

> It is widely agreed now that contextual information is a crucial factor determining how we make sense of utterances. The role of context is even more pronounced within a framework that assumes that the code is underspecified allowing for top-down inferential processes to narrow meanings down and adjust them to the specific context.
>
> Peleg et al. (2004: 172–186)

In interpreting an utterance, the hearer will select knowledge from context to process the utterance so that it gives at least adequate cognitive effects with minimal processing effort. It is our view that the same cognitive processes characterized in relevance theory allow us to retrieve appropriate meaning from art. Similarly, in interpreting visual art, the viewer will select knowledge from context to process the viewer art so that it gives at least adequate cognitive effects with minimal processing effort. We assume the displayed art to be relevant in its own right and therefore more worth processing, and that the meaning we retrieve from the visual inputs, perhaps with language plus image, yield significant cognitive effects and a smaller processing effort.

10.3 The systemic dimensions of culture

Viewing culture as a system requires that we articulate the relationship between its component parts, including cognition and knowledge, and where these connect with artifact, language, worldview, and the cultural models found with a way of life. The connection between these is to do with the (different kinds of) knowledge available to us as individuals and as a community, and how this is shared in a common ground.

Kronenfeld (2017: 1) argues that cognition refers to knowledge, and that cultural cognition is the shared pragmatic knowledge that includes our behavioral as well as conceptual knowledge. Indeed, anthropologists understand culture as a heterogeneously distributed collective system of pragmatic knowledge where different individuals know different parts of the cultural system. Cultural knowledge is shared knowledge within groups, but variable across different groups. Individual people may, of course, belong to a variety of such groups. Language has been viewed as a more systematic and organized system than culture, and therefore amenable to rigorous analysis, while culture has mostly been seen as a somewhat looser set of interrelated subsystems, and consequently, trickier to pin down. Both Kronenfeld and Daniel Everett (2013) view language as a social construct for use within a speech community, where local usage creates a socially defined context of understanding. Over the passage of time, the social usage often causes meaning changes for words in a language.

Culture knowledge provides us with an understanding of the different situations that unfold in society and life. As social animals, people live in a succession of different situational contexts. One of the functions of human cultures is to ascribe meaning to these situational contexts in real time. There are many different dimensions of the context of a situation, including time, place, agents and patients functioning as actors and undergoers, and the activities, dialogue, and purpose of the interactions. These dimensions found with a productive common ground (Kecskes and Zhang 2009), as we have seen characterized in Chapter 8, combine to produce the unique situational contexts that frame our lives. People prescribe meanings to situations, informed by context, and because human social life is complex, the myriad of situations and their contexts is associated with a wide variety of cultural meanings. The meanings of the various contexts of a situation create expectations for the actors and undergoers within the situation, in terms of what constitutes normal behaviors, including social roles, that each culture expects its members to engage in, in a culturally appropriate manner, given a specific situation. Social roles are like scripts in a play (Goffman 1956) since they delineate the types of behaviors that are expected in the context of a specific situation. Because cultures define the meaning of the context and situation, the roles and behaviors, and associated scripts within the contexts are culturally dependent. Cultural differences in the meaning of specific situations would lead us to recognize that there are cultural differences in the specific role expectations associated with different situations across cultures.

At the intersection of culture viewed as a system, and language, the framework of Cultural Linguistics as proposed by Sharifian (2011) characterizes the notion of "cultural cognition" to provide an integrated understanding of the notions of "cognition" and "culture" as they relate to language. Like Kronenfeld (2017: 16), Sharifian recognizes that the elements of a community's cultural cognition are not equally shared by speakers across that community, and, as such, cultural cognition is considered as a form of heterogeneously distributed cognition. Instead, speakers show variation and differences in their internalization of their community's cultural cognition.

Cultural cognition is considered to be dynamic and constantly renegotiated through contact between members of that community. It has been argued by Sharifian (2011: 23) that the construction, emergence, transmission, and perpetuation of cultural conceptualizations are phenomena best understood as constituting a complex adaptive system. Understanding "language" and "culture" from the perspective of complex adaptive systems affords important insights. A complex adaptive system is a system in which an understanding of the individual parts does not automatically convey a perfect understanding of the whole system's behavior. The study of complex adaptive systems is highly interdisciplinary with insights from many disciplines including computer science, artificial intelligence, agent theory, and natural and social and natural sciences. From a complex adaptive system perspective, "language" and "culture" are not viewed as entities independent of one another but rather as constantly interacting systems that form networks of overlapping, mutual influence.

The theoretical framework of Cultural Linguistics provides a basis for understanding cultural conceptualizations and their realization in language. Apart from language, cultural conceptualizations may also be instantiated in people's lives as art, literature, cultural events, rituals, non-verbal behavior, and emotion. We are particularly interested in the cultural conceptualizations instantiated in literature, and cultural events within our first case study, on Bloomsday, and rituals, in our second case study, on tea drinking in an Irish context involving offers and refusals with related practs and pragmemes. Cultural artifacts, then, such as our aforementioned painting, rituals, and language and gesture can be considered as instantiations of cultural conceptualizations. A premise of Cultural Linguistics is that many features of human languages encode or instantiate cultural conceptualizations, and that cultural conceptualizations are entrenched or embedded in many features of human languages. Cultural Linguistics provides a theoretical "toolkit" with which to analyze the relationship between language and cultural conceptualizations, via the notions of cultural schema, cultural category, and cultural metaphor. Cultural *schemas* (and subschemas) encode beliefs, norms, rules, and expectations of behavior and components of experience. Cultural *categories* (and subcategories) are the culturally constructed conceptual categories, for example, colors, emotions, attributes, foodstuffs, kinship terms, events, and so forth, that we find reflected in human languages and their lexicons. Cultural *metaphors* are cross-domain conceptualizations grounded in cultural traditions such as folk medicine, worldview, or a spiritual belief system.

10.4 Case study: Bloomsday as evidence of cultural systematicity

10.4.1 The Bloomsday celebration on 16th June

Bloomsday celebrates the life and work of the Irish writer James Joyce, in particular, his most famous novel, *Ulysses*. Bloomsday is celebrated on the 16th of June each year, in Dublin and elsewhere, this being the date in which the day's activities occur in the novel. This date had a special significance for James Joyce, as it was on 16th June 1904 when he first dated his future wife, Nora Barnacle. In this section, we provide an analytical case study of Bloomsday as an example of the systemic nature of culture within a cultural linguistics perspective. To understand Bloomsday, one needs to first understand (elements of) the novel *Ulysses* by James Joyce. The name of the day's event, Bloomsday (= Bloom's day), is based on one of the main characters of the novel, Leopold Bloom. While Joyce's *Ulysses* is a rich, complex, and funny book, Gilbert (1955: 3) provides a succinct summary of it:

> Ulysses is the record of a single day, June 16, 1904. That day was very much like any other, unmarked by any important event and, even for the Dubliners who figure in Ulysses, exempt from personal disaster or achievement. It was the climax of a long drought and the many public-houses of the Irish capital claimed most of the Dubliner's spare time and cash; the former, as usual, abundant, and the latter scarce, as usual. In the morning a citizen was buried; a little before midnight a child was born. At about the same hour the weather broke and there was a sudden downpour, accompanied by a violent clap of thunder. In the intervals of imbibing Guinness, Power or "J.J. & S" [John Jameson & Son] the Dubliners discoursed with animation themselves on their pet topic, Irish politics, happily bemused themselves with the singing of amorous or patriotic ballads, lost money over the Ascot Gold Cup. At about 4p.m. an act of adultery was consummated at the residence of one Leopold Bloom, advertisement-canvasser. A perfectly ordinary day, in fact.
>
> Gilbert (1955: 3)

Ulysses, then, is a novel about a day in the life of ordinary people in Dublin on 16th June 1904. The book was written by James Joyce in Trieste, Zurich, and Paris between 1914 and 1921. It tells in great detail many incidents of the life of Leopold Bloom and those interacting with him on that single day. As it turns out, the book was met with widespread scandal and controversy

Figure 10.1 Poster advertising Bloomsday activities.

when Joyce first published the novel *Ulysses* as a complete book in Paris in 1922. While it is now celebrated as a masterpiece of modern literature, it was subject then to heavy international censorship with attempts to suppress the book. Happily, these failed. The 16th of June has since become celebrated in Ireland (and internationally) as *Bloomsday* (Figure 10.1). Every year in Dublin on that date, hundreds of Dubliners dress as characters from the book, to assert a connection with the text and its events, including the characters Stephen Dedalus, James Joyce's literary alter ego, with his walking cane, along with Leopold Bloom wearing a bowler hat, and Molly Bloom wearing a petticoat. The celebration allows Dubliners to project a sense of community on the streets of Dublin in a festive carnival-like atmosphere. Despite its size with approximately 1.3 million people, and modern qualities, Dublin is felt to be an intimate people-centered city. Dubliners re-enact scenes from the novel in places mentioned in the novel at the appropriate time according to the schema, including, for example, Eccles Street, Sandycove's Martello Tower, and Ormond Quay.

One might ask: What then is it about *Ulysses* and Bloomsday that inspired ordinary Dubliners to re-enact the pathway, through the day, of the characters of the novel [CULTURAL SCHEMA]? While modelled on the schema of the events [EVENT SCHEMA], from the perspective of the worldview of the novel *Ulysses* [WORLDVIEW], Bloomsday involves a range of cultural activities [EVENT SCHEMA], including *Ulysses* readings and theatrical performances of scenes from the novel, pub crawls, and other events across Dublin. Enthusiasts are to be readily seen in the mode of dress [ARTIFACTS] from the Edwardian era celebrating Bloomsday while they retrace Bloom's route around Dublin via the various landmarks mentioned in the novel, such as Sweny's pharmacy[34] Glasnevin Cemetery, Hedigan's Brian Boru pub, and Davy Byrne's pub.

Literally, every year, hundreds of Dubliners dress as characters from the book [ROLE SCHEMA] to identify with the text within modern Irish culture [CULTURAL MODELS/WAY OF LIFE]. It is difficult to imagine any other masterpiece of modernism in the written work having such a centrality in the life of a modern European city. Frequently, readings of the entire novel, take place [LANGUAGE], in public, or broadcast on radio and the internet.

The events of the novel unfold across the day from early morning to very late at night and many different parts of Dublin are visited by the novel's characters. In an Irish, particularly Dublin, context, adaptations of cultural conceptualizations such as the BLOOMSDAY SCHEMA involve a reimagining of cultural categories such as the PARTY into the BLOOMSDAY PARTY, including the subcategories of BLOOMSDAY modes of Edwardian period dressing, BLOOMSDAY foods (Irish breakfast of sausages, rashers, toast; Gorgonzola cheese sandwiches with burgundy wine for lunch), and BLOOMSDAY drinks (Guinness, Irish whiskey, burgundy wine). These events within the novel are all echoed in the macro-event of BLOOMSDAY. It is a happy, celebratory day in the life of the city and enjoyed by many of Dublin's citizens.

10.4.2 The Bloomsday schema: wandering through Dublin

A central theme of wandering, or traversing a path across the day in the city of Dublin, prevails through the work, and indeed, across Bloomsday itself. The novel *Ulysses* has 18 episodes (=chapters) which are arranged in three

---

[34] http://sweny.ie/site/.

"movements", the *Telemachia*, *Odyssey*, and *Nostos*, which traverse a sequence of city locations. For our purposes, the important elements are the episodes and the locations in the schema indicated in Table 10.1, and the *time* they unfold in Dublin at a particular *location*. With the exception of the *Wandering Rocks* chapter, each reflects the episodes of Homer's *Odyssey*, from which Joyce has taken themes as well as a structure. The central character Leopold Bloom, Odysseus/Ulysses, wanders through a single day of the 16th June, during which he is, at all times, moving closer towards an encounter with another character in the novel, Stephen Dedalus, a self-absorbed artist. Finally, the third central character is Molly, wife of Bloom and a fading but popular soprano who likes to linger in her bed while dreamily letting her mind wander. Joyce modelled the structure of his novel *Ulysses* with a schema containing quite a considerable amount of detail. Several versions of this schema exist[35], and the two best known are the Linati schema and the Gilbert schema (Ellmann 1986: 186–190, Appendix 1).

The context for Bloomsday is activated on the date of 16th June and constructed in the ongoing interaction and is eventually shared by the Bloomsday participants in the construction of the Bloomsday common ground. We take Bloomsday to be an instantiation of culturally informed visual semiotic activity within the linguistic landscape of Dublin that provides an example of the systematicity of culture. Following Kallen (2014: 157), we take the linguistic elements in the linguistic landscape as interfacing between linguistic concerns, those of visual semiotics, and culture. Figure 10.2 shows elements of the novel *Ulysses*, recorded on the linguistic landscape of Dublin, from various chapters that are placed at the precise locations in the city.

Bloomsday demonstrates that the visual display of language can also add to our understanding of language, and identity, through expressive acts and artifacts in a cultural setting. In many ways, our application of the linguistic landscape paradigm is reminiscent of Goffman's frame analysis (Goffman 1956, 1974). It is a way of explaining and determining that which is salient in a given situation in the context of a given physical environment, or locale, as we see here with the Bloomsday celebrations across Dublin. According to Goffman, in relation to a frame as a conceptual schema:

---

[35] The first schema was provided by Joyce in 1920 to help his friend, Carlo Linati, understand the fundamental structure of the book and, consequently, this schema is known as the Linati schema for *Ulysses* (Ellmann 1986: 186–190). The second schema, the Gilbert schema for *Ulysses,* was produced by James Joyce in 1921 for another friend, Stuart Gilbert (1930 [1955]).

Table 10.1 The schema of Joyce's *Ulysses*.

Ulysses *episode/chapter*	Scene	*(Bloomsday) location*	*Time*
I. Telemachus	The Tower	The Martello Tower, Sandycove, Co. Dublin	**8 a.m.** – 9 a.m.
II. Nestor	The School	Clifton School, Dalkey. Co. Dublin	9 a.m. – **10 a.m.**
III. Proteus	The Strand	Sandymount Strand, Dublin 4.	10 a.m. – **11a.m.**
IV. Calypso	The House	7 Eccles Street, Dublin 7	**8 a.m.** – 9 a.m.
V. Lotus Eaters	The Bath	Sweny's Chemist, Lincoln Place, Dublin 2	9 a.m. – **10 a.m.**
VI. Hades	The Graveyard	Glasnevin Cemetery, Dublin 7	**11 a.m.** – 12 noon
VII. Aeolus	The Newspaper	Princes Street, Dublin	**12 noon** – 1 p.m.
VIII. Lestrygonians	The Lunch	Davy Byrne's pub, Duke St, Dublin 2	**1 p.m.** – 2 p.m.
IX. Scylla and Charybdis	The Library	National Library of Ireland, Kildare Street, Dublin 2	**2 p.m.** – 3 p.m.
X. Wandering Rocks	The Streets	Grafton Street, Dublin 2	**3 p.m.** – 4 p.m.
XI. Sirens	The Concert Room	Ormond Hotel, Ormond Quay, Dublin 7	**4 p.m.** – 5 p.m.
XII. Cyclops	The Tavern	Barney Kiernan's Pub (now The Claddagh Ring Pub), Little Britain Street Dublin 1	**5 p.m.** – 6 p.m.
XIII. Nausicaa	The Rocks	Sandymount Strand, Dublin 4	**8 p.m.** – 9 p.m.
XIV. Oxen of the Sun	The Hospital	National Maternity Hospital Holles Street, Dublin 2	**10 p.m.** – 11 p.m.
XV. Circe	The Brothel	The "Monto" nighttown area of Railroad St. Dublin 1	11 p.m. – **12 midnight**
XVI. Eumaeus	The Shelter	The cabman's shelter, Dublin 1	12 midnight – **1 a.m.**
XVII. Ithaca	The House	Bloom's house, 7 Eccles Street, Dublin 7	1 a.m.– **2 a.m.**
XVIII. Penelope	The Bed	Bloom's house, 7 Eccles Street, Dublin 7	—

Figure 10.2 Two plaques embedded in Dublin paths that celebrate *Ulysses*.

…definitions of a situation are built up in accordance with principles of organization which govern events, and our subjective involvement in them; frame is the word I use to refer to such of these basic elements as I am able to identify…

Goffman (1974: 10f)

Bloomsday, as a conceptual schema, organizes actions and experiences, and structures individual perception of events, building frames, and basic cognitive structures to guide one's perception of reality. We have seen that Bloomsday unfolds according to a schema with participants, temporal dimensions, and spatial locations. It is culturally motivated and shares a common understanding amongst its participants – a common ground. Context has a central role in Bloomsday, as a component of cognition in the determination of the conditions of appropriate knowledge activation (Bloom, *Ulysses*, Dublin, and so forth).

We stated that context includes cultural knowledge, general knowledge and shared communal beliefs, and the experience that arises from the resulting interplay of culture and social community. When the context for Bloomsday is activated and constructed in the ongoing interaction, it is eventually shared by the Bloomsday participants in their common ground.

In this view, common ground acts as a kind of decentralized knowledge system supporting the cognitive activation of a subset of relevant contextual knowledge. The types of knowledge characterized in common ground (Table 10.2), are diverse in that they relate to declarative, procedural, heuristic, meta, and structural knowledge, along a scale from volatile and dynamic to less volatile and less dynamic. We propose that the common ground pertaining to the celebration of Bloomsday by the various involved participants contains relevant knowledge on local dialogue, language, environment, recent events, historical knowledge, common sense, cultural knowledge.

Cultural cognitions may be best described as networks of distributed knowledge representations across the minds of people in cultural groups that form a common ground. In this case, it constitutes a network of distributed representations within the Bloomsday participants. The degree to which individuals in a community can participate in a group's conceptualized domain of knowledge determines their membership of the group, for example, some will have more, others less, knowledge of *Ulysses* and James Joyce. Cultural cognition is composed of *cultural conceptualization*s and *cultural categories*. Cultural conceptualization includes such things as cultural schemata of various types and cultural categories that embody group-level cognitive systems such as shared worldviews (Sharifian 2017). These different types of schema include EVENT schemata, ROLE schemata, IMAGE schemata, and PROPOSITION schemata. Earlier, we have seen examples of several types of schemata here within the Bloomsday celebration, including EVENT schemata and ROLE schemata. We have shown how these are activated across Bloomsday at different times and locations.

Cognition is that mental process of knowing, including such aspects as awareness, perception, reasoning, and judgment. To conceptualize is to form a concept or concepts. A concept is a way to classify the world in our mind. Classifying concepts allows us to optimally use our memory and to quickly make assumptions, predictions, and generalizations about the world around us. Take the simple example of the word "dog", in English. We know a dog is a four-legged animal, with fur, four legs, a wagging tail, and it barks. We rely on the concept of a [DOG], knowing that when I say the word "dog" one understands all of those things: four legs, a tail, fur, and barking. This is because all of these characteristics are associated with the concept [DOG]. Every concept is part of a hierarchical model of concept classification, which essentially means that there are more specific, and less specific, ways of classifying things. EVENT schemata are abstracted from our experience of certain events (Sharifian 2011: 8), while ROLE schemata function as knowledge structures that people have of specific role positions in a cultural group.

Table 10.2 Tentative structure and content of common ground (repeated from Table 8.4).

Structure of common ground	Contains	Volatility/ Dynamicity
Local dialogue	• Salient events and references within the dialogue chain	More volatile/ dynamic
Language	• Knowledge of the linguistic system	
Environment	• Shared knowledge of the entities, actions, and context of the local environment and which may prove relevant to the interlocutors within the dialogue • Meta and structural knowledge • Knowledge structures within our overall mental models • Schemata and frames	
Recent events	• Shared knowledge of the entities, actions in the context of the local environment • Declarative knowledge of concepts and facts	
Historical knowledge	• Shared cultural knowledge of (recent past to far past) historical context and associated entities, actions, and consequences • Declarative knowledge of concepts and facts	
Common sense	• General ontological knowledge about the world, its entities, and events • Heuristic and experiential knowledge • Schemata (Event, Role, Image, and Proposition) • Frames	
Cultural knowledge	• Ways of doing things in our community • Ways of behaving in our society • Common belief sets • Cultural values • Shared perspectives • Schemata and frames • Shared worldview	Tending to be non-volatile/ non-dynamic

IMAGE schemata provide structures for certain conceptualizations, for example, use of metaphors and metonymy, and PROPOSITION schemata act as models of thought and behavior, specifying concepts and the relations that hold among them. According to Mey (2008: 256), common ground is taken to have to do with what interlocutors have in common when it comes to cultural, linguistic, and other backgrounds. Typically, the background is defined in terms of shared knowledge, that is, the knowledge about the world that each interlocutor brings to the situation. In this case study, it is knowledge of Dublin and its environs, the novel *Ulysses* and its characters, the re-enactment of Bloomsday each year by the people of Dublin according to the novel's schema organized by time and location.

The people of Dublin celebrate this through connecting artifact, language, worldview, and way of life. The whole event category of Bloomsday is conceptualized as an Irish, especially Dublin, celebration. Bloomsday has been reconceptualized several times over the years – it started as a small, quite marginal, literary celebration over half a century ago, then, somehow, it seized the mind of the community and became popularized into a major Dublin cultural event, while capturing the popular imagination of Dublin's citizens.

10.5 Case study: The pragmatics of Irish tea culture

10.5.1 Tea drinking in Irish culture

Strange as it may seem, Irish people are the heaviest tea drinkers per capita in the world, after Turkey, averaging about six cups per day, with many people drinking even more. It has been calculated[36] that Irish people get through approximately 2.267kg (5 lbs) of tea per head every year[37], which places Ireland second place globally. Only Turkey gets through more tea, with an (astonishing) 3.17kg (7lb) per head consumed there. As part of Irish culture, it is not unusual that, after being invited into an Irish household, one will almost immediately find that tea will be offered. Additionally, once finished, you will be offered a refill of more tea,…and more tea. Irish people do consume a lot of tea!

As tea drinking is so embedded in Irish culture with certain ritualistic elements, it follows that there is a particular and definite etiquette [CULTURAL

---

[36] https://qz.com/168690/where-the-worlds-biggest-tea-drinkers-are/.
[37] Using data compiled by Euromonitor and the World Bank, *Quartz.*

SCHEMA], and language, related to it. This language use has several interesting pragmatic dimensions that we will explore here. The first part of the ritual is the tea making itself. First, the tea is (generally) brewed in a teapot, which should be warmed beforehand [PROCESS SCHEMA] by briefly swirling hot water around in it, after which the pot is emptied. This ritual act of *warming* the teapot first is commonly known as *"scalding"* the teapot. Then, placing the tea in the teapot, one must steep the tea – typically one bag per cup of tea – in water that has only just been brought to the boil.

In Ireland, having tea [CULTURAL ARTIFACT] in a household is always a priority. One must never run out of tea as this would constitute a minor, but significant, crisis. Additionally, it is a grave social error, significantly anti-social, in fact, to make one's self a cup of tea without offering to make tea for everyone else in your company. And, of course, to invite someone into one's house and not offer them tea is construed as somewhat offensive, or at least odd [CULTURAL WAY OF LIFE] and is often taken as a slight. Offering one's visitor a cup of tea forms part of the backbone of Irish hospitality.

As such, Irish tea drinking is a social activity and an important Irish custom that serves as a symbol of hospitality, camaraderie, and friendship. It is also a social ritual [EVENT SCHEMA] that initiates the start of a (long) conversation, serving to engage the host and the guest while pouring and serving, the tea as the conversational interlocutors relax and get comfortable themselves for an enjoyable discourse.

10.5.2 The language surrounding tea making and consumption

The language [LANGUAGE] surrounding tea making and tea consumption reflects Irish cultural nuances. Typically, and traditionally, Irish people *"scald the pot"* [EVENT SCHEMA] and then *"wet the tea"* rather than *"make the tea"*. One then allows [PROCESS SCHEMA] the teapot to *"brew"* or *"draw"* for about five minutes before serving. Tea drinking is very much a core part of Irish culture [CULTURAL WAY OF LIFE] and no visit to an Irish home would be complete if tea was not offered. From the householder's point of view [ROLE SCHEMA], the refusal by a guest to take tea, however polite, can be construed as strange and unsatisfactory. In Ireland, even on the warmest day, tea is never served cold. In an Irish home, tea is typically taken throughout the day: from breakfast, across the day, including over lunch and evening meal, up to very late at night.

As a visitor to an Irish home, one can expect to be offered [speech act: offer] tea within a few minutes of arriving. A particular ritual governs this.

Often the guest will politely refuse [speech act: refusal] the offer of tea on the *first ask*. Then, they will be asked a second time [speech act: offer], and often people politely say no here too (even though they would love a cup of tea) [speech act: refusal]. After the third ask [speech act: offer], one usually says "Yes, please a cup of tea would be wonderful" [speech act: acceptance], or something to that effect ("I'd love one, thank you" or "That sounds great"). Of course, if your guest says "no" the third time you offer tea, you can be assured that your guest does not actually want tea and you know that all participants have respected the politeness ritual. Then your host will put on the kettle to wet the tea and you will be on to another round of questions about whether you would like your tea black or with some milk, strong or weak, and if you would like a biscuit or scone to eat with it. The only exception to this politeness ritual [politeness] with Irish tea drinking happens in situations where you and your host are solid friends or family. In this instance, on the *first ask*, one simply says "yes" right away.

10.5.3 Tea drinking culture captured for comic effect

The Irish ritual dimensions of the culture of tea drinking have been captured to comic effect in the TV sitcom program, *Father Ted*[38], where the Irish obsession with tea is represented by one of the characters, Mrs. Doyle, the housekeeper, who seems to have dedicated her life to serving tea. Fr. Ted is about a number of hapless priests, the elderly, hideously debauched and incoherent alcoholic Fr. Jack Hackett, a childlike idiot priest called Fr. Dougal McGuire, and the central protagonist, Fr. Ted Crilly, the actual Fr. Ted, who is predisposed to worldly gratifications beyond his vocation as a priest, especially anything to do with large amounts of money. The trio of priests live on the remote and backward Craggy Island with their devoted and over-hospitable housekeeper, Mrs. Doyle, whose purpose in life is making tea and servitude. The atmosphere of the program is as if the absurd surrealism found in the Irish literary tradition of Samuel Beckett and Flann O'Brien was blended with the comedic world of Monty Python. While apparently anything can happen in their particular world, and frequently does, everything has its own internal logic based on how the characters react to

---

[38] The TV sitcom, *Father Ted*, was produced by the UK Channel 4 TV with Irish writers. The show successfully aired on TV in Ireland, Britain, and Australia. It may well be the case that the humour is so surreal and embedded in Irish culture that it would not be easily understood elsewhere (Linehan & Mathews 1999).

particular circumstances, where events and actions are usually taken to their ultimate bizarre conclusions. The humor of the TV show majors on repeatedly revealing Mrs. Doyle's tea-making habits. She makes tea for Ted, Dougal and Jack (three Catholic priests living together on the island) quite often, offering them a cup nearly every time she appears (*"Tea, father?" "Oh, you will, you will, you will."*). The insistence of Mrs Doyle, that everyone should have tea, is encouraged by her catch phrase *"… Go on, go on, go on!"* in a gentle caricature of that aspect of Irish hospitality. Mrs Doyle is quite simply obsessed with etiquette and the process of serving and drinking tea, and, from one script, she describes the process of making tea as:

> The playful splash of the tea as it hits the bottom of the cup. The thrill of adding the milk, and watching it settle for a moment, before it filters slowly down, turning the tea from dark brown to a lighter brown. Perching an optional Jaffa Cake on the side, like a proud soldier, standing to attention beside a giant…cup of tea[39].

Mrs Doyle's constant offering and re-offering of tea, and refusal to take a refusal, is one of the most famous running gags and has now become a meme. Her dedication to tea making is obsessive and often disturbing as, in the TV show[40], the behavior surrounding the tea ritual is taken to extremes.

10.5.4 The pragmatic strategy of a ritualized sequence of offers and refusals.

In the Irish tea offering ritual, we see an instance of the pragmatic strategy of a ritualized sequence set of OFFERS, REOFFERS, and REFUSALS, typically (but not always) with an eventual ACCEPTANCE, that plays an important role in Irish culture, as normal polite behavior, and is deeply ensconced in expressions of hospitality. An example based on Amador-Moreno (2010: 163 section 7.4), with the forms of Irish-English language, illustrates this (1). It is very common in Ireland to hear offers made using the form of a question/request (2).

---

[39] http://tvtropes.org/pmwiki/pmwiki.php/Series/FatherTed?from=Main.FatherTEd.
[40] https://www.channel4.com/programmes/father-ted.

(1)   Tea drinking offer and refusal

Speaker 1:	… will you have a cup of tea?	**Offer**
Speaker 2:	No thanks.	**1st Rejection/refusal**
Speaker 1:	Are you sure?	**Offer reissued**
	Do you want a bag of Taytos[41]	
	or something?	**Modified offer**
Speaker 2:	No thanks.	**2nd Rejection/refusal**
Speaker 1:	Are you sure?	**Offer reissued again**
Speaker 2:	No, I have to be back for around six.	**3rd Rejection/refusal**

(2)   Offer as question/request

'Will you have a cup of tea?'

Additionally, direct offers, using imperatives, are also to be found (3). When it comes to responding, the ritual refusal/rejection, the Irish-English assertion forms are often used. Some variations of these are included in (4).

(3)   Offer as IMPERATIVE

'Come on in and have a cup of tea'.

(4)   Reject/Refusal as ASSERTION

a.   'Ahhh, you're okay'.
b.   'You're grand'.
c.   'No thanks, it's grand'.
d.   'No bother at all'.

There is a tricky dynamic underpinning the offer–reoffer–refusal of the tea drinking schema, to do with politeness and face. From Barron (2005: 143), we know that offers may have face-threatening features in that their

---

[41] Tayto is a popular brand of potato crisps manufactured and sold in Ireland.

part-directive nature is similar to requests that may threaten the hearer's negative face. In virtue of offering, the speaker exerts pressure on the hearer to react to, and possibly to accept, the offer. According to Barron, the speaker's offer, although beneficial to the hearer, impinges on the hearer's privacy, lessens their freedom, and also encourages them to engage in an action that may place him/her under the speaker's debt. At the same time, the speaker's positive face is threatened because of committing to deliver a future action, which may not be accepted by the hearer. The concept of face has been used by Brown and Levinson (1987) as a device to explain politeness. For Brown and Levinson, politeness is universal, resulting from people's face needs. Positive face is the desire to be liked, appreciated, approved, and so on, whereas negative face is the desire not to be imposed upon, intruded, or otherwise put upon. Negative politeness addresses negative face concerns, often by acknowledging the other's face is threatened. Anytime a person threatens another person's face, the first person commits what is known as a face-threatening act. Commissives are categorized by Searle (1976: 11) as offers since they commit a speaker to some future course of action, the action being that denoted by the speech act. Similarly, while an offer is included in the set of commissive speech acts (Bach and Harnish 1979: 54) the set of acknowledgments include Thank, Accept, and Reject. According to Bach and Harnish, commissives express the speaker's INTENTION and BELIEF that the speaker's utterance obligates the speaker to do something where that something is identified within the speech act. Commissives, then, are acts of obligating oneself, or of proposing to obligate oneself, to do something specified in the propositional content, which may also specify conditions under which the action is to be done. In committing to do the action expressed via the offer, the speaker expresses the INTENTION to do the action and the BELIEF that their utterance commits them to doing it, under relevant specified conditions. These conditions may include the hearer's accepting the speaker's commitment to do the action or the hearer's not rejecting it.

10.5.5 The pragmeme as a situated speech act

The contribution of the actual situation is a key component in determining pragmatic meaning. The notion of pragmatic act, or pract, captures the requirement to account for the ways a situation determines what a speech act is actually about. A pragmeme is a situated speech act in which the norms of language, culture, and of society combine in determining meaning. It is sensitive to social expectations regarding the utterance situation. With respect to the Irish tea drinking culture, the pragmeme is realized in a variety of pragmatic acts, as situationally bound speech acts. The specific instantiation of the Irish tea offering schema may be represented by means of the pragmatic set in (5). Correct interpretation of practs relies on knowledge of the situational context as well as of the underlying pragmeme associated with a pragmatic act and this informs common ground. As we have seen with the Irish tea drinking ritual, pragmemes are linked with cultural assumptions and expectations (Capone 2010, Stalnaker 1998, Kecskes 2013, Wong 2010), the knowledge of which is essential for the correct determination of pragmatic meaning.

---

(5)   IRISH TEA OFFERING conceptual schema

Pragmatic schema: IRISH TEA OFFERING

Speech act/event: **[Offer**   (of   tea)]

Pragmeme 1:   [INSIST   ON   THE   OFFER   FOR   SEVERAL   ITERATIONS]

Practs (linguistic):   (1) "will you have a cup of tea?"
                                         (2) "Come on in and have a cup of tea".
                                         (3) "Ahhh, go on, go on … you will have some tea".

Pragmeme 2:   [REJECT   AN   OFFER N X   TIMES   BEFORE   ACCEPTANCE]

Practs (linguistic):   [When offered tea]
                                         (1) "Ahhh, you're okay".
                                         (2) "You're okay".
                                         (3) "No thanks, it's grand".
                                         (4) "No bother at all".

The basic premise underlying the approach taken here is that cultural conceptualizations, such as cultural schemas, cultural categories, and cultural metaphors, are important for understanding certain features of human languages at the interface of culture as a system and language as a system. Language and cultural cognition are dynamic systems that interact with each other.

10.6   Discussion

In this chapter, we have seen that language is an immensely complex behavior. Specifically, then, within the Bloomsday case study, we found evidence of cultural artifacts within the linguistic landscape. Bloomsday was shown to proceed according to a particular Bloomsday macro-schema, based on the schema underpinning the novel *Ulysses*, and this Bloomsday macro-schema provided the context for the activation of a wide variety of event and role schemata in the common ground of the participants of Bloomsday. Knowledge of Bloomsday was shown to be represented as distributed, as a complex adaptive system, over these participants. The various schemata within the Bloomsday macro-schema activated across different times and locations. With regard to the ritual pertaining to Irish tea drinking, common ground and context played an important role in the offer–reoffer–refusal of the tea ritual. Accordingly, this tea drinking social ritual allowed for schematized behavior. Cognitive conceptualizations of various kinds were activated in support of the speech acts of "offer, reoffer, and refusal". Additionally, practs and pragmemes were useful in characterizing these situated speech acts. These case studies provide evidence that support the argument of this chapter – that culture is systemic, knowledge is distributed, and common ground mediates this relationship between culture, context, knowledge, and language. All around us, language transforms our world and provides us with meaning in context.

11   Some final comments

At the start of this study, we had the stated aim of progressing the discussion on the sets of relationships between language, culture, knowledge, and context, and how they might influence and inform language in interaction. In advancing this exploration of the complex set of interrelationships, we provided a detailed theoretical characterization of each of the thematic domains. Our overall objective was to bring a new focus and a fresh perspective to these relationships across language, culture, and knowledge, through studying language in the linguistic landscape, the language found on artifacts and in art (as a special kind of artifact), knowledge and context, and the pragmatics of language in interaction. In this, we adopted a broad functional-cognitive approach within the study, that language is not an autonomous system and that its interactions with the domain areas are actually deeper, more wide-ranging and multifaceted than had perhaps been previously considered. We worked towards supporting the hypothesis that meaning in culture is facilitated by language and that language draws on context and shared knowledge, the cultural common ground, while cognitive processes retrieve a meaning from language in use. We also argued that these cognitive processes are exactly the same that apply to retrieving meaning from art, music, poetry, and language-based artifacts found within the wide linguistic landscape. We have motivated a definition of culture to include artifact, language, worldview, and the cultural models underpinning the way of life of a community. We noted that culture is different to civilization, where civilization is considered to be all of human society with its well-developed social organizations, and the social process whereby societies develop and organize. As we stated in the first chapter, civilization is the condition that exists when people have developed effective ways of organizing a society and care about art, science, and such like. Clearly, however, there is some overlap between culture and civilization. Culture was argued to have at least four major constituent dimensions (artifact, language, worldview, and cultural models/way of life), and we expressed this as (1):

> ## (1)   The constituents of culture
>
> 1.   [**ARTIFACT**]: A body of artistic and intellectual work.
> 2.   [**LANGUAGE**]: A means of spiritual and intellectual development.
> 3.   [**WORLDVIEW**]: The values, customs, beliefs, and symbolic practices by which people live as a community.
> 4.   [**CULTURAL MODELS/WAY OF LIFE**]: A way of life viewed at some moment in time.

We found that culture is about shared meanings, with language operating as the privileged medium through which we make sense of things. Meaning can only be shared through our common access to language. As such, language is central to our construction of meaning and has always been the key repository of cultural values and meanings. Culture therefore is concerned with the production and exchange of meaning between members of a social group, as it ranges over artifact, language, worldview, and way of life. It concerns the beliefs, values, rules, norms, symbols, and traditions that are common to a group of people. Importantly, language is able to do this because it operates as a representational system. In language, we use signs and symbols to stand for and represent our concepts, feelings, and ideas to other members of our society. We represent meaning in mental models of various kinds. Language is therefore the channel through which our thoughts, emotions, and ideas are represented in culture. Representation of this knowledge through language is central to the construction of meaning. As a means of communication, language is essential as it give us access to our knowledge repositories of art, science, and to all the knowledge and skills learned by people living in a cultural community. Culture is therefore at the interface of knowledge and language.

Insights were gained from our investigation of the linguistic landscape on how it contributes to the relationship between culture, common ground, and language, as languages are part of the cultural heritage and, as such, reflects our linguistic and cultural diversity. The linguistic landscape is that part of our environment where public displays incorporate language, acting and functioning as a form of sign. The visible use of language on signs in the public environment constitutes the linguistic landscape of a place. We included a case study on the linguistic landscape and cultural identity, and we touched upon issues of conflict that are manifest and discernible in the linguistic landscape. In our environment we noted that we are encircled by the artifacts of our society and our culture, and we interact with our world via these artifacts in many ways. Artifacts, digital or otherwise, enhance the quality of our lives, and frequently have significant culture value. These artifacts do, however, have a function, purpose, and a utility of some kind. They have the ability to preserve some cultural significance.

Culture is observed to provide the rich vibrant color and textural grain within our everyday lives, as a kind of social-collective-cognitive background in which we wrap all our beliefs, instincts, prejudices, sentiments, opinions, and assumptions. Culture, along with language, fuses the vital essence and heart of a people as a living community, maintaining and sustaining the repository of our shared knowledge. As a living vibrant thing, culture is (happily), always a work in progress. Embedded within culture is a worldview and every language gives expression to the distinctive worldview of a specific people. We saw that a worldview is a mental model of reality that functions as a theory of the world which we use for living in the world. It is a framework of our ideas and attitudes about the world, ourselves, and of life. The notion of worldview is important to how we perceive, conceive and experience, and act in the world. A worldview is the fundamental cognitive orientation of an individual and society encompassing the whole of the individual's or society's knowledge. The way of life was defined as the habits, customs, and beliefs of a particular person or group of people, as cultural models, and a style of living that reflects the attitudes of a person or group, and thereby reflects the cultural models of that society. An individual's lifestyle choice, along with their normal everyday activities, is broadly determined by their society and culture, while a way of life is developed and maintained by groups of people. An individual's own actions substantially intersect with social and cultural structures, while allowing for individual lifestyle choices.

The nature of knowledge and how it is represented was examined, along with context and its relation to discourse. Context draws on knowledge of the world and subsets of context may become relevant for discourse. We addressed how context and situation are important notions within pragmatic analysis, and how context helps to differentiate between *what is said* vs. *what is meant*, and utterance meaning. Consequently, the contribution of context to utterance meaning within language in use is now an area of considerable value within pragmatic analysis. We tackled the question of how theories of language might effectively characterize contextual knowledge and the cultural connection through examining performatives and speech acts, and we included a case study addressing the challenges of context in linguistic analysis of two speech acts.

A considerable discussion was undertaken in respect of the connection between context and common ground, how common ground reconciles the multidimensional relationship between culture and language in communicative interaction, and how culture informs language usage. We considered common ground to be a complex distributed structured entity important to the interface between culture, language, and knowledge, where knowledge includes ontology, knowledge representation, reasoning, cultural schemata, cultural metaphors, and cultural conceptualizations. We proposed a schematic structure for common ground and discussed the various kinds of knowledge contained within it, which we framed as a subset of the wider context of a situation. We then argued that a speech act must be interpreted in the local context of a given situation. We considered a situation to be a structured entity that functions as a unifying device to link semantics to events through to syntax, and onwards to utterance meaning. Common ground contains shared knowledge about the local dialogue, language itself, the environment, recent events, historical knowledge, common sense, and cultural knowledge. Within common ground, some forms of knowledge are less volatile and non-dynamic with broadly static but updateable components (concepts and facts), and some are more dynamic and volatile. Important to the relationship between context and common ground is the notion of salience. A special significance was given to the dynamic role that salience plays in the construction and maintenance of common ground, and the management of knowledge and information flow. We know that some pieces of knowledge become available to our attention in cognition, more so than other elements of knowledge, and thereby become salient. Salience can occur for both a speaker and a hearer, and when both interlocutors have a convergence of salience, the salient item enters common ground. Salience therefore selects entities of various kinds as candidates for inclusion into common ground.

In our exploration of culture and language in interaction, the role of language in culture was addressed. Here, we looked at art and artifact, and found that there are very many ways in which visual artists use language in visual art. Words can be used explicitly when they are included in, or on, the visual artwork. In medieval art, words frequently assume a prominent position. A primary example of this phenomena is medieval illuminated manuscripts, an art form that relies deeply on the consistent interdependence of graphics and language where words and image contribute equally to the resulting interpretation. In more contemporary visual art forms, use of overt words is easily recognized, and is widely accepted in the art by people. In other contemporary examples, such as pop art, modern cartoons, and MEMES, language is used as a visual semiotic linguistic device exhibiting a tight, unified, and significant interdependence with the images displayed. We analyzed and characterized elements of the application of language in the service of culture in one particular cultural narrative.

Specifically, we presented empirical case studies of facets of culture as a systemic model whose dimensions encompass culture, artifact, worldview, knowledge, common ground, and language. The four case studies provided in this study included: 1) the linguistic landscape and cultural identity; 2) meeting the challenges of context in linguistic analysis; 3) Bloomsday as evidence of cultural systematicity; 4) the pragmatics of Irish tea culture. We have mentioned the first two case studies earlier. In the final two case studies, we firstly examined the conceptualization of the cultural schema for the celebration of the Joycean Bloomsday in Dublin, as a language related ritual within the linguistic landscape, and secondly, the cultural pragmatic schema and pragmeme of "offers and refusal" relating to tea drinking in an Irish social context. Context and common ground mediates these relationships in important ways.

We initially posed several key questions for this study:

i.   What is CULTURE and cultural knowledge?
ii.   What is WORLDVIEW and way of life of a community, and how are these motivated by cultural models?
iii.   What are (cultural) ARTIFACTS and their function, and what cultural knowledge do they instantiate?
iv.   What language artifacts are found in the LINGUISTIC LANDSCAPE?
v.   What are the various kinds of KNOWLEDGE and their forms, and how might these be represented?
vi.   What is the relationship between language and CONTEXT?
vii.   How does context and COMMON GROUND inform utterance meaning in discourse?

Our functional-cognitive approach enabled us to address these questions across the various chapters. Our approach also enabled us to take a rounded perspective on the rich and complex set of relationships that are to be found to exist within and across culture and its constituent dimensions of artifact, worldview, linguistic landscape, knowledge, common ground, and language in interaction. What is important is the essential interrelatedness between all of these dimensions.

References

Abelson, R. 1981. Constraint, construal, and cognitive science. In *Proceedings of the Third Annual Conference of the Cognitive Science Society*. Berkeley, CA: University of California. 1–9.

Aerts, D., D'Hooghe, B., & Note, N. (eds.). 2005. *Worldviews, Science and Us: Redemarcating Knowledge and Its Social and Ethical Implications*. Singapore, Hackensack, NJ & London UK: World Scientific Publishing Company.

Aerts, D., D'Hooghe, B., Pinxten, R., & Wallerstein, I. (eds.). 2011. *Worldviews, Science and Us: Interdisciplinary Perspectives on Worlds, Cultures and Society*. Singapore, Hackensack, NJ & London UK: World Scientific Publishing Company.

Ager, M. 2009. Ethnography. In G. Senft, J. Östman & J. Verschueren (eds.) *Culture and Language Use*. Amsterdam: John Benjamins Publishing Company. 110–120.

Almor, A. 1999. Noun-phrase anaphora and focus: The informational load hypothesis. *Psychological Review* 106: 748–765.

Amador-Moreno, C.P. 2010. *An Introduction to Irish English*. Sheffield, UK: Equinox Publishing Ltd.

Ariel, M. 1990. *Accessing NP antecedents*. London: Routledge.

Ariel, M. 2001. Accessibility theory: an overview. In T. Sanders, J. Schilperoord, & W. Spooren (eds.). *Text Representation: Linguistic and Psycholinguistic Aspects*. Amsterdam: John Benjamins Publishing Company. 29–88.

Ariel, M. 2013. Centering, accessibility and the next mention. *Theoretical Linguistics* 39: 39–58.

Aristotle. *Physica*, 1930. *The Works of Aristotle*. D. Ross (ed.). Volume II. Oxford: Clarendon Press.

[Artifact]. 2018. *Stanford Encyclopedia of Philosophy*. Available at https://plato.stanford.edu/entries/artifact/ (accessed October 2019).

Auer, P. 2009. Context and contextualization. In J. Verschueren and J.-O. Ostman (eds.). *Key Notions for Pragmatics*. Amsterdam: John Benjamins Publishing Company. 86–101

Austin, J.L. 1962. *How to Do Things with Words: The William James Lectures delivered at Harvard University in 1955*, ed. by J. Opie Urmson & M. Sbisà. Oxford: Oxford University Press.

Bach, K. & Harnish, R.M. 1979. *Linguistic Communication and Speech Acts*. Cambridge, MA: MIT Press.

Backhaus, P. 2007. *Linguistic Landscapes: A Comparative Study of Urban Multilingualism in Tokyo*. UK, USA, and Canada: Multilingual Matters Ltd.

Baker, L.R. 2008. The shrinking difference between artifacts and natural objects. In *The American Philosophical Association Newsletters. Newsletter on Philosophy and Computers* 7(2): 2–5. Available at https://cdn.ymaws.com/www.apaonline.org/resource/collection/EADE8D52-8D02-4136-9A2A-729368501E43/v07n2Computers.pdf (accessed 13th January 2021).

Baker, P. 2016. Gender and sexuality. In J. Flowerdew (ed.) *Discourse in Context: Contemporary Applied Linguistics*. Volume 3. London: Bloomsbury Publishing. 1–27.

Barnes, J. 1984. *The Complete Works of Aristotle*. Bolingen Series LXXI. Princeton, NJ: Princeton University Press.

Barron, A. 2005. Offering in Ireland and England. In A. Barron & K. Schneider (eds.). *The Pragmatics of Irish English*. Berlin/New York: Mouton de Gruyter. 141–176.

Barthes, R. 1977. *Image–Music–Text*. London: Fontana.

Barwise, J. & Perry, J. 1983, *Situations and Attitudes*. Cambridge, MA: The MIT Press.

Beckner, C., Blythe, R., Bybee, J., Christiansen, M.H., Croft, W., Ellis, N.C., Holland, J., Jinyun, K., Larsen-Freeman, D., & Schoenemann, T. 2009. Language is a complex adaptive system: Position paper. *Language Learning* 59: 1–26.

Benatar, A., & Clifton, C. 2014. Newness, givenness and discourse updating: Evidence from eye movements. *Journal of Memory and Language* 71(1): 1–16. https://doi.org/10.1016/j.jml.2013.10.003.

Benedict, R. 1932. Configurations of culture in North America. *American Anthropologist* 34(1): 1–27.

Bennardo, G. & de Munck, V. 2014. *Cultural Models Genesis, Methods, and Experiences*. Oxford: Oxford University Press.

Bennett, J.W. and Tumin, M.M. 1949. *Social Life: Structure and Function*. New York: Alfred A. Knopf.

Blommaert, J. 2005. *Discourse*. Cambridge: Cambridge University Press.

Bloom, P. 2007. Water as an artifact kind. In E. Margolis & S. Laurence (eds.) *Creations of the Mind: Theories of Artifacts and Their Representation*. Oxford: Oxford University Press. 150–156.

Bloomfield, L. 1945. About foreign language teaching. *Yale Review* 34: 625–641

Boas, F. 1930. Anthropology. *Encyclopedia of the Social Sciences*. Volume 2. New York. 3–110.

Boas, F. 1938. *The Mind of Primitive Man* (Revised edition). New York: MacMillan.

Bose, N.K. 1929. *Cultural Anthropology*. Calcutta: South Asia Books.

Bowcher, W.L. 2018. The semiotic sense of context vs the material sense of context. *Functional Linguistics* 5: 5. https://doi.org/10.1186/s40554-018-0055-y.

Brewer, W. 1987. Schemas versus mental models in human memory. In P. Morris (ed.) *Modelling Cognition*. New York: John Wiley & Sons. 187–197.

Brown, P. & Levinson, S. 1987. *Politeness: Some Universals in Language Use*. Cambridge: Cambridge University Press.

Butler, C.S. 2003. *Structure and Function – A Guide to Three Major Structural-Functional Theories*. 2 Volumes (Studies in Language Companion Series). Amsterdam: John Benjamins Publishing Company.

Capone, A. 2010. On pragmemes again: Dealing with death. *La linguistique* 46(2): 3–21. DOI:10.3917/ling.462.0003.

Case, G.M. 1927. Culture as a distinctive human trait. *American Journal of Sociology* 32: 906–920.

Chafe, W. 1976. Givenness, contrastiveness, definiteness, subjects, topics, and point of view. In C.N. Li. (ed.) *Subject and Topic*. New York: Academic Press. 25–55.

Chandler, D. 2007. *Semiotics: The Basics* (2nd edn). New York: Routledge.

Chapman, S. & Routledge, C. (eds.) 2005. *Key Thinkers in Linguistics and the Philosophy of Language*. Edinburgh: Edinburgh University Press. 80–86.

Chazan, M. 2019. *The Reality of Artefacts: An Archaeological Perspective*. London and New York: Routledge.

Chein, M. & Mugnier, M-L. 2008. *Graph-based Knowledge Representation: Computational Foundations of Conceptual Graphs* (Advanced Information and Knowledge Processing). London: Springer-Verlag.

Chiarcos, C. 2009. Mental salience and grammatical form: Toward a framework for salience metrics in natural language generation. Dissertation. Universität Potsdam.

Chiarcos C, Claus, B. & Grabski, M. 2011. Introduction: Salience in linguistics and beyond. In C. Chiarcos, B. Claus, & M. Grabski (eds.). *Salience Multidisciplinary Perspectives on its Function in Discourse*. Berlin/New York: De Gruyter Mouton. 1–30.

Chomsky, N. 1965. *Aspects of the Theory of Syntax*. Cambridge, MA: MIT Press.

Chomsky, N. 2002. *Syntactic Structures*. Berlin: Mouton de Gruyter. DOI: 10.1515/9783110218329.

Clark, H.H. 1996. *Using Language*. Cambridge: Cambridge University Press.

[CnG-CAJ-UU report] Conradh na Gaeilge, the Committee for the Administration of Justice, and Ulster University. 2019. Comhairlí Áitiúla, Dualgais agus an Ghaeilge: Creatlach Comhlíonta. Local Councils, Obligations and the Irish Language: A Framework for Compliance. Available at https://drive.google.com/file/d/1vzxfKsmqMr_6mak2f8pCS3hQDb-ou4kf/view (accessed 12th December 2020).

Cowart, M. 2017. *Embodied Cognition. Internet Encyclopaedia of Philosophy*. B. Dowden & J. Fieser (eds.). Available at www.iep.utm.edu/embodcog/ (accessed 12th December 2020).

Crystal, D. 2014. *Language Death* (2nd edn). Cambridge: Cambridge University Press.

Davidse, K. 1987. M.A.K Halliday's Functional Grammar and the Prague School. In R. Dirven & V. Fried (eds.) *Functionalism in Linguistics*. Amsterdam: John Benjamins Publishing Company. 39–80.

De Busser, R. 2015. The influence of social, cultural, and natural factors on language structure: An overview. In R. De Busser & R.J. LaPolla (eds.) *Language Structure and Environment Social, Cultural, and Natural Factors*. Amsterdam: John Benjamins Publishing Company. 1–30.

De Busser, R. &. LaPolla, R.J. (eds.) 2015. *Language Structure and Environment Social, Cultural, and Natural Factors*. Amsterdam: John Benjamins Publishing Company.

Diedrichsen, E. 2020. On the interaction of core and emergent common ground in internet memes. *Internet Pragmatics*, special issue on the Pragmatics of Internet Memes. Amsterdam: John Benjamins Publishing Company. 223–259.

Dik, S.C. 1981. *Studies in Functional Grammar*. London and New York: Academic Press.

Dik, S.C. 1987. Some principles of functional grammar. In R. Dirven & V. Fried (eds.). *Functionalism in Linguistics*. Amsterdam: John Benjamins Publishing Company. DOI: 10.1075/llsee.20.05dik. 81–100.

Divjak, D. 2019. *Frequency in Language: Memory, Attention and Learning*. Cambridge: Cambridge University Press.

Dixon Hunt, J., Lomas, D. & Corris, M. (eds.). 2010. *Art, Word and Image: 2000 Years of Visual/Textual Interaction*. London: Reaktion Books.

Doyle, A. 2019. *A History of the Irish Language*. Cambridge, MA: Cambridge University Press.

Eco U. 1976. *A Theory of Semiotics, Advances in Semiotics*. Bloomington, IN: Indiana University Press.

Edelman, S. 2008. *Computing the Mind: How the Mind Really Works*. Oxford: Oxford University Press.

Elder, C.L. 2007. On the place of artifacts in ontology. In E. Margolis & S. Laurence. *Creations of the Mind: Theories of Artifacts and Their Representation*. Oxford: Oxford University Press. 33–51.

Elder, Cr. L. 2014. Artifacts and mind-independence. In M. Franssen, P. Kroes, T.A.C. Reydon, & P.E. Vermaas (eds.) *Artefact Kinds: Ontology and the Human-Made World*. Heidelberg: Springer. 27–44.

Eliot. T.S. 1973. *Notes Towards the Definition of Culture*. London: Faber & Faber.

Ellmann, R. 1986. *Ulysses on the Liffey*. Oxford: Oxford University Press. 186–190.

Ellwood, C.A. 1927. Primitive concepts and the origin of culture patterns. *American Journal of Sociology* 33: 1–313.

Everett, C. 2013. *Linguistic Relativity: Evidence Across Languages and Cognitive Domains* (Applications of Cognitive Linguistics [ACL]). Berlin: De Gruyter Mouton.

Everett, D.L. 2005. Cultural constraints on grammar and cognition in Pirahã: Another look at the design features of human language. *Current Anthropology* 46(4):621–646. DOI: 10.1086/431525.

Everett, D.L. 2013. *Language: The Cultural Tool*. London: Profile Books.

Fillmore, C.J. 1982. Frame semantics. In The LSOK (ed.). *Linguistics in the Morning Calm*. Seoul, Korea: Hanshin Publishing Company. 111–137.

Falk, S. 2014. On the notion of salience in spoken discourse: Prominence cues shaping discourse structure and comprehension. *TIPA. Travaux interdisciplinaires sur la parole et le langage*. http://journals.openedition.org/tipa/1303; DOI:10.4000/tipa.1303.

Firbas, J. 1971. *On the Concept of Communicative Dynamism in the Theory of Functional Sentence Perspective*. Brno Studies in English. Volume 7. Brno, Czechoslovakia: Brno University. 12–47.

Firth, J.R. 1957. *Papers in Linguistics, 1934–1951*. Oxford: Oxford University Press.

Firth, J.R. 1968. *Selected Papers of J. R. Firth, 1952–1959*, edited by F.R. Palmer. London: Longmans/Prentice Hall Press.

Firth, R. 1939. *Primitive Polynesian Economy*. London: George Routledge and Sons, Ltd.

Flowerdew, J. 2016. *Discourse in Context: Contemporary Applied Linguistics*. Volume 3. London: Bloomsbury Academic Publishing.

Ford, G.S. 1937. A sample comparative analysis of material culture. In G.P. Murdock (ed.) *Studies in the Science of Society Presented to Albert Galloway Keller*. 223–246.

Geertz, C. 1973. *The Interpretation of Cultures* (3rd edn). New York: Harper Collins Basic Books.

Gernsbacher, M.A. 1990. *Language Comprehension as Structure Building*. Hillsdale, NJ: Lawrence Erlbaum Associates.

Gernsbacher, M.A. 1997. Two decades of structure building. *Discourse Processes* 23(3): 265–304. DOI: 10.1080/01638539709544994.

Gilbert, S. 1955. *James Joyce's Ulysses: A Study*. New York: Random Books.

Giora, R. 1997. Understanding figurative and literal language: The graded salience hypothesis. *Cognitive Linguistics* 8(3): 183–206.

Giora, R. 1999. On the priority of salient meanings: Studies of literal and figurative language. *Journal of Pragmatics* 31: 919–929.

Giora, R. 2002. Literal vs. figurative language: Different or equal? *Journal of Pragmatics* 34: 487–506.

Giora, R. 2003. *On Our Mind: Salience, Context, and Figurative Language*. Oxford: Oxford University Press.

Givón, T. 1983. Introduction. In T. Givón (ed.) *Topic Continuity in Discourse: A Quantitative Cross-language Study*. Amsterdam: John Benjamins Publishing Company. 5–41.

Givón, T. 1989. *Mind, Code and Context: Essays in Pragmatics*. Hillsdale, NJ and London: Lawrence Erlbaum.

Givón, T. 1995. *Conversation: Cognitive, Communicative and Social Perspectives* (Typological Studies in Language). Amsterdam: John Benjamins Publishing Company.

Givón, T. 2001. *Syntax* (2nd edn). Amsterdam: John Benjamins Publishing Company.

Givón, T. 2005. *Context as Other Minds: The Pragmatics of Sociality, Cognition and Communication*. Amsterdam: John Benjamins Publishing Company.

Givoni, S. & Giora, R. 2018. Salience and defaultness. In F. Liedtke, & A. Tuchen (eds.) *Handbuch Pragmatik*. Stuttgart: J. B. Metzler. 207–213.

Glock, H-J. 1996. *A Wittgenstein Dictionary*. UK: Wiley-Blackwell.

Goddard, C. 2009. Cultural scripts. In G. Senft, J-O. Östman, & J. Verschueren (eds.) *Culture and Language Use*. Amsterdam: John Benjamins Publishing Company. 68–80.

Goffman E. 1956. *Presentation of Self in Everyday Life*. New York: Doubleday.

Goffman E. 1974. *Frame Analysis*. Cambridge, MA: Harvard University Press.

Goodenough, W.H. 1957. Cultural anthropology and linguistics. In P.L. Garvin (ed.) *Report on the 7th Annual Round Table Meeting in Linguistics and Language Study*. Washington, DC: Georgetown University Press. 109–173.

Goodenough, W.H. 1964. Cultural anthropology and linguistics. In D.H. Hymes (ed.) *Language in Culture and Society. A Reader in Linguistics and Anthropology*. New York: Harper & Row. 36–39.

Goranzon, B. & Florin, M. (eds.). 1990. *Artificial Intelligence, Culture and Language: On Education and Work*. The Springer Series on artificial intelligence and society. Berlin & Heidelberg: Springer-Verlag.

Gorter, D. (ed.). 2006. *Linguistic Landscape: A New Approach to Multilingualism*. Clevedon, Buffalo, and Toronto: Multilingual Matters Ltd. Available at http://link.springer.com/referenceworkentry/10.1007/978-0-387-30424-3_160 (accessed 14th October 2021).

Grandy, R. 2007. Artifacts: Parts and principles. In, E. Margolis & S. Laurence (eds.) *Creations of the Mind*. Oxford: Oxford University Press. 18–32.

Grice, H.P. 1967/1989. Logic and conversation. In H.P. Grice (ed.). *Studies in the Way of Words*. Cambridge, MA: Harvard University Press. 22–40.

Grice, H.P. 1969. Utterer's meaning and intentions. *Philosophical Review* 78: 147–77. Reprinted in H.P. Grice. 1975. Logic and conversation. *Syntax and Semantics 3: Speech Acts*, ed. by P. Cole & J. L. Morgan. New York: Academic Press.

Grosz, B.J., Joshi, A.K., & Weinstein, S. 1995. Centering: A framework for modelling the local coherence of discourse. *Computational Linguistics* 21: 203–225.

Grosz, B.J. & Sidner, C.L. 1986. Attention, intentions, and the structure of discourse. *Computational Linguistics* 12: 175–204.

Hall, E.T. 1959/1973. *The Silent Language* (reissue edn). New York: Random House/Bantam Doubleday Dell Publishing Group.

Hall, S. (ed.). 1997. *Representation: Cultural Representation and Signifying Practices*. Milton Keynes, UK: Open University Press.

Halliday, M.A.K. 1978. *Language as Social Semiotic: The Social Interpretation of Language and Meaning*. London: Edward Arnold.

Halliday, M.A.K. 2007. The notion of "context" in language education. In J.J. Webster (ed.). *Language and Education, Volume 9 in the Collected Works of M. A. K. Halliday*. London: Equinox. 269–290.

Halliday, M.A.K. 2014. *Halliday's Introduction to Functional Grammar* (4th edn), revised by C.M.I.M. Matthiessen. Oxon & New York: Routledge.

Halliday, M.A.K. & Hasan, R. 1989. *Language, Context and Text: Aspects of Language in a Socialsemiotic Perspective*. Geelong, Australia: Deakin University Press.

Harris, R.A. 1993. *The Linguistics Wars*. Oxford: Oxford University Press.

Hart, H. and Pantzer, A. 1925. Have subhuman animals culture? *American Journal of Sociology* 30: 703–709.

Hasan, R. 1995. The conception of context in text. In P.H. Fries & M. Gregory (eds.) *Discourse in Society: Systemic Functional Perspectives*. Norwood, NJ: Ablex. 183–284. http://dx.doi.org/10.1075/cilt.118.

Heaney, S. 2006. *Death of a Naturalist*. London: Faber & Faber.

Hicks, D. 2002. *Scotland's Linguistic Landscape: The Lack of Policy and Planning with Scotland's Place-names and Signage*. Paper at World Congress on Language Policies, Barcelona. Available at www.linguapax.org/congres/taller/taller2/Hicks.html (accessed 12th December 2020).

Hoebel, E.A. 1949. *Man in the Primitive World*. New York: McGraw Hill.

Horn, L.R. & Ward, G. (eds.). 2004. *The Handbook of Pragmatics*. Malden, MA & Oxford: Blackwell.

Horn, L. & Ward, G. (eds.). 2006. *The Handbook of Pragmatics*. UK: Wiley-Blackwell.

Humboldt, W. von. 1820. Über das vergleichende Sprachstudium in Beziehung auf die verschiedenen Epochen der Sprachentwicklung. In W. von Humboldt. *Werke in fünf Bänden*. Herausgegeben von. A. Flitner & K. Giel. 1963. Band III. Schriften. Zur Sprachphilosophie. 1–25. Wissenschaftliche Buchgesellschaft.

Humboldt, W. von. 1830–1835. Über die Verschiedenbeit des menschlichen Sprachbaues und ihren Einfluß auf die geistige Entwicklung des Menschengeschlechts. Berlin: Königliche Akademiw der Wissenschaften. In W. von Humboldt. *Werke in fünf Bänden*. Herausgegeben von. A. Flitner & K. Giel. 1963. Band III. Schriften. Zur Sprachphilosophie. 144–367. Wissenschaftliche Buchgesellschaft.

Huntington, E. 1945. *Mainsprings of Civilization*. New York: John Wiley.

Hymes, D. 1962. The ethnography of speaking. In T. Gladwin & W. C. Sturtevant (eds.) *Anthropology and Human Behavior*. Washington: The Anthropological society of Washington. 13–53.

Ichikawa, J.J. & Steup, M. 2017. The analysis of knowledge. *Stanford Encyclopedia of Philosophy*. Available at http://plato.stanford.edu/entries/knowledge-analysis/ (accessed 12th December 2020).

[Irish Language Act]. 2017. *Acht na Gaeilge: Pléchaipéis. Irish Language Act: Discussion Document*. Available at https://cnag.ie/images/Acht_Gaeilge_ó_Thuaidh/15MÁ2017_Plécháipéis_ar_Acht_Gaeilge_ó_Thuaidh.pdf (accessed 12th December 2020).

Jaszczolt, K.M. 2005. *Default Semantics: Foundations of a Compositional Theory of Acts of Communication*. Oxford: Oxford University Press.

Jaszczolt, K.M. 2011. Default meanings, salient meanings, and automatic processing. In K.M. Jaszczolt & K. Allan (eds.) *Salience and Defaults in Utterance Processing*. Berlin: De Gruyter Mouton. 11–34.

Jaszczolt, K.M. 2015. Default semantics. In B. Heine & H. Narrog. *The Oxford Handbook of Linguistic Analysis* (2nd edn). Oxford: Oxford University Press. 193–222. DOI:10.1093/oxfordhb/9780199677078.013.0009.

Jaszczolt, K.M. 2016. *Meaning in Linguistic Interaction: Semantics, Metasemantics, Philosophy of Language*. Oxford: Oxford University Press.

Jaszczolt, K.M. & Allan, K. (eds.). 2011. *Salience and Defaults in Utterance Processing*. Berlin: De Gruyter Mouton.

Johnson-Laird, P.N. 1980. Mental Models in Cognitive Science. *Cognitive Science* 4: 71–115.

Johnson-Laird, P. N. 1983. *Mental Models: Towards a Cognitive Science of Language, Inference, and Consciousness*. Issue 6, Cognitive Science Series. Cambridge: Harvard University Press.

Joyce, J. 2008. *Ulysses: The 1922 Text*. Oxford World's Classics. Oxford: Oxford University Press.

Kallen, J. 2014. The political border and linguistic identities in Ireland: What can the linguistic landscape tell us? In D. Watt & C. Llamas (eds.) *Language, Borders and Identity*. Edinburgh: Edinburgh University Press. 157.

Kant, I. 2008. *Critique of Pure Reason*. Translated by N. Kemp Smith. New York: St. Martin's Press. 41–48.

Kecskes, I. 2003. *Situation-based Utterances in L1 and L2*. Berlin: Mouton de Gruyter.

Kecskes, I. 2004. The role of salience in processing pragmatic units. *Acta Linguistica Hungarica* 51(3–4): 309–324.

Kecskes, I. 2010. Situation-bound utterances as pragmatic acts. *Journal of Pragmatics* 42(11): 2889–2897.

Kecskes, I. 2013. Intercultural encyclopedic knowledge, and cultural models. In F. Sharifian & M. Jamarani (eds.) *Language and Intercultural Communication in the New Era*. London: Routledge. 39–59.

Kecskes, I. 2015. Language, culture, and context. In F. Sharifian (ed.) *The Routledge Handbook of Language and Culture*. Oxon & New York: Routledge. 113–128.

Kecskes, I. & Zhang, F. 2009. Activating, seeking, and creating common ground: A socio-cognitive approach. *Pragmatics & Cognition* 17(2): 331–355. DOI 10.1075/p&c.17.2.06kec.

Kecskes, I. & Mey, J. (eds.). 2008. *Intention, Common Ground and the Egocentric Speaker-Hearer*. Berlin/New York: Mouton de Gruyter.

Klineberg, O. 1935. *Race Differences*. New York: Harper.

Kluckhohn, C. & Kelly, W.H. 1945. The concept of culture. In R. Linton (ed.) *The Science of Man in the World Crisis*. New York. 78–105

Kress. G. & van Leeuwen, T. 2006. *Reading Images: The Grammar of Visual Design* (2nd edn). Oxon UK: Routledge.

Kroeber, A.L. & Kluckhohn, C. 1952. Culture: A critical review of concepts and definitions. *Papers of the Peabody Museum of American Archaeology and Ethnology, Harvard University* 47(1): viii, 223.

Kroes, P. 2002. Design methodology and the nature of technical artefacts. *Design Studies* 23: 287–302. Available at www.elsevier.com/locate/destud and www.nomads.usp.br/documentos/textos/design_mobiliarios_objetos/arq_textos/KROES_Design_methodology.pdf (12th December 2020).

Kroes, P. 2012. *Technical Artefacts: Creations of Mind and Matter*. Dordrecht: Springer.

Kronenfeld, D.B. 1996. *Plastic Glasses and Church Fathers: Semantic Extension from the Ethnoscience Tradition*. Oxford: Oxford University Press.

Kronenfeld, D.B. 2008. *Culture, Society, and Cognition: Collective Goals, Values, Action, and Knowledge*. Berlin: Mouton de Gruyter.

Kronenfeld, D.B. 2017. *Culture as a System: How We Know the Meaning and Significance of What We Do and Say*. Routledge Studies in Anthropology. London/New York: Routledge.

Lakoff, G. 1984. *Classifiers as a Reflection of Mind: A Cognitive Model Approach to Prototype Type Theory*. Berkeley Cognitive Science Report No. 19. Berkeley, CA: University of California Institute of Human Learning.

Landry, R. & Bourhis, R.Y. 1997. Linguistic landscape and ethnolinguistic vitality: An empirical study. *Journal of Language and Social Psychology* 16(1): 23–49.

Langacker, R. 1987. *Foundations of Cognitive Grammar, Volume I: Theoretical Prerequisites*. Stanford, CA: Stanford University Press.

Lauer, H. 2009. A worldly view of worldview metaphysics. In N. Note, R. Fornet-Betancourt, J. Estermann, & D. Aerts (eds.) *Worldviews and Cultures. Philosophical Reflections from an Intercultural Perspective*. Dordrecht: Springer Science + Business Media B.V. 103–128.

Lemos, N. 2007. *An Introduction to the Theory of Knowledge*. Cambridge, MA: Cambridge University Press.

Levelt, W.J.M. 1989. *Speaking: From Intention to Articulation*. Cambridge, MA: MIT Press.

Lewis, D. 1979. Scorekeeping in a language game. *Journal of Philosophical Logic* 8: 339–359. (Reprinted in Lewis 1983. 233–249.)

Lewis, D. 1983. *Philosophical Papers*. Volume 1. Oxford University Press.

Libbrecht, U. 2009. Comparative Philosophy: A Methodological Approach. In N. Note, R. Fornet-Betancout, J. Estermann, & D. Aerts (eds.) *Worldviews and Cultures: Philosophical Reflections from an Intercultural Perspective*. Springer Science + Business Media B.V.

Lieve, O. 2011. Worldview as relational notion? Reconsidering the relations between worldviews, science and us from a radical symmetrical anthropology. In D. Aerts, B. D'Hooghe, R. Pinxten, & I. Wallerstein (eds.) *Worldviews, Science and Us: Interdisciplinary Perspectives on Worlds, Cultures and Society*. Singapore, Hackensack, NJ & London UK: World Scientific Publishing Company. 139–163.

Linehan, G. & Mathews, A. 1999. *Father Ted: The Complete Scripts*. London: Boxtree.

Locke, J. 1690/2014. *An Essay Concerning Human Understanding*. UK: Wordsworth Edition. Book II, Chapter 1, 121.

Lundberg, G. 1939. *Foundations of Sociology*. New York: Praeger Publishers Inc.

MacAulay, D. 1992. *The Celtic Languages*. Cambridge Language Surveys. Cambridge: Cambridge University Press.

Malinowski, B. 1923. The problem of meaning in primitive languages. Supplement I to C. K. Ogden & I. A. Richard (eds.) *The Meaning of Meaning* (8th edn, 1946/1989). New York: Harcourt Brace. 296–336.

Malinowski, B. 1931. Culture. *Encyclopedia of the Social Sciences* 4: 621–646. New York.

Malinowski, B. 1935. *Coral Gardens and Their Magic*. 2 volumes. London: Allen & Unwin.

Malinowski, B. 1944/1960. *A Scientific Theory of Culture and Other Essays*. New York: OUP.

Mey, J. 2008. "Impeach or exorcise?". Or, what is in the (common) ground? In I. Kecskes & J. Mey (eds.) *Intention, Common Ground and the Egocentric Speaker*. Berlin/New York: Mouton de Gruyter. 256.

Minsky, M. 1975. A framework for representing knowledge. In P.H. Winston (ed.) *The Psychology of Computer Vision*. New York: McGraw-Hill Book Company. 311–377.

Naugle. D.K. 2002. *Worldview: The History of a Concept*. Grand Rapids, Michigan USA & Cambridge UK: William B. Eerdmans Publishing Company.

[ND-NA]. UK Government and Irish Government. 2020. New Decade, New Approach. Available at https://static.rasset.ie/documents/news/2020/01/new-decade-new-approach.pdf (accessed 12th December 2020).

Nerlich, B. & Clarke, D.D. 1996. *Language, Action and Context – The Early History of Pragmatics in Europe and America, 1780–1930*. Studies in the Theory and History of Linguistic Science. Volume 80. Amsterdam: John Benjamins Publishing Company.

Nerlich, B. 1988. Philipp Wegener's (1848–1916) Theory of language and communication. *Henry Sweet Society for the History of Linguistic Ideas Bulletin* 11(1): 11–13, DOI: 10.1080/02674971.1988.11745345.

Nerlich, B. 1990. *Change in Language: Whitney, Bréal and Wegener*. Routledge History of Linguistic Thought Series. London and New York: Routledge.

Newmeyer, F.J. 1995. *Generative Linguistics: An Historical Perspective*. History of Linguistic Thought. London: Routledge.

Nolan, B. 2008. Modality in RRG: Towards a characterisation using Irish data. In Van Valin, R. (ed.) *Investigations of the Syntax-Semantics-Pragmatics Interface*. Studies in Language Companion Series 105. Amsterdam: John Benjamins Publishing Company. 147–159.

Nolan, B. 2012. *The Structure of Modern Irish: A Functional Account*. Sheffield: Equinox Publishing Company.

Nolan, B. 2013. Constructions as grammatical objects: A case study of the prepositional ditransitive construction in Modern Irish. In B. Nolan & E. Diedrichsen (eds.) *Linking Constructions into Functional Linguistics.* Studies in Language Companion Series 145. Amsterdam: John Benjamins Publishing Company. 143–178.

Nolan, B. 2014. Extending a lexicalist functional grammar through speech acts, constructions and conversational software agents. In B. Nolan & C. Periñán (eds.) *Language Processing and Grammars: The Role of Functionally Oriented Computational Models*. Studies in Language Companion Series 150. Amsterdam: John Benjamins Publishing Company.

Nolan, B. 2017. The syntactic realisation of complex events and complex predicates in situations of Irish. In B. Nolan & E. Diedrichsen (eds.) *Argument Realisation in Complex Predicates and Complex Events*. Studies in Language Companion Series 180. Amsterdam: John Benjamins Publishing Company. 13–41.

Nolan, B. & Diedrichsen, E. 2013. *Linking Constructions into functional linguistics.* Studies in Language Companion Series 145. Amsterdam: John Benjamins Publishing Company.

Note, N., Fornet-Betancout, R. Estermann, J. & Aerts, D. (eds.). 2009. *Worldviews and Cultures: Philosophical Reflections from an Intercultural Perspective.* Springer Science + Business Media B.V.

Nöth, W. 1990. *Handbook of Semiotics.* Advances in Semiotics. Bloomington, IN: Indiana University Press.

Noveck, I.A. & Sperber, D. 2004. *Experimental Pragmatics.* Hampshire UK: Palgrave Macmillan

Nunberg, G., Sag, I.A. & Wasow, T. 1994. Idioms. *Language* 70(3): 491–538.

Ó Dochartaigh, C. 1992. The Irish language. In D. Macaulay (ed.) *The Celtic Languages.* Cambridge: Cambridge University Press. 11–99.

Ó Siadhail, M. 1989/1991. *Modern Irish.* Cambridge: Cambridge University Press.

Ogburn, W.F. & Francis Nimkoff, M. 1940. *Sociology.* Boston, MA: Houghton Mifflin.

Osgood, C. 1942. *The Ciboney Culture of Cayo Redondo, Cuba.* Yale University Publications in Anthropology, no. 25. Department of Anthropology, Yale University. Yale University Press; London: Oxford University Press.

Östman, J.-O. & Simon-Vandenbergen, A.-M. 2009. Firthian Linguistics. In G. Senft, J.-O. Östman, & J. Verschueren (eds.) *Culture and Language Use.* Amsterdam: Benjamins Publishing Company. 140–145.

Oyserman, D. 2015. Culture as situated cognition. In R. Scott & S. Kosslyn (eds.) *Emerging Trends in the Social and Behavioral Sciences.* John Wiley & Sons, Inc.

Peirce, C.S. 1882a. On junctures and fractures in logic. MS 427. In C. S. Peirce, 1989. *Writings of Charles S. Peirce, A Chronological Edition*, v. 4. Peirce Edition Project. Bloomington, IN: Indiana University Press. 391–399.

Peirce, C.S. 1882b. Letter, Peirce to O. H. Mitchell (L 294). In C.S. Peirce, 1989. *Writings of Charles S. Peirce, A Chronological Edition*, v. 4. Peirce Edition Project. Bloomington, IN: Indiana University Press. 391–399.

Peirce, C.S. 1897. *On Signs* [R]. MS [R] 798.

Peirce, C.S. 1989. *Writings of Charles S. Peirce, A Chronological Edition*, v. 4. Peirce Edition Project. Bloomington: Indiana University Press. 391–399

Peirce, C.S. n.d. "Representamen" (pub. 18.08.13-18: 27). In Bergman, M. & S. Paavola (eds.) *The Commens Dictionary: Peirce's Terms in His Own Words* (new edn). Retrieved at www.commens.org/dictionary/entry/quote-signs-r-4 (12th December 2020).

Peleg, O., Giora, R. & Fein, O. 2004. Contextual strength: The whens and hows of context effects. In I.A. Noveck & D. Sperber (eds.) *Experimental Pragmatics.* Hampshire UK: Palgrave Macmillan Ltd. 172–186.

Pojman, L.P. 2001. *What Can We Know? An Introduction to the Theory of Knowledge* (2nd edn). Belmont, CA. USA: Wadsworth Thomson Learning.

Preston, B. 2014. Ethnotechnology: A manifesto. In M. Franssen, P. Kroes, T.A.C. Reydon, & P.E. Vermaas (eds.) *Artefact Kinds: Ontology and the Human-made World*. Heidelberg: Springer. 145–165.

Pritchard, D. 2018. *What is This Thing Called Knowledge?* (4th edn). Oxon and New York: Routledge.

Quinn, N. & Holland, D. 1987. Culture and cognition. In N. Quinn & D. Holland (eds.) *Cultural Models in Language and Thought*. Cambridge: Cambridge University Press. 3–42.

Radcliffe-Brown, A.R. 1949. White's view of a science of culture. *American Anthropologist* 51: 503–512 .

Recanati, F. 2003. *Literal Meaning*. Cambridge: Cambridge University Press.

Recanati, F. 2010. *Truth-Conditional Pragmatics*. Oxford: Clarendon Press.

Recanati, F. 2012. Contextualism: Some varieties. In K. Allan & K.M. Jaszczolt (eds.) *The Cambridge Handbook of Pragmatics*. Cambridge: Cambridge University Press. 135–149.

Redfield, R. 1940. Unpublished lectures quoted in *Sociology* by W. F. Ogburn, & N. Meyer Francis. Boston: Houghton Mifflin Company. 25

Rescher, N. 2003. *Epistemology: An Introduction to the Theory of Knowledge*. Albany, NY: State University of New York Press.

Reuter, L.B. 1939. *Race and Culture: An Outline of the Principles of Sociology*. New York: Barnes & Noble.

Ridgeway, C. 2006. Social structure and interpersonal behavior: a theoretical perspective on cultural schemas and social relations. *Social Psychology Quarterly* 69: 5–16.

Riegler, A. 2005. Inclusive worldviews: Interdisciplinary research from a radical constructivist perspective. In D. Aerts, B. D'Hooghe, & N. Note (eds.) *Worldviews, Science and Us: Redemarcating Knowledge and Its Social and Ethical Implications*. Singapore, Hackensack, NJ & London UK: World Scientific Publishing Company. 20–37.

Rosengren, K.E. (ed.). 1994. *Media Effects and Beyond Culture, Socialization and Lifestyles*. London: Routledge.

Rouse, I. 1939. *Prehistory in Haiti*. Yale Publications in Anthropology, No. 21. New Haven, CT: Yale University Press.

Rubdy, R. 2015. Conflict and exclusion: the linguistic landscape as an arena of contestation. In R. Rubdy & S. Ben Said (eds.) *Conflict, Exclusion and Dissent in the Linguistic Landscape*. UK: Palgrave Macmillan.

Ryle, G. 1949/2002. *The Concept of Mind*. Chicago, IL: University of Chicago Press.

Sapir, E. 1921/1949. *Language: An Introduction to the Study of Speech*. New York: Harcourt, Brace & World Inc.

Sapir, E. 1929. The status of linguistics as a science. *Language* 5: 207–214. (Reprinted in Sapir, 1949. 160–166) .

Sapir, E. 1949. *Selected Writings of Edward Sapir in Language, Culture, and Personality* (ed. D.G. Mandelbaum). Berkeley, CA: University of California Press.

Schank, R.C. 1975. The structure of episodes in memory. In D.G. Bobrow & A. Collins (eds.) *Thinking: Readings in Cognitive Science*. Cambridge: Cambridge University Press. 421–432.

Schank, R.C. & Abelson R.P. 1975. Scripts, plans, and knowledge. In Johnson-Laird, P.N. (ed.) *Representation and Understanding: Studies in Cognitive Science*. New York: Academic Press, Inc. 237–272.

Schank, R.C. & Abelson, R.P. 1977. *Scripts, Plans, Goals and Understanding: An Inquiry into Human Knowledge Structures*. Hillsdale, NJ: Lawrence Erlbaum.

Schroeder, M. 2016. *Value Theory. Stanford Encyclopedia of Philosophy*. Available at https://plato.stanford.edu/entries/value-theory/ (accessed 12th December 2020).

Scollon, R. & Wong Scollon, S. 2003. *Discourses in Place Language in the Material World*. Oxon UK: Routledge.

Searle, J.R. 1969. *Speech Acts*. Cambridge MA: Cambridge University Press.

Searle, J.R. 1976. A classification of illocutionary acts. *Language in Society* 5(1): 1–23. doi:10.1017/S0047404500006837.

Searle, J.R. 1995. *The Construction of Social Reality*. London: Penguin Books.

Searle, J.R. 2007. Social ontology and the philosophy of society. In E. Margolis & S. Laurence (eds.) *Creations of the Mind: Theories of Artifacts and Their Representation*. Oxford: Oxford University Press. 3–17.

Searle, J.R. 2009. Language and social ontology. In C. Mantzavinos (ed.) *Philosophy of the Social Sciences: Philosophical Theory and Scientific Practice*. Cambridge: Cambridge University Press. 9–27.

Senft, G. 1996. *Classificatory Particles in Kilivila*. New York: Oxford University Press.

Senft, G., Östman, J-O., & Verschueren, J. (eds.). 2009. *Culture and Language Use*. Amsterdam: Benjamins Publishing Company.

Senft, G. 2007. *Bronislaw Malinowski and Linguistic Pragmatics*. Lodz Papers in Pragmatics 3. 2007: 79–96. DOI 10.2478/v10016-007-0006-7

Senft, G. 2009a. Introduction. In G. Senft, J-O. Östman, & J. Verschueren (eds.). *Culture and Language Use*. Handbook of Pragmatics Highlights 2. Amsterdam: John Benjamins Publishing Company. doi:10.1075/hoph.2.01sen. 1–17.

Senft, G. 2009b. Bronislaw Kasper Malinowski. In G. Senft, J-O. Östman, and J. Verschueren (eds.) *Culture and Language Use*. Handbook of Pragmatics Highlights 2. Amsterdam: John Benjamins Publishing Company. 210–225. DOI: 10.1075/hoph.2.19sen.

Serangi, S. 2009. Culture. In G. Senft, J-O. Östman, & J. Verschueren (eds.) *Culture and Language Use*. Amsterdam: Benjamins Publishing Company. 81–104.

Sharifian, F. 2011. *Cultural Conceptualisations and Language: Theoretical Framework and Applications*. Cognitive Linguistic Studies in Cultural Contexts. Amsterdam: John Benjamins Publishing Company.

Sharifian, F. 2015a. Cultural linguistics. In F. Sharifian (ed.) *The Routledge Handbook of Language and Culture*. Oxon & New York: Routledge. 473–492.

Sharifian, F. 2015b. Language and culture: Overview. In F. Sharifian (ed.) *The Routledge Handbook of Language and Culture*. Oxon & New York: Routledge. 3–18.

Sharifian, F. (ed.). 2015c. *The Routledge Handbook of Language and Culture*. New York/London: Routledge/Taylor and Francis.

Sharifian, F. 2017. *Cultural Linguistics: Cultural Conceptualisations and Language*. Amsterdam: John Benjamins.

Sharifian, F. & Palmer, G.B. 2007. *Applied Cultural Linguistics: Implications for Second Language Learning and Intercultural Communication*. Cognitive Linguistic Studies in Cultural Contexts. Amsterdam: John Benjamins Publishing Company.

Silva-Fuenzalida, I. 1949. Ethnolinguistics and the Study of Culture. *American Anthropologist* 51(3): 446–456.

Silverstein, M. 1975. Linguistics and anthropology. In R. Bartsch & T. Vennemann (eds.) *Linguistics and Neighbouring Disciplines*. Amsterdam: North-Holland Publishing Co. 157–170.

Sowa, J.F. 1984. *Conceptual Structures: Information Processing in Mind and Machine*. Reading, MA: Addison-Wesley.

Sowa, J.F. 1987. Semantic networks. In S.C. Shapiro (ed.) *Encyclopedia of Artificial Intelligence*. Wiley. 1011–1024.

Sowa, J.F. 1997. Matching logical structure to linguistic structure. In N. Houser, D. D. Roberts, & J. Van Evra (eds.) *Studies in the Logic of Charles Sanders Peirce*. Bloomington and Indianapolis: Indiana University Press, 418–444.

Sowa, J.F. 2008. Conceptual graphs. In F. van Harmelen, V. Lifschitz, & B. Porter (eds.) *Handbook of Knowledge Representation*. Amsterdam: Elsevier. 213–237, Chapter 5.

Sperber, D. & Wilson, D. 1986/1995. *Relevance: Communication and Cognition* (2nd edn). Oxford: Blackwell Publishers.

Sperber, D. & Wilson, D. 2005. Pragmatics. In F. Jackson & M. Smith (eds.) *Oxford Handbook of Philosophy of Language*. Oxford: Oxford University Press.

Stalnaker, R.C. 1978. Assertion, *Syntax and Semantics 9*, New York: Academic Press. Reprinted in R.C. Stalnaker, *Context and Content*. Oxford: Oxford University Press 1999. 78–95.

Stalnaker, R.C. 1998. On the representation of context. *Journal of Logic, Language, and Information* 7. Reprinted in R.C. Stalnaker. 1999. *Context and Content*. Oxford: Oxford University Press.

Stalnaker, R.C. 1999a. *Context and Content*. Oxford: Oxford University Press.

Stalnaker, R.C. 1999b. Introduction. In R.C. Stalnaker (ed.) *Context and Content*. Oxford: Oxford University Press.

Stalnaker, R.C. 2014. *Context*. Oxford: Oxford University Press.

Steward, J.H. 1950. *Area Research: Theory and Practice*. Social Science Research Council, Bulletin 63.

Swidler, A. 1986. Culture in action: Symbols and strategies. *American Sociological Review* 51(2): 273–286. Available at www.csub.edu/~rdugan2/ SOC%20477%20Culture%20readings/culture%20and%20action%20tool%20 kit%20swidler.pdf (12th December 2020).

Talmy, L. 1995. The cognitive culture system. *The Monist* 78: 80–114.

Talmy, L. 2000. *Toward a Cognitive Semantics. Volume 2: Typology and process in concept structuring*. Cambridge, MA: MIT Press.

Talmy, L. 2007. Attention phenomena. In D. Geeraerts & H. Cuyckens (eds.) *Oxford Handbook of Cognitive Linguistics*. Oxford: Oxford University Press. 264–293.

Thomasson, A.L. 2007. Artifacts and human concepts. In E. Margolis & S. Laurence. *Creations of the Mind: Theories of Artifacts and Their Representation*. Oxford: Oxford University Press. 52–73.

Truncellito, D. 2007. *Epistemology. Internet Encyclopedia of Philosophy*. Available at www.iep.utm.edu/epistemo/ (12th December 2020).

Tylén, K. & McGraw, J.J. 2014. Materializing mind: The role of objects in cognition and culture. In M. Gallotti & J. Michael (eds.) *Perspectives on Social Ontology and Social Cognition*. Studies in the Philosophy of Sociality 4. Dordrecht: Springer Science+Business Media. DOI 10.1007/978-94-017-9147-2_10. 135–149.

Tylor, E.B. 1871. *Primitive Culture: Researches into the Development of Mythology, Philosophy, Religion, Art, and Custom. The Origins of Culture*. Volume 1. London: John Murray.

Tylor, E.B. 1877. *Primitive Culture: Researches Into the Development of Mythology, Philosophy, Religion, Languages, Art and Customs*. Volume 2. New York: Henry Holt and Co.

Underhill. J.W. 2009. *Humboldt, Worldview and Language*. Edinburgh: Edinburgh University Press.

Underhill, J.W. 2011. *Creating Worldviews: Metaphor, Ideology and Language*. Edinburgh: Edinburgh University Press.

van Dijk, T.A. 2008. *Discourse and Context: A Sociocognitive Approach*. Cambridge: Cambridge University Press.

van Dijk, T. A. 2009. *Society and Discourse: How Social Contexts Influence Text and Talk*. Cambridge: Cambridge University Press.

van Dijk, T.A. 2014. *Discourse and Knowledge: A Sociocognitive Approach*. Cambridge: Cambridge University Press.

van Dijk, T.A., & Kintsch, W. 1983. *Strategies of Discourse Comprehension.* New York: Academic Press.

Vega-Encabo, J. & Lawler, D. 2014. Creating artifactual kinds. In M. Franssen, P. Kroes, T.A.C. Reydon, & P.E. Vermaas (eds.) *Artefact Kinds: Ontology and the Human-Made World.* Heidelberg: Springer. 105–124.

Wallis, W.D. 1930. *Culture and Progress.* New York: McGraw-Hill.

Wegener, P. 1885/1991. *Untersuchungen über die Grundfragen des Sprachlebens* (Investigations into the Fundamental Questions of the Life of Language). Reprint from the 1885 edition (Classics in Psycholinguistics). Amsterdam: John Benjamins Publishing Company.

White, L.A. 1943. Energy and the evolution of culture. *American Anthropologist* 45(3-1): 335–356.

White, L.A. 1949. Ethnological theory. In R.W. Sellars, V.J. McGill, & M. Farber. *Philosophy for the Future.* New York: Macmillan. 357–384.

Whorf, B.L. 1940. Science and linguistics. *Technology Review* 42: 229–231, 247–248.

Whorf, B.L. 1950. An American Indian model of the universe. *International Journal of American Linguistics* 16: 67–72.

Whorf, B.L. 1956/1984. *Language, Thought and Reality: Collected Writings* (ed. by J.B. Carroll). Cambridge, MA.: MIT Press.

Wilson, D. & Matsui, T. 2012. Recent approaches to bridging: Truth, coherence, relevance. In D. Sperber & D. Wilson (eds.) *Meaning and Relevance.* Cambridge: Cambridge University Press. 187–209.

Wilson, R.A. & Foglia, L. 2015. *Embodied Cognition.* In E. Zalta (ed.) *Stanford Encyclopaedia of Philosophy.* Available at https://plato.stanford.edu/entries/embodied-cognition/ (accessed 12th December 2020).

Wissler, C. 1929. The Validity of the Culture Concept. *American Journal of Sociology* 35: 204–219.

Wittgenstein, L. 1922/1961/2001. *Tractatus Logico-Philosophicus* (2nd edn). Oxon: Routledge Classics.

Wittgenstein, L. 1969. *Schriften 1: Tractatus Logico-Philosophicus.* Frankfurt: Suhrkamp.

Wittgenstein, L. 2009. *Philosophical Investigations.* German-English edition with P. Hacker & J. Schulte (4th edition). Translated by G.E.M. Anscombe. UK: Wiley-Blackwell.

Włodarczyk, A. & Włodarczyk, H. 2006. SUBJECT in the Meta-Informative Centering Theory. Instytut Slawistyki Polskiej Akademii Nauk. *Cognitive Studies | Études cognitives* 7: 39–64.

Wodak, R. 2016. Political discourse analysis – Distinguishing frontstage and backstage contexts. A discourse-historical approach. In J. Flowerdew (ed.) *Discourse in Context: Contemporary Applied Linguistics*. Volume 3. Bloomsbury Publishing. Kindle Edition. 321–346.

Wong, J. 2010. The "triple articulation" of language. *Journal of Pragmatics* 42(11): 2932–2944. DOI: 10.1016/j.pragma.2010.06.013.

Zeman, J. 1977. Peirce's Theory of Signs. In T. Sebeok (ed.) *A Perfusion of Signs*. Bloomington, IN and London: Indiana University Press. 22–39.

Zwaan, R.A. & Radvansky, G.A. 1998. Situation models in language comprehension and memory. *Psychological Bulletin* 123: 162–185.

Index

CPSIA information can be obtained
at www.ICGtesting.com
Printed in the USA
JSHW041148160322
23717JS00001B/5